# THE SECRET WORLD OF RED WOLVES

T. DELENE BEELAND

# THE SECRET WORLD OF RED WOLVES

The Fight to Save

North America's Other Wolf

THE UNIVERSITY OF NORTH CAROLINA PRESS

CHAPEL HILL

This book was published with the assistance of the
WACHOVIA WELLS FARGO FUND FOR EXCELLENCE
of the University of North Carolina Press.

Designed by Sally Fry
Set in Quadraat and MetaPlus type
by Tseng Information Systems, Inc.
Manufactured in the United States of America

The paper in this book meets the guidelines for permanence
and durability of the Committee on Production Guidelines for
Book Longevity of the Council on Library Resources.

The University of North Carolina Press has been
a member of the Green Press Initiative since 2003.

Library of Congress Cataloging-in-Publication Data
Beeland, T. DeLene.
The secret world of red wolves : the fight to save North
America's other wolf / T. DeLene Beeland. — 1 [edition].
pages cm
Includes bibliographical references and index.
ISBN 978-1-4696-0199-1 (hardback : alk. paper)
ISBN 978-1-4696-2654-3 (pbk.: alk. paper)
1. Red wolf—North America—Conservation.
2. Wildlife conservation—North America.  I. Title.
QL737.C22B43  2013
599.773097—dc23
2012034397

FOR MATT ERTL, my husband: thank you for deferring one of your dreams so that I might pursue mine.

# CONTENTS

# PHOTOGRAPHS, MAPS, AND FIGURES

## Photographs

## Maps

## Figures

# PREFACE

Compared to other wolves, the red wolf is on the smallish side. But don't let its size fool you. This creature has a vast and complex story, the depth and breadth of which continue to surprise and fascinate me. Until now, the details of its story have not been recorded in one volume for general audiences. Bits of its history exist in academic papers and book chapters, various children's books, and works that focused on the initial efforts to reintroduce the species to a small part of its historic range. But the book you hold in your hands is the first to fold all the elements of the red wolf's extraordinary story into a single narrative for nonexperts. It traces this unique animal from its hypothesized origins to its modern management and even glimpses into its future. This is a story of science, nature, history, and the human aspects of conservation projects. But more than anything, it is the story of real people who were inspired, and who continue to be inspired, to think differently and to innovate new biological field methods because of the red wolf's dire plight. It is a story both of the red wolf's natural history and of the people working to recover it.

This is also the story of how I came to understand what red wolves are today and what they may have been historically. My initial interest in red wolves was sparked shortly after I graduated from the School of Natural Resources and the Environment at the University of Florida, where I studied interdisciplinary ecology. While working on my thesis—an investigation of stakeholder beliefs and values regarding the controversial Mexican gray wolf reintroduction program that is taking place in the American Southwest—I became aware of the amazing ecological role that wolves play in our environment. As I learned more about wolves, I became intrigued by their position at the crux of science, economics, politics, culture, natural-resources management, and public perception. During my thesis research, I continually bumped into miscellaneous papers about red wolves and began saving them to read later. When later finally came, I was instantly electrified by red wolves' mysterious past and by the fact that, while we know a great deal about these animals, there are still so many important questions yet to be answered.

When I searched for further information, I was sorely disappointed to learn that there were no current, comprehensive, general-audience books about the red wolf. It surprised me that a story involving an animal as polarizing and charismatic as a *wolf* could be left unwritten. The red wolf's story is lesser known than that of its more media-savvy western cousin, the gray wolf, but it's certainly no less compelling. In fact, I find it more so—perhaps because of the red wolf's brush with extinction and its saga of being perpetually controversial. I feel incredibly fortunate that the editors at UNC Press agreed that this was a story worth telling.

To write this book, I was granted unparalleled access to the U.S. Fish and Wildlife Service's Red Wolf Recovery Program, where I shadowed several of their field biologists over the course of more than two years. The program enjoys the good fortune of having had an extremely stable staff over time. As of 2013, Chris Lucash has remained with the program for twenty-seven years, Michael Morse for twenty-five years, and Art Beyer for twenty-three years. Ford Mauney has worked on it for twelve years, and, as the newest field biologist, Ryan Nordsven has eight years of experience. The program's recovery coordinator position tends to turn over more frequently, but the current coordinator, David Rabon, has put in four years; previously, he worked on a Ph.D. examining factors contributing to red wolf mate selection, which gives him an additional eleven years. Compared to other wolf recovery programs, the stability, cohesiveness, and longevity of the red wolf team over several decades is remarkable. The continuity and depth of program knowledge and memory that these professionals share is irreplaceable. In light of all they know about red wolves, my own contributions to documenting this story feel quite small. I feel that in many ways, I have only borrowed their thoughts and experiences and woven them together here in these pages.

On September 14, 2012, the Red Wolf Recovery Program celebrated its twenty-fifth anniversary. I like to think that the publication of this book is a fitting, if belated, commemoration of the program's quarter-century anniversary, as well as a heartfelt thank-you gift to the red wolf recovery team for helping to make the completion of this work possible.

This story is, to the best of my knowledge, true and accurate. It has undergone fact-checking by myself and by a few volunteers. UNC Press also subjected it to a blind external review undertaken by several experts.

Sources for this book include a combination of primary interviews and field observations (interviewees are listed in the back), historical research, biologists' field notes, scientific literature, popular media, government documents, and red wolf program newsletters. Wherever feasible, I attribute material and quotes to their source(s) if the material was not something I uncovered in an interview. However, in cases where accounts of program events have been included in several different references over time (for example, in popular media, academic writings, and program newsletters), I did not attribute any particular source when condensing the material for the book.

A few chapters deserve further mention about sources. Chapter 9 is a literature review of sources detailing wolves in the eastern United States; none of the information presented is my original reporting, although I do my best to retell what's already been reported in a unique way. This chapter draws upon a variety of primary and secondary sources, but one substantive reference for records after 1900 is an article written by Ronald Nowak titled "The Red Wolf in Louisiana" (1967), which provides a rich and detailed account of southeastern wolves.

Chapters 10 and 11 include a fresh take on historical events. The majority of this material is sourced from the personal archive of Curtis Carley and, to some degree, the recollections of his widow, Sara Hanson Carley. Records in Carley's archive include his original monthly field reports from the Beaumont Field Station, correspondence, internal reports, notes from his public talks and slide shows, and the occasional personal journal entry.

Chapter 12 draws upon a variety of sources to reconstruct past events. Main sources for this chapter include interviews and conversations with Warren Parker, Chris Lucash, Art Beyer, Neil Hutt, Michael Stoskopf, and Lisette Waits; program newsletters and government reports; and events recorded in Jan DeBlieu's book, *Meant to Be Wild* (1991).

Chapter 8 also deserves special mention. This chapter attempts to outline the debates over red wolf origins. It is by no means a comprehensive analysis of all the scientific literature that has been published on red wolf genetics; rather, it is meant to characterize the competing origin models and the disagreement among experts as to which of these may be correct.

All of the places and names in this book are real, but there are two special cases. In general, the red wolf program names pack territories based on geographical references. The dominant breeding animals that occupy these territories may change over time, but the pack names stay the same. In two cases, the program biologists had begun using the names of private landowners to reference the packs. To protect the privacy of these individuals, I agreed to alter these pack names to older, geographically based names. Here, then, they are called the New Lakes pack and the Newlands pack.

I should also note that world authorities on mammals disagree as to what red wolves are. While some experts classify them as a subspecies of the gray wolf, others classify them as their own species. There is a long history of viewing them as something *other* than gray wolves, however. Because I find the evidence compelling that red wolves are a separate species from gray wolves—or at the very least, that the historic source population of southeastern wolves was its own species, from which the modern population was bred—I use the name *Canis rufus*. It is my hope that this story will entertain, educate, and inspire all who are interested in North America's native fauna, and especially its dwindling but magnificent predators.

# THE SECRET WORLD OF RED WOLVES

# PART I
## The Red Wolf Today

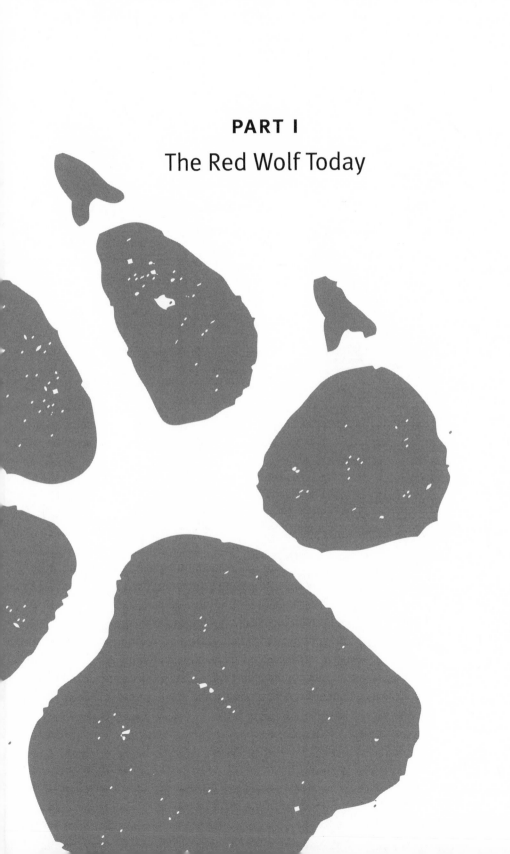

If wolves are animals of savage and demonic qualities, as myth and folklore portray them, then red wolves have been doubly damned. They are despised, on the one hand, by people who think of wolves as bloodthirsty and sinister, yet they are often overlooked by those who might be expected to rush to their defense.

JAN DEBLIEU, *Meant to Be Wild: The Struggle to Save Endangered Species through Captive Breeding* (1991)

## CHAPTER 1

# Red Wolves of the Albemarle Peninsula

Red wolves are cryptic animals. Some people believe they arose as a unique New World canid and loped through southeastern North America. To them, these mysterious creatures are living symbols of the region's diverse natural heritage. Other people believe that red wolves are man-made constructs of nature that have interbred, for an unknown period of time, with another maligned and often misunderstood canid: the common coyote. Like wolves the world over, red wolves bear the burden of people's myths and misinformation about them. Folklore has taught us that wolves are cunning killers, yet red wolves are viewed as unnaturally meek. Like many myths, these contrasting visions hold only granules of truth.

But what is the truth about red wolves? For the curious minded, facts can be difficult to suss out because the trail of scientific literature on these creatures begins at the precise point in time when the species was straddling the gulf between survival and extinction. Long before early naturalists and scientists began to take serious notice of red wolves, European settlers and early Americans were busy exterminating native predators from eastern forests. When biologists finally began studying them formally in the twentieth century, red wolves were "ninety-nine miles down a one-hundred-mile-long road to extinction," according to former U.S. Fish and Wildlife Service (FWS) biologist Curtis J. Carley. And Carley should know, because he put a good amount of elbow grease and late nights into coaxing them back from the brink. Red wolves are now one of the most endangered canids in North America and the world. After flirting with extinction in the 1970s, they were bred in captivity and reintroduced to a forested and swampy region of northeastern North Carolina known as the Albemarle Peninsula. This land is a mere single-digit fraction of their historic southeastern range.

These days, most people will never catch a glimpse of a wild red wolf. This extremely rare and elusive canid is famously wary of people, and it also is mainly nocturnal. Those folks who do spy a red wolf in the wild are insanely lucky. I count myself among them.

A common misconception is that the red wolf has fur similar in color to the bright auburn of a red fox. Even its Latinized name, *Canis rufus*, entices our mind's eye with red-hued promises. But a red wolf's coat mainly varies from tawny to beige to black speckled. The red is relegated to cinnamon-colored hairs that tinge the backs of its ears and the tops of its muzzle. This is not the showy red of a scarlet tanager. Rather, it is the muted red of American red squirrels and red-tailed hawks. The red wolf's pelage is under-laid with light brown fur but punched through in spots with the organic red of a moist, decaying hardwood tree. In some, the reddish coloring runs across the shoulders and zips like racing stripes down the legs. The forelegs of most red wolves lighten in overall color compared to their torsos, but some also have black bars. You might think of the name "red wolf" in a com-parative sense, too, because its overall hue is indeed red when compared to the slate coloration of the western gray wolf. Historically, some wolves in Louisiana and Florida were seen with black coats, though the genes driv-ing this morph are now lost to the red wolf—and our viewing pleasure—forever.

Red wolves are lanky. Their lean, long-legged carriage suggests a muscled greyhound's proportions more than an archetypal wolf's. They have long ears and a snout that is much broader than a coyote's. Males range in size from fifty-five to eighty-five pounds, which fits snugly in between a coyote (fifteen to forty pounds) and a gray wolf (seventy to 120 pounds). Female red wolves may weigh anywhere from forty-two to sixty-five pounds. Their short and shaggy ruff is a reminder that southeastern wolves do not need the thick, winterized fur of their northern and western cousins. Most have white fur under their chins that creeps up to line their upper lips and lighter fur around their eyes that sometimes hints at an almond shape. From a dis-tance, this adds to the perception that their eyes are slanted. Their backs and tails are often a mix of light and dark hairs, while the undersides of their legs are comparatively lighter. Many hold their ears at a characteristic forty-five-degree angle, which results in a head shape reminiscent of an in-verted triangle. Their tail tips appear to be daubed with charcoal, and, like gray wolves, they often hold their tails out and parallel to the ground while trotting or running.

The name "red wolf" was originally what people in central Texas called the small wolves with which they shared the land. It is said that these wolves had a reddish color, though some historians have wondered if perhaps their coats were simply reflecting the late-afternoon Texas sun. People in other areas had other names for them, but the term "red wolf" became popularized in the mid-twentieth century, and the name soon stuck for all of the Southeast's diminutive forest wolves.

The first time I stumbled across the name "red wolf," I thought it must have been a mistake. Like everyone else, I knew of gray wolves. But a *red* wolf? At the time, I was searching through scientific literature on predator reintroductions for my master's thesis, which examined stakeholder beliefs and values in the Mexican gray wolf (*C.1. baileyi*) reintroduction program in Arizona and New Mexico. I was stunned to learn that the very first wolves reintroduced in the United States were red wolves and not the gray wolves of Yellowstone, as I had naively assumed. I was instantly intrigued, but I had little time to pursue this curiosity. Yet as my thesis research deepened, I continually bumped into papers about *C. rufus*, and so I began to stash them in a file labeled "To Read Later." After graduation, I happened to move to North Carolina, four hours inland from the Albemarle Peninsula where reintroduced red wolves were making a comeback. My festering curiosity cracked wide open.

The Albemarle may appear, at first glance, to be an odd place to nurture a rare canid back to self-sustaining numbers. Take out a U.S. map and look at North Carolina. Trace your finger along the state's deeply sinuous coastline and notice how a gnarled, bulging piece of earth juts eastward into the center of a skewed, V-shaped archipelago known as the Outer Banks. This projection is the Albemarle Peninsula. It is bounded on three sides by water: the Albemarle Sound to the north, the Croatan Sound to the east, and the Pamlico Sound to the south. These sounds, plus a few rivers, form a natural barrier partially hemming in the wolves, but they are free to leave the peninsula at its western neck where the Albemarle melts into the upper coastal plain. And some wolves do leave.

The peninsula itself is a patchwork of small family farms, large corporate farms, state game lands, and national wildlife refuges. Here, there are more dirt roads than paved ones. It's not a wilderness, and it's not pristine. It's a landscape altered by humans, complete with a naval bombing range, highways, small towns, fishing villages, scattered rural homes, and intricate landscape-scaled plumbing that bleeds vast swamps and wetlands of their freshwater.

The Albemarle's main visitors are wildlife watchers, fishermen, and hunters of deer, bear, and waterfowl. The nearby Outer Banks, on the other hand, is an East Coast travelers' hot spot. Nags Head, Kill Devil Hills, and Cape Hatteras National Seashore are well-known vacation destinations: every year, an estimated 5 million tourists flow through the ecologically fragile coastal islands. Three-fifths of these tourists flock to the beaches in the high season, which runs from late May to September. The lion's share of them originate from North Carolina, Virginia, Pennsylvania, Maryland, and Washington, D.C. Some visitors arrive by car on routes that cut across the peninsula. The Albemarle Peninsula and the Outer Banks are geographically close, but they are worlds apart socially and economically. Most tourists only pass through the peninsula on U.S. Highway 64 en route to the Atlantic Ocean. They probably think of it as nothing more than an eighty-mile-long, two-lane, fifty-five-mile-per-hour annoyance impeding their arrival at the beach. As they cut through Alligator River National Wildlife Refuge, tourists may not even notice the series of yellow caution signs that declare: "Red Wolf Crossing Next 10 Miles."

In the late summer of 2009, I was one of the many tourists on my way to the Outer Banks. But I wasn't there for a seaside vacation, as alluring as that seemed. I was visiting, for the first time, to learn about federal efforts to recover the red wolf. With few places to stay on the mainland peninsula itself, I opted to stay in Nags Head. My visit to the red wolf recovery area was spurred by a series of questions: How are the red wolves managed, and what are the species' main conservation challenges? How is the FWS dealing with the red wolf's propensity to hybridize with coyotes, now that coyotes have infiltrated all of North Carolina? Is the recovery program working? But more than anything, I wanted to know why so few people, other than a handful of specialists and scientists, seemed to know much about red wolves. When I first moved to North Carolina and met other writers, science communicators, wildlife lovers, and outdoorsy people — many of whom had lived in the state for decades — I peppered them with questions about red wolves. Some expressed wide-eyed wonderment that a *wolf* inhabited their state. Others shook their heads and called them hybrids. How is it, I wondered, that an animal as charismatic, symbolic, and polarizing as a wolf can fly under the radar of so many people?

The evening I arrived in Nags Head, I entertained myself with a walk on the beach. I considered whether, historically, red wolves had ever traversed the Outer Banks themselves. Only a few hundred years ago, long before people developed these coastal barrier islands with condos and homes squashed up against bulbous beach dunes, there would have been impenetrable scrub and sea oats. The shore birds I spied skittering in the sand and darting from the rhythmic surf surges would have been more numerous. And maybe, just maybe, red wolves had trotted through the maritime thicket and nosed around red bays, sweet gums, scrubby live oaks, and lob-

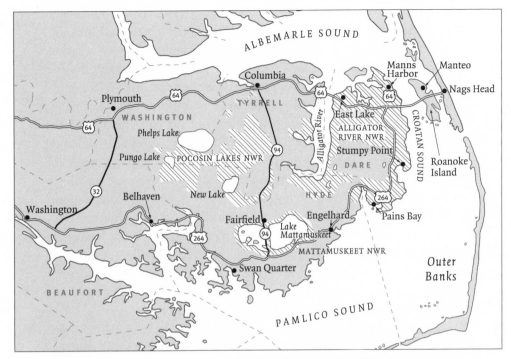

The Red Wolf Recovery Area. When the red wolf was first reintroduced in 1987, its recovery area comprised only Alligator River National Wildlife Refuge. Today, it encompasses most of the Albemarle Peninsula.

lolly pines intent on scaring up rabbits for a quick meal. Maybe they visited the beaches to forage for delicacies like stranded fish or seasonal turtle hatchlings. It's hard to say. Scientists have so few reliable historic observations from which to know their behavior and ecology at the time of European contact, and so few fossils of red wolves from which to tease their ancient natural history. There's really no reason to think they used the coastal barrier islands; but then again, there's also no reason to assume they didn't. Wolves are excellent swimmers.

Today, biologists talk about the red wolf in terms of two different populations: a captive population of about 200 individuals and a wild population that fluctuates between 100 and 120 individuals grouped within about twenty-nine different family units. The captive population stems from fourteen of the last wild red wolves known to have lived in the Southeast. They were bred to safeguard the species from extinction, and individuals from this population eventually were reintroduced into the wild. Actually, it's not quite accurate to say "into the wild" because the natural habitat within their restoration area, like many places in our country, is now fundamentally transformed by human activities. The captive population lives dispersed throughout forty-one zoos and licensed facilities across the nation.

The land used for the FWS's Red Wolf Recovery Program spans five North Carolina counties: Dare, Tyrrell, Hyde, Beaufort, and Washington. All together, the program utilizes 680,000 acres of federal and state public lands. With the help of private landowners who are cooperating with the FWS, and who collectively add another 1.002 million acres of land, a total of 1.7 million acres are available for red wolves to live, hunt, and breed. The three largest pieces of public land in the recovery program are the Alligator River National Wildlife Refuge (154,000 acres), Pocosin Lakes National Wildlife Refuge (110,106 acres), and Mattamuskeet National Wildlife Refuge (50,180 acres). The land in between these tracts contains private homes and small farms, plus state game lands and conservation lands. Nearly 60 percent of the red wolf reintroduction area is privately owned, and 40 percent is public land—a subversion of the idea that large carnivores need a core refuge of entirely public land mostly devoid of people.

Red wolves survive on the Albemarle Peninsula by catching raccoons, otters, muskrats, rabbits, squirrels, rats, birds, and even lowly bullfrogs and mice. They've been known to make off with a few domestic chickens and goats, too. Historically, they likely preyed on beaver, though this wetland-engineering animal is now absent from much of its former range. Red wolves also take down white-tailed deer. Their deer-eating ways may irritate the local hunters, but one of their dinner-menu items provides a valuable ecological service: red wolves eat nonnative nutria. Nutria are large rodents that live in wetlands and are native to South America. Their Latin genus name, *Myocastor*, is a blending of two words: mouse and beaver. Nutria use their four-clawed digits to dig out roots, and they have a huge appetite for vegetative matter. Every day, they eat enough plants and roots to equal about 25 percent of their twelve-pound body weight. Such an appetite wields destruction upon sensitive wetlands, but red wolves help to limit the the nutria population.

A wild red wolf might live for four to eight years in the Albemarle. One female lived to be thirteen years old. She was the matriarch of the Milltail pack for most of her life. When she aged, she was kicked out of her territory by a younger and stronger female, but she eked out a living elsewhere. In 2010, just before she died, she wandered back to her old territory and was later found to have passed away peacefully near her old den site. It was a first-of-its-kind behavior observed by the recovery team. This wolf was one of the lucky ones. Many red wolves die from human-related incidents, like being shot or getting mowed down on one of the many roads that incise the peninsula. Some also die from aggression with other red wolves, from infections due to mange, and from uterine infections. Other, rarer causes of death include getting eaten by alligators, being injured in a hurricane, drowning, or encountering pure random bad luck, such as the poor wolf that choked on a raccoon's kidney while eating the procyonid for dinner. A red wolf born and raised in the captive breeding program may live to ten or fifteen years of age.

From what we can piece together from their natural history, red wolves evolved in North America. Some people think they arose in the East, independently from gray wolves, from an archaic canid lineage shared with coyotes. Others think they arose as a relatively recent hybrid from the interbreeding of gray wolves and coyotes. Before European settlement, red wolves are thought to have ranged from the mid-Atlantic South to modern-day Florida, inland along the Gulf Coast states into central Texas, and from there north and throughout the Ohio River valley. They dwelled in eastern Kansas, eastern Oklahoma, Missouri, Indiana, and southern Illinois, extending west only to where prairies erupted in the midcontinental plains. They shared their range with another large, native obligate carnivore: the eastern cougar. Sadly, the eastern cougar is now extinct, while the red wolf barely managed to keep a toehold on existence.

Today, the red wolf's present and future are tied to the Albemarle Peninsula. The area harbors a unique beauty and ecological sense of place. The land lies below the Atlantic Flyway and beckons hundreds of thousands of migratory waterfowl from the skies. Tundra swans, snow geese, wood ducks, American black ducks, ruddy ducks, hooded mergansers, and northern shovelers descend upon its wetlands during their migrations. But birds are not alone in favoring the Albemarle; the area is also home to one of the densest populations of black bears east of the Mississippi. Bobcat, foxes, raccoons, river otters, beavers, flying squirrels, big brown bats, barred owls, pygmy rattlesnakes, marsh rabbits, long-tailed weasels, peregrine falcons, and cerulean warblers all use the peninsula's farmlands, estuaries, lakes, marshes, swamps, variety of forests, and a unique habitat called a pocosin.

"Pocosin" is a word from the Algonquian Native American language that translates to "swamp on a hill." Pocosins are very flat but tend to be a little more elevated than surrounding areas. They are defined by a layer of poorly draining peat soil—mostly composed of decaying leaves, sticks, and other vegetative matter—that holds water like a sponge and releases it slowly to

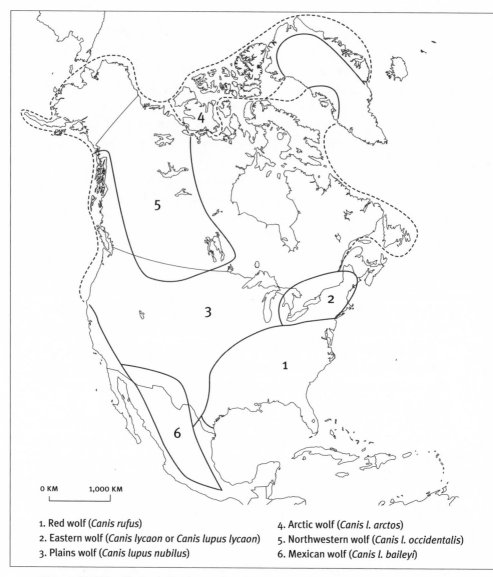

1. Red wolf (*Canis rufus*)
2. Eastern wolf (*Canis lycaon* or *Canis lupus lycaon*)
3. Plains wolf (*Canis lupus nubilus*)
4. Arctic wolf (*Canis l. arctos*)
5. Northwestern wolf (*Canis l. occidentalis*)
6. Mexican wolf (*Canis l. baileyi*)

Historic Wolf Distribution in North America. The red wolf was once thought to range north of Pennsylvania due to specimens from New York and Maine that were assessed by Ronald Nowak to be *Canis rufus* by their physical features. However, genetic analyses recently grouped these specimens with *Canis lycaon* (eastern wolf). (Adapted from Ronald M. Nowak, "Wolf Evolution and Taxonomy," in *Wolves: Behavior, Ecology, and Conservation*, edited by L. D. Mech and L. Boitani, 239–58. Chicago: University of Chicago Press [2003]. Reprinted by permission of University of Chicago Press.)

nearby areas. It can take a hundred years to form one inch of peat. Pocosin Lakes National Wildlife Refuge, on the Albemarle Peninsula, harbors deposits of the black matter ranging in depth from a few inches to ten feet. Pocosins of eastern North Carolina used to form the southernmost end of the Great Dismal Swamp. If you walk through one, you'll find thick and dense growth of low brush and evergreens, such as loblolly and pond pine, red bay and sweet bay, greenbrier, and wax myrtle. The area is also laced with freshwater streams. Some of these streams appear black, but if you scoop a cupful of their water, it could pass for luminous, golden-brown iced tea.

Every place is unique if you consider the special forces of geology, time, and climate that helped to create it. The Albemarle Peninsula is a part of the lower coastal plain, which stretches from Virginia down to South Carolina and inland to about Interstate 95 in North Carolina. The topography of the lower coastal plain formed during the Ice Ages of the last 2.6 million years. At the beginning of the last Ice Age, about 25,000 years ago, sea levels plummeted to about 400 feet below today's present levels. As the climate warmed around 18,000 to 10,000 years ago, floodplain forests formed as rivers drained to the sea from the comparatively elevated piedmont. Longleaf pine savannas sprawled across North Carolina's coastal plain. On the Albemarle Peninsula, pond pines grew in the developing pocosins, and loblolly pines were sprinkled in among swamp black gums, cypresses, and Atlantic white cedars that spread throughout the tidal and nonriverine swamps. In the wet hardwood forests, laurel oaks, swamp chestnut oaks, and cherrybark oaks dominated. Red wolves likely used these forests and swamps, living and hunting within them.

The most powerful landscape feature of the Albemarle Peninsula today is the ever-present interplay of low-lying land and water. Bogs, swamps, and freshwater and estuary marshes blanket the area like a patchwork quilt of ecosystems connected by a common attribute: water. Water formed it; water sustains it; and in the future, water could be the force that reclaims large swaths of this land for the sea.

Though the peninsula is unique ecologically, it is also an economically depressed region—a string of sparsely settled counties and small towns that time and development seem to have forgotten, a place where farming communities encompass vast stretches of corn, soy, and cotton fields and hold out against agribusinesses. In winter, when the agricultural fields are cleared and laid bare, the land appears dismal and bleak. But come May, June, July, and August, it swells green with fecundity. The sultry, humid summer air can feel as thick as a wet cloak, and biting bugs don't seem to care too much which season it is. Visitors are just as likely to see dilapidated wooden shacks decaying on their foundations or abandoned fishing vessels listing on their hulls in a side yard as they are to see upscale brick homes with manicured lawns. There are pockets of rural tranquility, small towns where people make a good living, take great pride in their well-kept homes and public spaces, and enjoy country living with access to fertile hunting and fishing grounds. Yet time does seem to have forgotten other places in the peninsula. Or perhaps more accurately, some places may have wanted to be forgotten. The first time I passed through communities here, I felt like I was entering a time warp to the 1950s. It wasn't just the midcentury ranch houses and beat-up old Ford work trucks that created this aura. It was also the mindset of folks I met—people who quickly sized me up as someone who had grown up with either concrete or grass under her feet.

Many people who live here earn their living connected to the outdoors: farming, managing land, guiding, and fishing. Some citizens hear the howls of red wolves at dusk and dawn; others find their tracks and scat. Farmers working atop tractors and combines have the best seat in the house when it comes to wolf watching, because red wolves will often patrol the perimeter of agricultural fields and wait for the farm machinery to flush out tasty rodents and rabbits. There are people who live here who may be unaware they share their land with wild wolves. There are also residents who are convinced these wolves were let loose to the wrong area. Some citizens resent the wolves' presence, although their reasons often vary. And there are those who quietly tolerate the red wolves, even those who find their own existence enriched by sharing their farm fields and woods with a native southeastern predator.

To me, the Albemarle Peninsula is a place of rich contrasts: a land of conserved ecosystems fragmented by heavy farming and of natural and rural beauty marred by poverty. Of course, it is also unique because it is the only spot in the entire world where red wolves live by their own wild cunning, shoehorned between the North Carolina upper coastal plain and the Atlantic Ocean. It was into this water-riddled and sparsely settled landscape that four pairs of red wolves were released within Alligator River National Wildlife Refuge on September 14, 1987. Their reintroduction was nothing short of a biological, political, and sociological miracle.

Hundreds of years earlier, the war against eastern wolves had begun when Europeans arrived in the New World and unpacked their Old World fears, myths, and folklore regarding these wild canids. When people encountered the East's wolves, they lumped them in with mythologies based on Old World gray wolves, *Canis lupus*, which paint wolves as cunning livestock stalkers and murderers that will stop at nothing to shred flesh for a blood meal. The East's wolves were persecuted and exterminated as settlers pulled the forests down around them. Later, they were targeted by federal programs bent on destroying predators.

By the early 1900s, the remaining beleaguered red wolves interbred on a large scale with coyotes in the extreme southwestern portions of their range in central Texas and the Ozarks. These interspecies couplings were the metaphorical last gasp of their survival instinct. Some researchers think that it was only after red wolves had been largely eliminated from their historic range that coyotes crept eastward and claimed the transformed landscape, now empty of wolves, for their own. Coyotes proved much more resilient and adaptable by living near farms and even within towns and cities. In short, they tolerated and even thrived in close proximity to people, a habit that red wolves simply never acquired.

By the time scientists noticed, there were nearly as many, if not more, red wolf–coyote hybrids on the landscape than there were pure red wolves. Yet, a few red wolves remained. They held the physical characteristics of the species, as far as we are able to determine them to have been. These animals retreated to the swamps and no-man's-lands of far southeastern Texas and southwestern Louisiana. The last of their kind, they were pushed up against the Gulf of Mexico in coastal habitat too bug- and tick-laced for people to desire. Enough survived to give the species a new start, with the guiding hands of humans and science. But the rest—nearly a quarter of a continent's worth of wolves and their pups—were lost to poisons, wolf hounds, traps, bullets, and dynamite. It's mind-boggling to imagine how a large mammal that was once so widespread could be lost to near extinction in such a short time.

Before the red wolf was declared functionally extinct in the wild in 1980, the FWS spearheaded a program to breed the predator in zoos and sanctuaries across the nation. It was a daring, first-of-its-kind experiment and a desperate step to prevent losing the species entirely. The red wolf stock utilized for this captive breeding program was plucked from among the last known wild red wolves captured in the 1970s in Texas and Louisiana. At the time, there were many unknowns about captive breeding of carnivores. It was not the first or the last time that efforts to save the red wolf would push scientific boundaries. Today's wild red wolves that inhabit the Albemarle Peninsula can trace their pedigree to the captive breeding program. The Red Wolf Recovery Program believes their program marks several firsts:

*Canis rufus* was the first listed species for which the FWS chose to control a functional extinction in the wild with the purpose of later reintroducing animals bred from captive stock; it was the focus of one of the earliest, if not the first, FWS captive-breeding programs of carnivores; it was the first wolf to be reintroduced in the United States; and it has the distinction of being the first wolf in the lower forty-eight states to be shot with a tranquilizer dart from a helicopter, which is now a widespread management practice. Because the recovery efforts to save the red wolf have continually pushed the envelope of established wildlife science, those studying it seem to be always poised on the leading edge of their field.

The red wolf was also included in the first batch of species listed under the Endangered Species Act (ESA) in 1973, and it was even included in toothless legal lists that predated the ESA in 1967. It became one of the original flagship species the FWS sought to restore, along with the Florida panther, the grizzly bear, the Sonoran pronghorn, and the Caribbean monk seal. Today, we take these sorts of recovery programs for granted as a catchall safeguard to stave off extinction for many imperiled species; and for the most part, we demand that these programs work. But when the red wolf program was launched, the FWS had no idea if success was even achievable. There was nothing for them to measure their planning and efforts against. As luck would have it, the initial phases of the recovery program coincided with a point in history when a newfound awareness of environmental degradation gripped the nation's conscience in the 1970s, and the FWS enjoyed fairly widespread support for their actions. The roots of the Red Wolf Recovery Program helped create a blueprint for captive breeding programs for the black-footed ferret, the California condor, and the Mexican gray wolf. Without the FWS, the red wolf would be grouped in the same category as the Tasmanian wolf, the quagga, the passenger pigeon, the dodo, and the golden toad—all recently declared extinct. Nothing would remain of it except a few teeth, bones, and hides preserved in museums, and maybe a few undiscovered fossils lodged somewhere in dank soil.

Today, red wolves embody the crisis that large predators face globally: a restriction of their historic range, a landscape that has changed radically since the time they first evolved, and the blooming presence of people and our roads, farms, homes, and cities. But red wolves also suffer from the added misfortune in their recent history of a devastating identity crisis. Not an identity crisis of their own making, but rather humanity's inability to identify them scientifically. Ever since biologists first began studying red wolves, they have been stumped by their taxonomy and their exact relationship to other wolves and wild canids. The public's perception of red wolves also remains murky, clouded by accusations of genetic impurity due to their habit of hybridizing with coyotes.

How can science ask society to conserve that which it doesn't fully understand?

When I first began learning about red wolves, this was the question that kept coming back to me. It was intriguing enough that I decided to commit a significant amount of my time to documenting what red wolves are today; exploring how the wild population is managed; and understanding the contradictory concepts of the species' origins, its past history in the East, and what its main conservation challenges are heading into the future.

The morning after my beach stroll, I set out to meet a red wolf biologist named Ryan Nordsven. He had agreed to show me Sandy Ridge, which is a secure facility where the recovery program holds wild red wolves that are sick or being held for other reasons. A few wolves that are part of the captive breeding program are also kept there permanently. But the facility's location is somewhat of a secret, and I was supposed to go first to the FWS's Red Wolf Recovery Program headquarters in the small town of Manteo. Manteo is on Roanoke Island, a low and narrow, kidney-bean-shaped island wedged in the sounds between the Albemarle Peninsula and the Outer Banks. It is smothered in live oaks, and its perimeter is bordered by thick marsh grasses. From Manteo, the red wolf biologists make tracks across the whole peninsula. As I drove through the marsh and into town, my hope was that Ryan or one of the other biologists might let me tag along as they worked with the world's only population of wild C. rufus. Little did I know then how deep Ryan and the others would ultimately take me into the secret world of red wolves.

## CHAPTER 2
# A Morning at Sandy Ridge

It's only sunup, but if I'm lucky, I might see my first wild red wolf by sundown. My mind buzzes with anticipation. Golden, late-summer morning light licks at the coastal marshes surrounding Roanoke Island. Wide expanses of cord grass and black needle rush create a textured canvas for the sun's amber rays. The low, beige marsh grass is punctuated by mounded islands of green scrub, pine trees, and hardwood hammocks. Their presence indicates changes in elevation and soil just substantial enough (probably only an inch or two) for trees to carve out a living in the estuary. In the distance, pine trees taper out into the marsh at the horizon line until their trunks are visible singly, like a row of slim men marching to sea. I arrive at the Red Wolf Recovery Program's office and enter the foyer. Only a few paces from the door stands a dog-sized articulated skeleton. A small sign beneath it reads: Red Wolf, *Canis rufus*. With the flesh gone, it is easy to see how the wild canid balances on its toes. Scientists call this posture digitigrade, which means the animal walks perched on its digits rather than with the metatarsals (middle foot bones) flat on the ground, as both bears and humans do.

The program staffer who arranged my field trip to Sandy Ridge greets me. She waves me to a government truck parked out front and ferries me to the facility which is within Alligator River National Wildlife Refuge. We pass estuarine wetlands and freshwater marshes. The truck barrels down stark white refuge roads made of crushed shells and gravel. Low-lying wetlands spread out on either side. Dark piles of scat stand out in stark relief to the white gravel about every 200 feet. Some of the droppings look crumbly and dry, but others appear wet. Fresh. They are also large, a good eight ounces or more. They are the markings of American black bears. We follow the bear piles for about a mile and then turn onto another gravel road. A yellow and black swallowtail butterfly darts along the road ahead. I will it to move. Too late—our champagne-colored bumper mows it down. We enter a part of the refuge cut off to visitors by a locked swing-arm gate, and then we mow down another lackadaisical swallowtail. But we stop to admire a turtle. Slick rouge stripes behind its eyes glisten like wet paint and give it away as a painted turtle, common in North Carolina. We park beside a rustic wood cabin with an orange stubby river kayak leaning on its end in a screened porch. A small pond lies about twenty feet from the cabin's steps. A pileated woodpecker drums a rat-a-tat tune that reverberates in the surrounding woods. The staffer carefully points out that this area is not open to the public and that they don't typically allow tours of the facility. I vow to soak in all the day's details.

Sandy Ridge is an outdoor holding facility where the Fish and Wildlife Service keeps a few captive red wolves beneath a dense canopy of hardwood trees. Wild wolves are brought here temporarily to recuperate from wounds or sickness. The cabin houses a rotating cadre of barely paid interns, usually students seeking wildlife management experience. They live here for twelve weeks at a time with no potable water, plumbing, or electricity and a stipend of a few hundred dollars a month for groceries. They also get access to a government truck. Given the ruggedness of the surrounding woods, the remoteness of the location, and the lack of communications, access to a truck is a huge selling point—as is working directly with the red wolves. The interns feed the wolves of Sandy Ridge and clean their pens. They also administer medicine to its wild visitors. The current caretaker is taking a rare day off, and one of the red wolf biologists, Ryan Nordsven, is tending the animals this morning.

I can't see the holding pens from the clearing by the cabin, but the woods are so dense, they may be only thirty feet past the tree line and I wouldn't know. I walk down a dirt road leading from the cabin to the wolf pens. Deer flies dart around my bare legs. As I approach a ten-foot-high chain-link fence, a man waves and opens the gate from the inside. As I pass through, I notice a second chain-link fence about six feet inside the perimeter of the first.

"I'm Ryan," the man says. "So you're the writer who's here to learn about red wolves?"

"Yes, as much as I can," I reply. He shakes my hand while holding a shovel in his other hand. Ryan has sandy brown hair, a closely trimmed goatee, and blue eyes set in Scandinavian features. He's six feet tall, well muscled, and looks like he could wrestle a wolf to the ground with each hand and still have strength left over. By now it is late morning, and the sun's heat presses down. We amble into the shade of several large loblolly pines and live oaks. The interior of Sandy Ridge is comprised of about sixteen holding pens for wolves, fifty-by-fifty feet each, plus several outbuildings.

Outside the perimeter fence, the hardwood forest of the refuge grows thick and dense. Gum, pine, oak, bay, and red maple trees compete for limited space, light, and nutrients. Their vegetative mass presses against the fence's metal weave. Inside the perimeter, some trees and lots of brush have been cleared to create workspace, but many tall trees remain and provide shade.

Each pen is enclosed with fencing that angles inward at the top to prevent the occupants from climbing out. The pens are built on bare soil and are open to the forest canopy above. Natural vegetation grows inside, and some pens have privacy screens. Ryan explains that the screens make the red wolves feel more protected and prevent them from seeing each other. Because the wolves are so territorial, being in close proximity or even visual proximity to each other can stress them. The fencing also runs unseen for several feet into the pen's underground interior, parallel to the ground, so they cannot tunnel their way out. Not that they don't try.

Ryan jams the shovel into the ground, blade first, and leaves it standing upright. "One of the things the caretaker does is pen inspections, and so they're responsible for walking each pen and checking for digging holes and filling them in. I was just filling in a hole in that back corner right before you arrived." He points to his left. "Some of them are real diggers."

"Do any dig themselves out?" I ask.

"Yeah, last year we had some real escape artists," he says. "There's a pen with three sisters over there, and one dug through some rusted-out skirting at the fence base in the rear of the pen. We got a call from the caretaker to come quick because they'd all three gotten out. It took a while to catch them, but we eventually got them back in and the hole patched."

I point to the double fencing and ask if it was designed to keep the wolves in. No, Ryan says; wolves used to come up to the fence and cause trouble, so the team created a double-layered fence to protect the captive wolves inside. Plus, in the program's very early days, free-roaming red wolves approached a fenced pen and injured a female red wolf inside by catching hold of her leg through the chain link. They shredded her flesh to ribbons. Her injuries were so severe that she was euthanized.

Ryan tells me that at the simplest level, the program's work boils down to keeping track of which red wolves are paired together, determining which wolves are holding a territory and where, and checking to make sure that the animal's telemetry radio collars work. Telemetry is a remote-sensing method that allows the biologists to track individual animals wearing collars that emit a unique radio frequency. By knowing each collar's unique frequency, the scientists track each wolf's movement from the air or the ground with minimal invasiveness. Each week, the biologists fly at an altitude of 500 to 3,000 feet over the recovery area. They record where the packs are and where animals within each pack spend their time. The aerial work helps them map out wolf territories, interactions between animals, and even an individual animal's behavior.

Starting in January or February, the red wolf team spends a lot of time verifying which wolves are spending time together in an effort to interpret if paired breeders might produce puppies. Then in late March and early April, they begin scrutinizing the female wolves' movements to see if they stick to a specific area. If the female stays in the same spot for several days, there's a good chance she's preparing a den for puppies or that she's given birth. Throughout the month of April, the team spends nearly every day out in the field trying to track down suspected dens to document if there are puppies and, if so, how many. Once they find a den, they draw blood samples from each puppy. The samples are then screened by a geneticist, who looks for the presence of some seventeen genetic markers that are used to distinguish red wolves from other wild canids. The markers help determine whether the modern wolves are descendants of the fourteen red wolves that were used to found the captive breeding program. For the past decade or so, the results of these genetic tests have dictated, along with an extensive pedigree database, what the program considers to be a true red wolf versus a hybrid red wolf–coyote cross. In cases where the biologists know the identity of one wolf in a breeding pair but not the other, the genetic tests are crucial for assessing the pair's offspring.

Puppy season takes the whole month, and the recovery program team might spend all of May wrapping up their search for dens. In late May and June, sometimes they spend time revisiting a few select dens and working with veterinarians to surgically implant radio transmitters in puppies that are about six weeks old. Because puppies are too small for radio collars, the finger-sized transmitters function like an internal radio collar. This helps the team track the animals as they grow. Red wolf puppies grow very fast; their skulls reach nearly 90 percent of their adult length by six months of age. Their canines erupt and are fully emerged by the end of their first year, when their skulls also complete their growth. The biologists back off from tracking the dens or trapping any of the wolves during the summer months when it's too hot. When the coolness of fall settles in, the team begins trapping the year's new arrivals—pups that have grown to nearly adult size—to fit them with radio collars. They also trap to survey all of the canids in specific areas, especially if it is an area where they may be unsure whether the canids present are wolves, coyotes, or feral dogs. That usually keeps the team occupied until January, when they again start the cycle of tracking breeding pairs.

"We only have red wolves here at Sandy Ridge now," Ryan says. "Summer is our slow season. But by fall, this place will be packed with wolves and coyotes."

"Why do you hold coyotes here?" I ask.

"If we know one is holding a territory, we trap it, sterilize it and put a radio collar on it," Ryan explains. "They stay here at Sandy Ridge while they recover, and then we release them back to their territory." By sterilizing coyotes that set up territories in the red wolf recovery area and then tracking them, the red wolf biologists protect the red wolf's unique genome from hybridization with coyotes. But a sterile coyote doesn't solve the red wolf's propensity for running with and mating with coyotes. It only prevents conception. It is an elaborate birth-control scheme to ensure the survival of an endangered species.

One of the quirks of the genus *Canis* is that the various species within it can interbreed and produce fertile offspring. Historically, hybridization of the last wild red wolves with coyotes was the single biggest threat that prompted the FWS to begin capturing the last wolves for breeding in captivity. When the first red wolves were reintroduced to Alligator River in 1987, the nearest coyotes were 500 miles west. Experts thought it would take them eight to ten years to pad their way to the coast—plenty of time, they thought, for red wolves to build up a big population and keep the invading coyotes at bay. But coyotes soon infiltrated the red wolf's recovery area in the early 1990s. Suddenly, the Red Wolf Recovery Program had a problem on its hands: red wolves were once again hybridizing with coyotes.

"Why don't you just trap all the coyotes out of the recovery area?" I ask.

"Even if we could remove them all, then more coyotes would likely just come in and take their territories," Ryan replies. Plus, the team simply doesn't have the manpower to trap all of the coyotes off the peninsula, though they put significant effort into patrolling certain areas to keep coyotes out. Coyotes are too adaptive and elusive for a large-scale trapping program to work permanently. In one of their biological quirks, coyotes are known to have more offspring survive to adulthood when their population is persecuted through lethal control efforts. The rascals can live on practically nothing, and they are prolific breeders to boot.

Red wolves, like all wolves, develop and defend a home range, which is also known as a territory. You might think of a territory as a private hunting ground with specific boundaries. A territory might be patrolled by a single adult red wolf, but more often it is defended by a mated pair. The pair will attack, and even kill, other red wolves and coyotes that they find in their home range. They mark their boundaries with scent posts, which are basically spots where they squirt a little urine onto a tree or other object at sniffing height or on the ground; they also use scent from their anal glands or excrement placed where it will be noticed.

A red wolf pack is usually a breeding male and female and often includes yearling wolves born the season before. But breeding pairs and pack territories are temporal. Pairs sometimes split up and bond with new mates. Territorial boundaries are fought over and redefined. The dynamics are ever changing. On average, today's red wolf territories range in size from about thirty-seven to sixty-eight square miles. The amount of prey present in a given area, and the type of habitat within it, contribute to territory size—as do the energy requirements of the wolf maintaining it—so these numbers vary greatly. The East's ecologically productive forests and swamps may be one reason why red wolves have smaller territories than gray wolves. Red wolves' comparatively smaller stature, which equates to lower energy requirements, is another reason.

The feeling of ten different needles drilling into my ankle distracts me. Biting flies and mosquitoes have zeroed in on us under the shade of the loblolly, where we are both sweating freely. "This is really the worst time of year to be out here," Ryan says in an apologetic tone. Deer flies alight in waves as I swat at my legs. "Fall and spring are beautiful, but summer is brutal. We get ticks, chiggers, deer flies, mosquitoes . . . you name it."

"I can tell. I can't believe I thought shorts would be okay." My deep-woods experience is, I realize now, a bit rusty.

"You ready to see some wolves?" Ryan asks. He sounds like a proud parent. I nod.

The only live red wolves I'd seen previously were display animals on exhibit at the Museum of Life and Science in Durham, North Carolina, and the North Carolina Zoo in Asheboro. I hop up and we stroll to a nearby pen, where two male red wolves pace nervously. It is hard to look at a leggy red wolf and not escape the thought that these animals are built to run. Their legs appear proportionally longer than those of a gray wolf. The brothers before me are about five feet long, if you include the tail. Burnt-umber red spreads out from their ears to their shoulders. Their muzzles look long and strong, their chest and waist are less heavyset than a gray wolf's, and their tail is less bushy.

"They look like they're all legs," I say.

"They are a little more leggy than a coyote is, in comparison to their frame," Ryan says. "Especially in summer, when their coat is shorter. It makes them look a lot longer and leaner."

Even though the brothers run along the fence in repetitive circles, they barely make a sound. I stand five feet away and yet can't hear them pant. The sound of leaves stirring under their paws barely registers. Their movements are anxious, yet silent.

We move on to the next pen, which holds a breeding pair and a three-month-old pup. We tiptoe around a corner to a break in the privacy screen. I peek through and see a male jammed against the back corner. He presses his body against the fence's metal weave. The female paces furiously about ten feet in front of him. They stare at us. She paces back and forth, back and forth. Their pup spots us and then bolts along the far wall. He scrambles with his chest low to the ground, like a spooked house cat. He wriggles nose first between the fence and his dad, his ears pressed back. The little guy clasps his tail against his anus.

"I can't believe they're so afraid of us," I say.

"Yeah, even the ones that grow up in captivity often do not ever lose their fear of people," Ryan says. "It's just some basic wild instinct that they maintain, that they haven't lost." Even though these animals are fed three times a week by human hands, they still get agitated when a person approaches. As I watch, the three-month-old puppy pushes deeper into his dad's side. I feel guilty that our presence is causing such unease; then Ryan, along with the biting deer flies, prods us to move on.

We walk to a shed, talking, and Ryan slips on a yellow leather work glove. Only then do I realize that the sawed-off leg of a white-tailed deer lies at our feet. He leans down and picks up the appendage just above the narrow black hoof. "We have a wild red wolf in a rear pen, while she recovers from mange," he explains. While the biologists feed Kibbles 'n Bits to the captive wolves, they can't do that with the wild ones that are temporary guests at Sandy Ridge. After all, they wouldn't want to have wild red wolves sauntering up to a home and leaping up onto the back porch trying to get at a bowl of Kibbles. So they feed the wild wolves frozen meat logs, called carnivore logs, which are carefully designed for wild animals. Or the wolves might get fairly fresh roadkill, if it is available, which is what this wolf is about to dine upon. "Roadkill is like gold for us. Anytime we see it on the side of the road, we just have to have it," Ryan jokes, as he carries the sawed-off leg. "If we don't have a use for it at the time we find it, then we'll just put it in the walk-in freezer and save it for later." (Months later, when the freezer breaks down, I witness him cart a dead deer in his pickup bed for three days in a row, hooves sticking straight up.)

I follow Ryan past the shed to the rear of the facility. The shrubs close in a bit more. I hear a steady tweet and scan the brush. A streak of sunflower yellow and a wisp of gray and white settle down on a branch. A prothonotary warbler splays its tail feathers, flashing blacks and whites like piano keys. This large forest warbler prefers wooded swamps and flooded bottomland forests. The handsome yellow bird flies off as we approach. Ryan opens the door to the sick wolf's pen. For a moment, I think he might chuck the deer leg inside and leave it at that, but he gestures for me to follow him in. I trust that he isn't leading me into a dangerous situation, so I duck behind him. The pen's inside has more trees and shrubs within it than the others I've seen. There are more places for a wolf to hide.

"We'd gotten reports of a wolf with mange, so we'd been trying to trap her since Christmas," he whispers. "We finally got her about six weeks ago. She had one of the worst cases of mange I've ever seen. You wouldn't believe it, but she didn't have a hair left on her body when we got her."

Mange is an infection caused by parasitic sarcoptic mange mites, a relative of ticks, that burrow into living tissue and lay their eggs. At only $\frac{1}{64}$ of an inch long, the oval-shaped beasties can do a whole lot of damage. They tunnel through the top layer of their hosts' skin and emit a substance that triggers an allergic reaction. Excessive scratching can lead the host to wound itself with lesions, which then become infected. The biologists treat their mange-ridden red wolves with antibiotics and Revolution, a pesticide of the ivermectin family commonly applied to domestic dogs. This wolf is healing up nicely, Ryan says.

I scan the pen but don't see any movement. Oak leaves litter the ground, along with bits of bone. The mandible of a deer lies chin down in a patch of leaves. I begin to notice other bones once I look for their shape and color. Some are tinted green with algae. A tart stench assaults my nostrils: rotting flesh. The partial remains of her carnivore log is strewn on the ground. Decomposers like beetles must prefer this pen to the others, where the occupants dine only on Kibbles.

"Where is she?" I whisper.

"She's in the dog box," Ryan whispers back. He sets the deer leg down gently and approaches a waist-high metal box. He explains that they use these boxes to capture the animals to give them vaccination shots or medicine. The red wolves seek refuge through an opening in the side of the box. They feel protected in the cavernous, den-like interior. However, all the biologists have to do is flip a door to shut this opening, and then pry off a lid that allows access from the top. This is what Ryan does. He bids me to come closer, and I peer over the top of the gunmetal gray box. The red wolf lies on her side, panting from the heat. Small bubbles of saliva edge her tongue. Flies swarm off open sores on her forearms, where the mites and her scratching has sparked an infection. She squints balefully at the sudden intrusion of daylight and peeks over her shoulder at us. Tiger stone eyes, deep amber, meet mine for a split second, then cut away. I notice her right ear is ragged and tattered but well healed. Perhaps she'd fought with something, long in the past. Her coat appears to be a uniform beige and is still growing in. When a red wolf loses its fur to mange, its coat grows back in as a creamy beige because pigment-producing cells are destroyed when the skin becomes highly inflamed. She looks resolute in her misery, or perhaps it is simply the endurance of a wild animal that knows the pattern of survival.

"We've got to get rid of these bugs," Ryan says, upset about the flies hovering near her sores. In that instant, I admire the responsibility he feels for taking care of the red wolves. It is one thing to administer routine vaccines and medical injections but quite another to want to remove flies from his patient's wounds.

I gaze at the wolf's lean body, curled into a ball in the hot metal box. My eye catches something pink near her tail, then something dark moves.

"She's so scared of us, she's pooping," I blurt out.

"That's what they do when they're scared," Ryan says. He slowly lowers the lid on her box so that it would not clatter and further rattle her. She now has her privacy back, even if it is a hot, metallic, fly-filled hell. She has the whole fifty-by-fifty-foot pen to roam around, and yet this two-by-three-foot box is where she chooses to be. I begin to get a glimpse of how hard it must be to spend your career conserving an animal that doesn't lose an ounce of affection on you, an animal that you are responsible for keeping fed, whole, and healthy while it makes it abundantly clear through its body language that it would rather be anywhere else on earth than near you.

"They are scared to death of people," Ryan says as we exit the pen. "As scared as some people are of being face-to-face with a wolf, you can pretty much guarantee that they are more scared of you."

I agree. What I'd witnessed led me to question whether red wolves are behaviorally hardwired to be different than their cousins, the western gray wolves. When I was working on my master's degree, I not only heard Mexican gray wolves howling in the wild, but I also got to see four that were kept in captivity at the California Wolf Center in Julian, California. These wolves were slightly smaller than their cousins from the northern Rocky Mountains, but they seemed to harbor the same "don't mess with me" posture as the more-northern gray wolves. When I approached them at their fenced enclosure, they paused from running laps and looked straight at me, as if assessing who I was and if I were a threat. But something in their body language was different from the red wolves I'd just seen. Somehow, the red wolves appeared more anxious, more stressed, by my presence. Their body language screamed that they wanted to dive for cover, hide their bodies, and melt into the refuge of the forest. At Sandy Ridge, in the span of a few minutes, I'd witnessed behavior completely at odds with the way the public conceives of "fearsome" wolves. I'd seen two adult red wolves and a pup pushed into a tizzy because we peeked around a privacy screen at them, and I'd seen a somewhat ill adult female so scared of me that she shat her own bed.

After my morning at Sandy Ridge, I visit downtown Manteo for lunch at Poor Richard's, a popular mom-and-pop sandwich store. It sports a back porch near some docks on the north curve of Shallowbag Bay. Sitting on the porch, eating a sandwich, I spy an aged, faded sign nailed to a dock piling. It reads "Fly the Wolf" in green lettering, with a silhouetted howling wolf sitting above the W. The *Wolf*, it turns out, was a parasailing boat operated by Kitty Hawk Kites, a local kite and kayak rental business. But tourists who purchased tickets to fly above the *Wolf* likely hadn't the faintest idea that there really *were* wolves within a fifteen-mile drive. Though from the little I'd seen, the imperiled canids had zero interest in the tourists.

On the other hand, the locals who live on the Albemarle Peninsula are mostly aware of the presence of the red wolf, but not all of them believe it is a rare species. Some believe that red wolves are hybrid animals that have crossbred themselves out of existence, and that because they are hybrids, they deserve no special protection. The red wolf's natural history is entangled with that of the coyote's; the two species are close cousins. Some critics have argued that what was the red wolf in the past has already gone extinct, and that what remains is not a species unto itself. Others argue that the animal living in the Albemarle Peninsula today is the closest thing we have left to what red wolves once were. It's a raging debate with high stakes.

Trying to understand red wolves is a prime example of what's called the "species problem." This phrase refers to the centuries-old struggle of biologists to define exactly what species are. No current definition works when applied across all taxonomic kingdoms. What defines species in one group—let's say birds—can fail to define species of another group, such as microbes. One of the most widely applied species definitions is the Biological Species Concept, which states that populations that can interbreed and yield fertile offspring are the same species, and populations that can't interbreed are different species. This idea uses reproductive barriers to delineate a population or group of populations as a species. But this concept encounters problems when applied to groups of organisms that obviously differ from each other but are still capable of interbreeding. In the genus *Canis*, wolves (*C. lupus* and *C. rufus*), dogs (*C.l. familiaris*), and coyotes (*C. latrans*) can mate and produce fertile hybrid offspring. Yet most biologists agree that *Canis* includes different species. This means that they see your dog as a different species from a gray wolf, and a gray wolf as a different species from a coyote.

When species exist and their reproductive barriers are porous, what criteria can biologists use to define them? And what to do with organisms that readily hybridize, such as the red wolf? Defining what a red wolf is has been one of the sticking points marring the creature's conservation plight ever since scientists began noticing it was going extinct in 1962, when it was first documented to have widely hybridized with coyotes. Because study of the red wolf was lacking even before this happened, a clear understanding of what a red wolf may have been in the past—and how it interacted with the coyote—versus what it is today has proved extremely difficult to untangle.

If she was lucky, the wild red wolf I'd seen at Sandy Ridge would be released back to the wild in a few weeks to reclaim her territory and further her species through breeding. But first, her sores needed to heal. This particular wolf has a lot riding on her creamy shoulders. She had originally been released in Pocosin Lakes National Wildlife Refuge, where a male red wolf had paired with a female coyote after its mate had been shot. The biologists removed the coyote before placing her in an acclimation pen within the male wolf's territory. They hoped that the wolves would grow accustomed to each other, bond, and mate. But she fell ill with mange before breeding season, and the team had to capture her for treatment, so she hadn't yet bred. Now, the biologists held hope that when they released her, she'd re-pair with the male red wolf, still holding his territory, and that the two would make pups. (A cartoon in the biologists' headquarters shows a male red wolf sidling up to a female, who eyes him warily. "C'mon baby, the species is counting on us," reads the bubble above his head.)

This little scenario illustrates clearly two of the biggest stumbling blocks the program has met in recent years, the first being the red wolf's tendency to hybridize with coyotes under certain conditions. My day talking to Ryan, and my previous research, confirmed what I had suspected before visiting Sandy Ridge: the reintroduced red wolf population had hit a plateau. Only it wasn't clear why this had happened, and I questioned if hybridization had played a role. In 1990, three years after the first wolves were reintroduced, the population grew to eighteen collared wolves. In 1995 it grew to seventy-four, and by 2000 the population had reached 128. It topped out in 2001 at 131 animals. But by 2003 this number had fallen back to 119, and it had hovered around 120 ever since. (These numbers include all of the collared red wolves and their puppies.) Puppy production had also petered out at between forty and forty-five pups per year since 2003. Granted, there were a dozen or more red wolves on the landscape that were uncollared, so these numbers reflect only the known red wolves, but program staffers say they are confident they have kept 75 to 90 percent of the population collared. Likewise, the number of breeding pairs initially rose over time, from less than five in 1993 to a high of twenty-one in 2003. By 2010 this number fell to fifteen or so breeding pairs. After early successes in saving the animal from extinction, the program was languishing at around 120 wild red wolves and twelve to fifteen breeding pairs.

The growth of the population was not entirely natural, in that the FWS had released captive-bred wolves for eight years after the first four pairs were released in 1987. Some scientists wondered if perhaps the Albemarle was saturated, meaning that perhaps all the good red wolf habitat was occupied by packs, and there was no more space for additional red wolves to hold territories. If true, that could explain the population leveling off. But the FWS biologists strongly disagreed with this assessment. They believed there was still space for more red wolves in the Albemarle Peninsula. They quietly pondered whether illegal killings made their red wolves more susceptible to hybridizing with coyotes, and that that was what kept their population numbers suppressed.

The FWS had developed an aggressive management plan to deal with invading coyotes, but just as FWS scientists were evaluating their tools for success, there was an uptick in red wolves dying illegally from gunshot wounds, which was the second-biggest stumbling block to the recovery program. The program biologists believed they were hampered by too many red wolves getting shot or simply vanishing without a trace in an undetermined fate. They believed that if they could grow the population, a stable network of packs could be created and the wolves would then ward off invading coyotes. The red wolf field team believed that if more wolves would survive to the next year, their management plan might work. But to really understand the current recovery program and the biological and social obstacles facing it, I needed a more intimate look at what the red wolf biologists do throughout the year. In early 2010, I asked the red wolf program's fifth coordinator, David Rabon, if I could shadow his biologists in the field throughout the coming year.

He graciously said, "Yes."

## CHAPTER 3

# The Search for Spring's Pups

Springtime brings a flush of new leaves and new crop shoots to the Albemarle's woods and farm fields. It also brings a new batch of red wolf puppies. For the biologists of the Red Wolf Recovery Program, puppy season is akin to one giant and protracted Easter egg hunt. The five-member field team fans out across the peninsula for six to eight weeks and searches for small, well-camouflaged treasures stashed expertly in the deep woods.

Red wolves form pair bonds in January and then mate in February or early March, and some sixty days later, pups arrive in April or early May. Pregnant females dig a subterranean den or scrape out a shallow depression above the ground under deep forest cover. There is often an intense two- or three-week-long period when the bulk of the breeding females give birth at the same time. Some biologists call this a birth pulse. But whether you use that fancy term or simply call it puppy season, for the field team, it means boots-on-the-ground searches from sunup to sundown almost every day for weeks at a stretch. Litters may be as small as one or two pups or as large as eight or nine. Female red wolves can breed as young as nine months old, but the majority wait until they are about twenty-one months old. Males generally get the urge to breed in their third season, at about thirty-three months old.

To supplement the wild population, the red wolf program has pioneered the process of fostering captive-born red wolves. Fostering has become a tried-and-true method of shuttling individuals and their genes from the captive-bred population into the wild population. Between 2002, when the first puppies were moved from the North Carolina Zoo in Asheboro to Alligator River, and spring 2010, twenty-six red wolf puppies were fostered into the wild. On April 30, 2010, I'm fortunate enough to witness the thirteenth time that the Fish and Wildlife Service fosters captive-born puppies into the recovery area.

That morning, Erin Hennessy, a Lincoln Park Zoo animal keeper, had boarded a red-eye flight from Chicago to Virginia with a carry-on holding two rare red wolf puppies. Erin stowed the black mesh bag safely by her feet, her fellow passengers none the wiser about her endangered cargo. The siblings nestled against each other and grunted softly. They were so young, their eyes were still sealed shut. The pups were born at the zoo, where Erin's duties included caring for the red wolves and bears. She'd nursed these two since their birth twelve days prior. Erin had landed in Virginia and headed by car to the red wolf recovery area. It was about noon. Her day had begun at three o'clock in the morning when she and a vet prepped the pups for travel. The babies had not eaten since.

In the Albemarle, the red wolf biologists have been busy locating and documenting all the dens this season. By the time I arrive, Ryan has worked ten days in a row, which is typical for this time of year. We drive down U.S. Highway 264 south and west from the program's headquarters. Along the way, we pass canals filled with black water. Ryan points out alligators, turtles, and great blue herons. Near Lake Mattamuskeet, we follow dirt roads until we reach another highway. He pulls over onto the shoulder near a farm entrance. Here, we wait for Erin to arrive with the puppies so that we can guide her over a series of dirt roads to the targeted den site. The midday sun pours down on the truck and heats the interior.

I roll down the window and strain to look past the tree line at expansive agricultural fields.

"This farm's owners have cooperated with us for a long time," Ryan says. "They don't mind the wolves on their land."

"So what's going to happen here today? You're going to go in on foot and find her den, then place the zoo-born pups in it?"

"Pretty much. The biggest thing is just finding the den site itself."

"Do the wolves ever reject the foster puppies?" I ask.

"I think the maternal instinct is just so strong at that point, it doesn't matter if they're not her own pups. We've never found any evidence that the pups are rejected." He shrugs. "I just hope we find her today. And I hope it doesn't get much hotter than this."

In a former life, Ryan may have been a Viking. He hails from robust Norwegian stock that settled in the Dakotas, and he is not entirely comfortable in the sweltering North Carolina early summer heat. His six-foot-one frame is designed for colder climes, and today the heat is oppressive. But he is more concerned about the pups overheating than he is about himself.

"Wait a second. You guys don't know where the den is?" I ask.

"Well, we know from aerial telemetry where the female has been localizing her movements, but after we walked in on her last week and found her pups, she moved the den to a new spot."

"Walking in" on a mother red wolf is hard to do. The wolves often pick areas covered in dense brush and thorns. Plus, after the biologists visit a wild den, the female nearly always moves her litter to a new den. Keeping track of the den locations requires the red wolf team's constant surveillance. More often than not, a female red wolf will use a new den each season, and she may use multiple dens in a single season. Some dens are dug as mini holes only a few feet deep, but sometimes the wolves will burrow six to twelve feet or more into the bank of an agricultural field or canal. There are photos showing biologists crawling body-deep into den tunnels, with only their feet left exposed to the sun.

Where there is dense vegetative cover, red wolves may simply scrape out a shallow bed on the ground and keep their pups aboveground in an earthen "bowl depression." Red wolf females that birth a litter will move their pups often, even when the biologists have not disturbed the den. The biologists perform frequent telemetry monitoring, trying to maintain contact every few days with all of the collared wolves they suspect may produce litters. In 2010 the biologists are keeping tabs weekly on the den sites of fourteen bonded pairs in the hope that they have bred.

When they found the New Lake pack's den in Tyrrell County the week before, they realized that the female wolf's litter was almost exactly the same age as a litter at the Lincoln Park Zoo. The team shifted into high gear to arrange for fostering a few of the zoo's pups. The biologists only risk fostering when certain criteria align, and among the most important of these is finding puppies that are less than two weeks old and that have not yet opened their eyes fully. The wild and zoo-born puppies should be about the same age, usually within one to three days of each other. Age was not the only reason the team had singled out this nine-year-old New Lake breeding female, though. She had accepted foster pups the year before, which gave them a measure of certainty she would do so again. Plus, she'd birthed a small litter this spring (just two puppies), so they figured she could feed two more mouths.

In the early days of using fostering to augment the wild population, the biologists returned to the natal den site a day after they slipped the captive-born pups into it to search for evidence that the female had taken the fosters with her as well. They never found evidence suggesting that the foster pups were abandoned. Plus, by tagging the fosters with unique radio-frequency ID chips called PIT tags (for "passive integrated transponder") placed under their skin, the program biologists ruled out the possibility that the foster mothers ate the intruder pups. The foster animals grew into yearlings and often turned up in the biologists' traps the following fall—known without a doubt by their telltale embedded chip.

After waiting about twenty minutes, we spot the truck carrying Erin and the zoo pups. Ryan pulls his truck off the shoulder and leads her onto the farm. We bump across a dirt access road between agricultural fields edged by an unruly sea of wax myrtle bushes and pine trees. It hasn't rained in a month. Aerosolized peat billows from our wheel wells like ash erupting from a volcano. We are only a short distance from the main highway, but crop fields surround us. Ryan turns right onto a small dirt road marked by two large dirt piles. The road bisects two more agricultural fields containing tiny green shoots in long, even rows. A few hundred yards from the road is a patch of low-lying wax myrtle scrub punctuated by tall pine trees. It is an island of wildness amid the vast, orderly farm fields. The land here closely approaches the Pocosin Lakes National Wildlife Refuge. The Albemarle Peninsula is dotted with conservation easements, and more than 400,000 acres are conserved. In swampy areas, such as here, patches of land are conserved in the federal Wetlands Reserve Program. These conserved islands of native habitat provide crucial resources for many animals, including red wolves. Flyovers with aerial telemetry have narrowed down the New Lake female's most recent location to this scrub patch, but the biologists have to look for her on foot. And they have to find her: they have no backup plan for the foster pups if they fail to locate her den today.

We bump across a dike and enter the scrub patch. Inside the tree line, we find program biologists Chris Lucash and Ford Mauney awaiting us. Chris has been a biologist on the program since before the first red wolves were officially released in Alligator River National Wildlife Refuge. Restoring red wolves is his life's work. He is a wiry, lean man with dark, close-cropped hair and a carefully trimmed beard. His observant brown eyes do not miss a single thing. His experience and knowledge have earned him seniority and deep respect among the staff. Ford has worked on the program on and off since the early 1990s, when Chris hired him. He has a medium build and shy eyes. He knots his long, dark-brown, wavy hair into a ponytail and tucks it beneath a hat. The biologists pull on their protective canvas field shirts and telemetry gear as soon as they spot us. Not a minute to lose. It's nearing one o'clock and everyone knows the pressure is mounting to get the zoo pups tucked safely in the wild den. Finding a den is as much an exercise in patience as it is skill. Going into it, no one ever knows if the task will take ten minutes or two days.

Chris walks over and introduces himself to Erin. He assesses the pups' size and sex, and questions her about their birth and siblings. When Erin tells him that the female dam who birthed them had born nine pups in all but that three had died from staph infections, Chris immediately asks what bedding the zoo used.

"It's a wooden substrate with straw on top," Erin says.

"Try dirt," Chris advises. "We've been messing with this for thirty years, and we've found that shoveling good, clean dirt in there is the best thing." The newborn puppies' paws are too delicate for wooden or concrete floors, he tells her, but they deal with dirt just fine.

Chris fingers a stiff hair plug over the male pup's shoulder blades and asks if the puppies have received ID chips. Erin replies that they have. The chips are inert until they are activated externally by a scanner that makes them emit a frequency. The scanner converts the frequency into a code of letters and numbers, like a bar code. The zoo vet used a bonding agent to protect the puncture where the chips had been placed, and it matted the hair over their wounds. The matted plugs would fall off when their hair grew and shed.

"Ryan, get the scanner and let's make sure our equipment reads their chips," Chris says. He cradles the puppy in the shaded cab of the pickup truck. Ryan pulls a palm-sized plastic device out of his bag and points it over the wolf's shoulders. It beeps. He reads the code from a digital screen, carefully checking each character twice. Chris transcribes the code in his notes. This one code is the only way the biologists will be able to link this animal, if they find it later in its life, to its life history information in their database. Tagging the puppies with these ID chips is crucial, because the biologists will have a blackout of data on them for a year or two while the pups are growing. Knowing the pedigree of each animal is vital to preserving the genetic integrity of the red wolf population. If they are lucky enough to trap one of these wolves when it's grown, they will use the scanner to identify it, then fit it with a radio collar.

Chris places the pup back in the carrier. The pair squirm into each other. They mew and grunt. The male hiccups, and his diaphragm convulsions jiggle his sister.

Chris and Ford decide it will be best to locate the den first without taking the puppies. They reason that they'll move more quietly without the carrier. Plus, the temperature is approaching ninety degrees, and it is risky to keep the pups in the sun. Erin and I remain with the pups in the shade while the three biologists set off into the shrub. They hold their telemetry antennae aloft like torches and listen hard to the pinging in their headphones. When they hold the antennae in an upright T position, they determine the direction of their quarry. But sometimes they switch and hold the antennae with their arm parallel to the ground, with the antennae in a sideways T position, which tells them distance. Their minds translate the loudness of the sounds, via headphones attached to the antennae, into direction and distance like bats using echolocation to find their prey.

The female wolf's tracks lead along a ditch blanketed in rich black peat, then veer into the myrtle. The biologists follow the flat shore of a drainage canal that contains dark, tannin-laden water. They pick their way through bleached stubs of shrub stems and small tree trunks. It is easier terrain than where some of the den-locating activities took them.

They pause here and there, waiting, trying to move soundlessly and to give the mother wolf time to confuse their sounds with that of a passing deer. The black, dried-out peat lifts in a fine, silent mist around their rubber boots and gaiters. It also muffles their footfalls. Chris signals for the team to cut left, where her tracks do, and they creep into the sea of green wax myrtles. The pinging is loud now. They are close. Ford unplugs the antennae cable to his receiver and shows Chris the disconnected end. This means they are close enough, within thirty feet or so, that he hears her frequency without the amplification of the antennae. They creep along, trying to breathe as quietly as possible. They communicate only with looks and hand signals.

They never hear the wolf dash from her den. But the telltale pinging of the telemetry tells them she is off and running. They shed their gear, fan out on foot, peer into the bushes, and scan the ground. They often rely on wolves' tendency to dig in and stay with the pups until the last moment. Ford kneels down and crawls under the myrtle canopy, scanning. And just like that, he finds it. The den is a small yawn of an opening, a cool pocket of earth cradling two red wolf puppies a little less than two weeks old. They are the color of dark, moist dirt, and they blend into the excavated hole. Only their wriggling, shaky forms give them away.

Now that the team knows where the den is, they double back to the trucks and fetch the puppies, as well as Erin and me. We trek back along the dark water canal and retrace their steps. No one worries about being quiet this time. They lead us to a spot where a sea of green wax myrtle bushes blend one into the other. Only the best-trained eyes might note an upside-down V notched in the canopy, near two tall sprigs of grass where the wolves had worn the twigs smooth with their comings and goings.

Chris nods at Erin and points at the notch. "Want to do the honors?" he asks.

Her face lights up, and she clasps her hands together. She nods, *Yes, yes.*

Chris plucks the puppies from the carrier and places one in each of her hands. When, after a moment, it becomes obvious that Erin needs at least one hand free to lower herself beneath the bushes, I take one of the puppies and she ducks in after Ford. The pup is warm in my palm. His tail is about the size of my pinky. I can hold him safely with just one hand, but I cradle him with two. I crawl in after her. It is five to seven degrees cooler under the network of tightly spaced, tiny myrtle leaves.

Ford, who is perched above the den on the hill, reaches into the opening and fishes out the male. When fostering pups, the team has made it a standard practice to take urine or excrement from the wild pups and rub it into the fur of the captive-born pups. The female may be more accepting of the foreign pups, the thinking goes, if they smell like her own.

"Let's see how much pee you got," Ford says. He tickles the baby wolf's underside. The pup wiggles its spine, and its little limbs flail in an uncoordinated fashion. Its head wobbles back and forth, mouth slightly agape in protest. Pink gums are visible, along with a tiny pink tongue. It looks for all the world like it's trying to bark or yelp, but all that comes out is a squeaky, unsteady whine. A few gold drops dribble down on the pup Erin holds in her hands. Ford keeps tickling, but the pup doesn't have much juice to give. He returns the male and scoops out its sister. She is much larger than her brother. He rubs her privies and honey-colored pee rains down freely. She mutters a protest. Her head waggles from side to side.

"Aw, you got lots of pee!" Ford exclaims, rationing the river of urine between the pup in Erin's hands and the one in mine. Pee washes over puppies and hands alike. We rub the urine into the pups' fur as an acrid, sharp odor reaches my nose. With the zoo-born pups duly christened to the wild, we lower them into the den. Now there are four red wolf puppies in the cool pocket of earth. The puppies nose and tunnel into each other. They shake and feebly haul themselves atop one another. The natal pups are darker than their new siblings. Their fur is the color of dark peat, but their heads show a large helping of auburn hair, the color of dried pine straw lit with a summer's sunset. The Chicago pups are slate gray and have traces of white on their paws, but they have the same characteristic auburn heads. One of the zoo-born pups wanders from the puppy pile and crawls on jerky legs to the front den wall. We watch as he tries to haul his feeble limbs up the soil embankment. He gets only far enough for sunlight to sparkle off his pee-streaked fur. Having stretched himself as far as he can, he loses his balance and careens to one side, then crawls back to the swarming puppy pile. His sister, meanwhile, has crawled atop the two natal pups and come to a rest with her back legs stretched out over both the other pups' back ends. They settle, after awhile, into a ball against the den's inner wall. Everyone crowds around and watches the baby wolves. I feel privileged to be here, and I'm hopeful that these four will grow up and one day have puppies of their own.

"Let's go," Chris directs, pushing himself up from the lowered position he'd been in while videoing the puppies tumbling into each other. "We don't want to keep her from them." The team would have been happy to crouch around this small hole in the earth and watch the pups a while longer, but Chris was right for shooing us away. The biologists try to interfere with the wild dens only as much as they must. Young pups depend on their mothers to regulate their body temperature, and they didn't want to keep the mother away. Practice and repetition had shown them that the adult red wolves never flee too far from the dens when the biologists show up. They usually stay close, within a few hundred yards.

In 2009 Chris coauthored a study examining whether biologists' actions at den sites had any long-lasting negative effect upon the wild puppies in terms of their development and survival. The study's lead author, Karen Beck, then a postdoctoral candidate at N.C. State University, had pushed to do the study for years but met with steep resistance. The dogma of wolf experts around the world at the time was that any human interference with a wolf's den would result in the mother killing the pups. The red wolf team was hesitant to place their endangered wolves at risk. But Chris was game to test the conventional wisdom. After studying puppies from twelve wild litters between 1999 and 2004, the research team found that handling neonatal puppies did not result in the mothers' abandoning them, and that it did not negatively affect the puppies' survival. (The dogma about interfering with wolf dens was so entrenched, however, that the research team faced obstacles getting their study published until 2009.) Having this information allowed the management team to develop protocols to obtain blood samples from all the puppies of every litter they can locate. It's an invasive process for any wild animal, let alone an endangered one, but getting the blood samples has also become a vital monitoring step to prevent the offspring from coyote and wolf crosses from getting into the red wolf population.

The team slides out from the myrtle's undercanopy of branches, which is layered like a petticoat. We blink in the bright sun and hike back to the trucks. The men joke with the lighthearted relief of a job well done. The biologists enjoy the feeling of doing something to help their charges, a cherished sentiment of something going well for the wolves. These moments are a reservoir of strength to draw upon later, when they find vehicle-battered red wolves on the shoulders of highways and refuge roads or wolves dead from blood loss and bullet holes.

The team isn't always as lucky as they are on this day. As I soon find out, discovering a single den can also take days. The next day, we look in vain for the Swindell pack's den in an island of woods between a farmer's field and a clear-cut swath west of Lake Mattamuskeet. The wind is all wrong, and it blows our scent right to the breeding female. We reek of tick spray and sweat. She flushes too early, and we aren't clear if we're even near where her pups may be. "You never know, you may luck out," Ford says, wading into the brush. We search for hours in the hot and muggy timber block, duckwalking beneath bramble so dense that we must squat. We worm our way, stomachs writhing over twigs and dirt, beneath mats of thorns. Gnats hover everywhere skin is exposed. I spot several shallow pine-straw beds where the female, male, and yearlings likely had lain recently. Bits of fur still cling to them. Myrtle, blackberry bushes, and carpets of dried ferns press all around. Twigs dig into my side and back. It is difficult to see more than twenty feet in any direction. The wolves like tight spaces with heavy vegetative cover for their den sites. The harder it is to reach, the more secure they feel.

We also search in vain for the Pocosin Lakes pack in a flat landscape devoid of trees, where the ground is dry as a bone and small ferns have desiccated into brown, shriveled curls that crackle and snap, like brittle November leaves, beneath every footfall. We hoof over dried marsh grasses in a wide open coastal plain that feels as hot and exposed as a frying pan. In fact, we aren't too far from an area off the Alligator River that is named The Frying Pan. We search for hours and hours, looking for a small hole in the ground with pups inside. We find stringy, brittle wolf turds and scuffle skids that mark where otters played on a canal embankment. Not a bush, log, or briar patch goes unchecked. It's easily in the high eighties, and everyone's canvas field shirts sag heavily with sweat. By early evening, my head swims from the heat. Two days pass, filled with searching. Often, this is how the denning season goes for the biologists.

On my third day, Ryan, Chris, and I head back to the Swindell pack's haunts to try again. The timber stand this pack uses tapers into a thin strip of woods sandwiched between a clear-cut and an unused agricultural field packed with tall, drought-withered grasses. The evening before, Ryan and Chris conferred with Art Beyer, another red wolf biologist, who had spotted the female running into this timber block during aerial surveys. They know from her telemetry locations that she uses this bit of woods regularly, and her movements indicate she has pups.

We park a few hundred feet to the south. The wind is just right today. It comes from the northwest and blows our scent downwind from where we suspect the den is. Chris dons his field jumpsuit and boots, and Ryan pulls on a heavier shirt and gaiters. I tug on a heavy canvas shirt. Chris shushes me when I speak too loudly. They turn on short-range telemetry kits, and we approach through the clear-cut. The black soil is deformed into thigh-high welts from earth-moving equipment. Pings from the radio collars tell them that the male is south of the female, who is farther up the wood line. Because the male wolf and the yearlings will often sit with the pups while the female goes off to hunt or rest elsewhere, the biologists must choose which wolf's signal to focus upon. This morning, they can't decide which wolf might be with the pups. Chris whispers a game plan to Ryan.

"I'm going to walk up on the male," Chris says. "You walk farther up and get a bead on the female. Wait a few minutes before you go in—give me some time to find him first because the wind will wash your scent south right back on top of him, okay? If the pups aren't with him, I'll just keep moving north toward her and find you."

Ryan nods his agreement, and Chris slips into the woods. The density of the vegetation encloses around him within a few feet from the tree line. Chris, having spent twenty-five years using telemetry to track wolves, can interpret the pings like most people read road signs. His body melts behind thick vines, woody growth, and an abundance of wax myrtle bushes that crowd the understory.

Ryan and I walk north along the clear-cut. He listens for the female, holding his telemetry antennae high. He waves the unit this way and that, searching the radio waves for the best strength. It begins raining. He paces up and down a fifty-foot stretch of the tree line. Where the female wolf's signal is the strongest, he scratches a large X in the dark muck with his boot heel. We wait in the light drizzle. Minutes tick by. Finally, Ryan motions for me to follow him into the woods. We creep deliberately, slowly, and I plant each step where he does. After about ten yards, he drops onto his hands and knees and crawls beneath a cluster of thorny devil's walking sticks. I trail him as if playing a silent game of follow the leader. We pause here and there to let the wolf confuse our sounds with a foraging squirrel. He uses vine clippers to snip through several large branches obscuring our way. Soon, Ryan pulls the cable from his antennae and shows me that he can hear her with just the receiver box. We are close. I try not to breathe. She is within thirty feet. Then the pinging in his headphones tells him she is running. We don't hear or even see her flush. It is like tracking a ghost.

"Look around and see what you can find," he says, shedding his gear. "It's probably very near to where we are standing."

A very dense thicket sprouts twenty feet ahead. Vines and brush block our way. We crawl and clip our way to it. Myrtle stalks no wider than a broom handle sprout everywhere. They are so dense that eight or more grow in a square foot. Ryan peers into the outcrop of myrtle stalks, the branches unified like a fortress. Two little milky eyes stare back at him, peering up. Two little erect ears wobble on a shaky head. Within the dense brambles, a mass of several puppies crawls around in a bowl depression. Their ears are erect and their eyes are open. The first pup has wandered away from the other three.

"They're mobile!" he calls to me. "Try to get around in here." We have to get to them fast, before they scatter and can't be found again. They are at least a week older than expected. I try to enter the copse from the side. Ryan crashes through the mass of twigs and stretches his arms out, grabbing at the pups before they go helter-skelter. One pup sees Ryan coming and yelps in fear while trying to out-crawl him. The other puppies, alarmed by their sibling's alarm yelp, begin to squeal. Ryan presses two pups gently against the ground. They shriek. He pins the third with his other hand, but the fourth puppy scrambles away. I finally wiggle into the copse and nab it. I glance at Ryan, wondering what to do now that our hands are full of squirming red wolf puppies.

"They're a lot bigger than the last ones," I say.

"Yeah, they must be four weeks old. She must have dropped this litter early. Can you sit with your legs out to hold them?"

Without a subterranean den, we had to corral them somehow. Inside the copse, there is barely room to move. I drop down to a sitting position with my legs splayed out, and the pups wiggle en masse against my thigh. Their noses press against my pant leg. They calm down and begin to nuzzle into each other. Dirt streaks their coats, which range from coal to warm gray. Their heads are covered in dense auburn fur, and all of them have now closed their milky-gray eyes. I stare at them in disbelief at the thought that, not so long ago, settlers threw dynamite into wolf puppy dens. Their muzzles appear foreshortened and out of proportion to the long and wide jaws they will grow into one day. Something compels one pup to move closer and closer to me until the little wolf wedges its nose firmly into my groin. The other pups trail behind it, tunneling between each other and pawing their way over one another until all four are piled together between my legs. I try not to think about the fact that suddenly I am a temporary nursemaid to some of the world's rarest wolves while their mother likely paces a few dozen yards away. Adjusting the puppies is futile, as they seem hardwired to nuzzle their way into the warmest, tightest spot they can find.

The brambles, while thick on the outside, form a natural opening in the middle that is just large enough for a wolf to circle around in. The mother had dug a very shallow earthen dish—only a few inches deep—to keep her babies in.

"Doesn't seem like much of a den," I remark. "I thought we'd find another big hole in the ground."

"It varies," Ryan says. "Sometimes we find them in these bowl depressions, usually where the woods are thicker and the ground is flatter, like here. But sometimes they're in holes. When the ground is sloped, they'll dig back into the slope. That's the most typical kind of den. But we've found them in storm culverts, too. It's all over the map."

Ryan sets to work pulling out rubber gloves, blood-sample supplies, and ID chips. Chris snaps and cracks his way to us. He crawls through the copse and curses at the dense vegetation. Finally, he reaches the inner sanctum, where there is barely enough room to sit Indian style jammed up against Ryan's legs and mine. Roomy for a wolf, maybe, but cramped for three human adults.

"What a sorry little den," Chris remarks. He glances at the scratched-out dirt bed and porous brush overhead. Rain drips through, wetting our heads. "Is she nearby?"

"Somewhere over there." Ryan gestures behind us. "She's not going far, though, you can be sure of that. These guys squealed their guts out."

I notice that one pup has a knot of exposed, hairless tissue by its ear. Chris picks him up to examine the skin. Sometimes tick bites get infected and cause such wounds, he says. He puts the pup down and says he's not concerned about it.

Chris and Ryan work quickly, not wanting to stress the pups or the adults any more than needed. They pull out data sheets and record the sex of each pup—two males and two females. They take blood samples. The blood will be shipped to a genetics laboratory in Idaho to verify that the pups are pure red wolves and are not a hybrid litter. Next, they insert the pups with PIT tags using an eighteen-gauge hypodermic needle.

"Looks like they were feeding when she split," Chris says. He fingers the edge of a pup's rigid stomach.

"Helps to find them with a belly full of milk," Ryan replies.

When the puppy processing is done, we pack up the equipment, and I pile the pups back in the bowl depression, lining them up head-to-tail and tail-to-head so that they can nuzzle into each other until their mother returns. We crawl out of the copse, pick up the discarded gear, and search for the largest animal trail we can find to carry us out of the woods. Within minutes, we are standing in the sun of the clear-cut. The morning's rain showers have cleared. We walk south across the black soil and toward the trucks, glad to have finally found the Swindell pack's well-hidden puppies. One more den is checked off their list. The morning's rain has softened the muck, and our boot prints mingle with the prints of raccoons, bobcats, deer, and wolves. Seeing the mixed prints, I am struck by the thought that man is as much a part of this landscape as the red wolf is.

It is clear from the short time that I'd shadowed Ryan and Chris that much of their time is spent doing muddy-boots wildlife management—literally tracking their quarry. Finding pups always gave Ryan's mood a boost. He was happy when things seemed to be okay, because this wasn't always the case.

In 2007 the team had taken a red wolf caretaker named Christy with them into the field to locate a den. Christy had worked hard all spring, and the team wanted to reward her with a field day where she could help find dens. They found two dens, then Ryan decided to try for one more. Aerial flyovers revealed that this particular red wolf was moving around a little but largely sticking to one place. Ryan, Ford, and Christy crept up on her, but instead of finding a new mother, they found the wolf lying on her side, half paralyzed and frightened to death. She was very thin, and she tried to pull herself to her feet when she saw them. She struggled, then collapsed. She was obviously ill, so Ford picked her up, slung her across his shoulders, and took her back to his truck. They drove an hour and a half to a vet, who peered at a radiograph of her abdomen and discovered a bullet. They had no choice but to euthanize her. Ryan felt terrible about exposing Christy to the truism that fieldwork could turn so rapidly from good to bad.

In the weeks after my visit, the team found a few more dens. There was one last female wolf they suspected might have a litter, but they couldn't find her and were unable to determine if she had bred with a known red wolf, a hybrid, or a coyote. More than a month later, a graduate student named Justin Dellinger was doing field research when he spied a pup in the area where the likely litter was thought to be. He ran it down, tackled it gently, and was able to get a blood sample. When the team received the genetic result a week later, it showed the pup as negative for being a hybrid, to everyone's relief.

This season, there were twenty-nine packs, which are defined by holding a territory and having at least one red wolf as a breeder. However, eleven of these are wolf-coyote or wolf-hybrid pairs. One of the biologists' management goals is to convert all twenty-nine of these pack territories into known wolf-wolf pairs. (A wolf-hybrid pair is rare; perhaps only one or two exist per year, usually in the far western section of the recovery zone where management is less intensive.) Going into puppy season, both breeders were alive in only fourteen of the eighteen known wolf-wolf pairs; in the other four pairs, one of the breeders had died, typically after being shot during the previous year's hunting seasons. The team documented that the fourteen wolf-wolf pairs produced forty-two red wolf puppies from nine litters, a moderately low puppy crop for the program. One additional litter was later found, but the blood tests revealed these pups were hybrids. The team had to euthanize the whole batch, a task no one relished.

The real test, though, would be how many of the red wolf pups showed up in the team's traps the following fall. Although they sometimes had veterinarians place abdominal transmitters in pups that were six weeks or older, they didn't do that this year. For the most part, the program remained ignorant of the puppies' fates until they were juveniles and showed up in the fall and winter trapping efforts. Generally, the biologists do some trapping immediately after puppy season, but once the heat of summer arrives, they back away from fieldwork because it's too hot and stressful for the animals.

But the growing warmth of the sun also brings hordes of tourists converging on the Outer Banks, and each year, hundreds of them come to the Albemarle to listen to red wolves howl at night.

## CHAPTER 4
# Howling Summer Nights

One Wednesday evening in late August, I pull my car into the parking lot of the Creef Cut Wildlife Trail just off Highway 64 and find that it is packed with people. Sunset is only about thirty minutes away, and so is the second-to-last red wolf howling session of the year. A golden-pink hue soaks the surrounding trees in a warm glow. Though most of the visitors milling around don't know it, the parking area connects to a network of gravel refuge roads that lead to the penned red wolves of Sandy Ridge. Families and couples stand in clusters by their cars. One woman cradles a sleeping baby. Retirees mill around, and young couples sit on their trunks and sip colas. Each of these sixty people paid seven dollars for tonight's howling safari. They are a tiny fraction of the 200,000 tourists who visit the Outer Banks each week during the summer.

I park on the grass and stroll to the two tables that are set up near the trailhead. I skirt the lines of people waiting to buy red wolf bumper stickers and plush toys and approach a table laden with interpretive materials. A coyote pelt lies side-by-side with a red wolf pelt so people can visually compare them. Next to the pelts is a telemetry receiver kit and a collar. The collar has a bit of heft to it; the large battery pack causes the weight to feel lopsided in my hands. Wolves that weigh less than forty-five pounds, usually juveniles or small females, receive a collar that weighs 400 grams (.88 pounds). Wolves that weigh more receive a larger collar that weighs 500 grams (1.1 pounds). The weight difference translates to more battery power, and the weightier collars last longer in the field. Plaster casts of red wolf prints also lie on the table; tourists pick them up and trace the foot and toe pad indentations with their fingers. A leg-hold trap catches my eye. The red wolf program uses only soft-catch traps, which means the mouth of the trap is flat and lined in rubber. This creates clamping pressure without slicing the animal's skin. My finger trails over the leading edge of the trap, and I remember when Ryan showed me how these work a few months back.

"The truth is, I hate that we have to trap them," Ryan had said out of the blue one afternoon when we were wrapping up fieldwork. "Even though we use the soft-jaw traps, trapping can be a pretty cruel thing to do to an animal. But we try to do everything we can to make it as safe and humane as possible. Here, I'll show you how the trap works."

He walked around to the back of his truck. There must have been thirty traps piled in the bed. He hauled out one that was weathered and dusted in red clay. It was shaped like the half moon of a closed Venus flytrap. Dark rubber coated the flat edge of the jaw's inner rim. He splayed it open into a full circle by pushing down two side flaps, called lifters. He pressed a gloved hand into the pan in the trap's middle. The half-moon segments flew shut, clamping firmly onto his fingers near the second knuckles. My stomach hurtled to my feet.

"I mean, it doesn't hurt. As you can see, it's on there real tight," he said, tossing his trapped hand left and right to demonstrate the clamping strength. "I can't say it feels good—I mean, I *feel* it—but I'm not bleeding or anything. I do this when I give talks to groups, and I keep it on a minute or two."

Ryan waved his hand around, and the chain attached to the trap clattered like a metal whip across the sand. It looked medieval. Ten feet of chain connected the trap to something called a drag, which looked like a boxy metal anchor with two pointed prongs turned in opposing directions. When a wolf steps into a buried trap and it clamps down on her foreleg or paw, the drag is how the biologists find the animal. As the wolf struggles to get out of the trap or find cover, the drag literally leaves a trail of marks through the brush. The terminal prongs dig into dirt or break off twigs, like giant fingernails scratching out a path in the earth that signal, It went this way. Once trapped, a red wolf will instantly seek out cover. They generally dash for the nearest tall grass, thicket, or timber stand. They may try to keep moving, but the drag will generally get caught on something, forcing them to hunker down and wait; or they get too tired of fighting the constant friction, and they stop to rest. Sometimes, they cross the numerous canals in the Albemarle and seek refuge on the other side.

Historically, wolf trappers staked traps in the earth so that a trapped animal was stuck at a single location. This made it easier for the trapper to find his quarry, but it caused a great deal of stress for the animal. Stake-trapped animals often struggle so violently against the metal clinching their legs that they severely injure themselves. By not staking their traps, and by adding features like a drag with a coil spring and swivel—which reduces the strain from the pointed prongs when it's being dragged—the red wolf program allows a trapped animal to continue moving and to seek refuge.

In theory, this makes the trapping experience less stressful, both physically and mentally, for the animals. It can also make them harder to locate.

"Please take it off," I blurted. The sight of the metal trap biting Ryan's hand shot adrenaline up and down my spine. Even though he claimed it didn't hurt, I still expected geysers of blood to spout at any second. Ryan paused, clearly taken aback. Then he grinned like a jester and doubled over in laughter at me. When he freed himself and slipped off the glove, a faint purple pressure mark wrapped around his fingers. He often demonstrated this to groups sans glove.

Back in the parking lot of Creef Cut Wildlife Trail, I step away from the soft-catch trap to allow other tourists to examine it. A volunteer of the Red Wolf Coalition is pointing out several of the trap's safety features to a young couple who gaze at the metal clamp with skeptical looks and furrowed brows.

"Everybody, gather around!" a middle-aged blonde woman shouts. She climbs up the side of a pickup truck and stands in the bed. She welcomes everyone and introduces herself as Kim Wheeler, the executive director of the Red Wolf Coalition.

"Who has seen a red wolf in the wild before?" she asks. "C'mon, hold up your hands." She looks from face to face. Everyone's arms stay down.

"Who's seen a coyote before?" she asks. Nearly two dozen hands shoot up. "They're similar, but different looking," she remarks, and then she goes on to explain how red wolves have comparatively wider snouts, and their legs are much longer. A red wolf's tail will come down to about mid–hind leg, she says, while a coyote's tail will look like it's hitting the ground; this is because, while their tails are roughly the same length, a red wolf has much longer legs.

"The first time I saw a red wolf pelt, I was expecting it to have 'I Love Lucy' red hair," Kim confesses from the pickup. "But it's not like that. They're colored more like a coyote, tawny and beige and gray and black, but with red on their ears and shoulders. It's more a cinnamon red than a rose red, though."

Two ibises fly over the crowns of nearby pines, their white feathers reflecting the salmon pink sunset. Kim briefs the group on the red wolf's near demise, the beginning of the captive breeding program, and its subsequent reintroduction to North Carolina's Alligator River National Wildlife Refuge. "This is the only wild red wolf population in the world," Kim says, and the crowd responds with murmurs of oohs and aahs. It makes me reflect upon how little people know about the program and the species in general. She breezes through the high points in the animal's natural history with the self-assured confidence of someone who has delivered the same speech several dozen times. Kim is the lone staff member of the Red Wolf Coalition, and she has been for several years. She has run the howling sessions for five years, relying on help from the Fish and Wildlife Service and various volunteers whenever they could offer it. She has the routine down pat, but she also knows how to make it feel special for first-time visitors.

A ripple of murmurs passes through the crowd when a black bear lumbers out of the woods to the left of the parking lot. It sits on a paved trail, looking at us. It is slim and small and appears young. The bear stands on its haunches and swats at the lower branches of a gum tree, playing with the gum balls that fall. People gasp. But Kim can't see the bear from her vantage point, so she keeps on her spiel of how the program manages land within the Albemarle for invasive coyotes. The crowd's attention is divided between her and the bear. A few people duck away and snap pictures of *Ursus americanus* as it waddles away down the Creef Cut Wildlife Trail.

Kim switches gears to covering the red wolf's behavior and social structure.

"How many wolves does it take to make a pack?" she asks.

People in the crowd call out: Seven! Eight! Twelve!

"How about just two?" Her answer-cloaked-as-a-question is met with perplexed silence. "It only takes a breeding male and female to compose a pack," she says. It used to be that biologists used the term "alpha wolf" to describe the top male and female wolves in a pack, she explains, which were also usually the breeding pair. But these terms fell out of fashion over time. In 2008 famed wolf biologist L. David Mech wrote an article titled "Whatever Happened to the Term Alpha Wolf?" in which he explored concepts of dominance and aggression that people connote with the word "alpha." Mech argued that the "alpha" term gives a false impression that certain animals fight their way to leading a pack, and that perhaps aggression keeps them at the head of their pack. He also recognized that wolf packs mirror our own family units in that they are led by a breeding male and female, and the members of the pack are typically the breeders' offspring. Because the act of breeding is more integral to elevated social status than is aggression alone, biologists have abandoned "alpha" in favor of calling the heads of packs "breeders" or a "breeding pair." Red wolf packs are composed of a breeding pair plus one to two generations of offspring. This may total six to eight wolves, although some packs may be smaller or larger. (The program is not sure of the size of a naturally occurring red wolf pack because the wolves are so affected by human-caused mortalities.) Often, the yearlings help with raising the litter produced after them, but they usually disperse from their natal territory around two years of age, when they reach sexual maturity. There are cases when red wolves may disperse from their natal pack earlier than two years. For example, if a mature male red wolf displaces a breeding male red wolf, then the new breeding male may chase off the pups born to the previous male sooner than they would have dispersed had their father stayed head of the pack.

Kim asks if there are any questions.

Someone in the crowd raises a hand and asks, "Were the farmers upset when the wolves were introduced here?"

"I'm not sure that they were upset, but they had a lot to learn," Kim replies. "Red wolves are good for farmers, because wolves eat nutria and nutria harm their crops."

A child who looks about ten years old raises his hand. Kim calls on him. "Do wolves ever have kids with coyotes?" he asks.

She explains that sometimes when a red wolf can't find a suitable mate, they've been known to have a litter with a coyote. The hybrid litter is always found by the Fish and Wildlife Service and they euthanize the puppies. The lady next to me gasps and asks under her breath why they couldn't just let the hybrid pups live? Others in her group shake their heads, seemingly disgusted. It's a fine line for the FWS to be open and honest with the public about why they euthanize hybrid litters. On the one hand, animal lovers like the ones next to me have a hard time understanding that emotions can't guide management of hybridization. Hybrid litters can't be allowed to stay in the red wolf recovery area because their presence jeopardizes the genetic integrity of the red wolf's recovery. Nor can they be adopted out from animal shelters because they are wild and don't make good pets. This leaves the red wolf program little wiggle room. When they find a litter that is documented to be of hybrid origin, they destroy it. The biologists' hearts grew heavy and their shoulders sagged when they learned they had a hybrid litter on their hands; no one wanted to kill a few wild animals in order to save others.

The warm colors of dusk have long faded to the cool blue of twilight by the time Kim wraps up the questions. Two bats fly in erratic lines overhead, and the last rays of light bleed away. Calls from insects, frogs, and birds rise in decibels with every passing minute. Nighttime is unquiet in these parts.

Kim tells us to follow the lead car onto the refuge, where we'd eventually see a man with a flashlight who would instruct us where to park. I recognize a red wolf program staffer who was there to help out and cop a ride with her. As it turns out, we are the lead car, the first in a column of traffic streaming onto the darkened refuge. People pile into their vehicles, turn their lights on, and set off in concert. Kim takes up the rear of the column. A half moon is visible, large and low in the sky vault.

Kim and the staffer trade useful information on hand-held walkie-talkies. "Black bear on left, just past the next intersection," the staffer tells Kim. A few moments later, I can just make out the curved silhouette of a bear sitting in the left lane ahead. It lumbers off into the vegetation, and by the time we reach where it had been, the dark behemoth has melted into the night. We see four more black bears over the ensuing miles. Two are mammoth specimens. They gaze slack jawed from the roadside as we approach and then retreat into the refuge marsh grasses. Some of the bears that appear younger turn and scurry away quickly, their feet scuffling in rapid flat-footed succession. And those are just the ones we see. Who knows how many are in the trees and thickets where our daytime-loving eyes can't spy them. While I'd carefully sprayed for mosquitoes before heading out that evening, I'd not given much thought to bears. Stars punctuate the deep-sapphire dusk sky like white glints sparked from a jewel. Bats swoop and swerve in jagged flight patterns that crisscross our high beams. The people-packed Outer Banks where I'd been just ninety minutes earlier feel a hundred miles away. Just outside our car door lay slumbering turtles and alligators, scavenging bears, and more wildlife than we might be prepared to encounter.

We soon arrive at the sandy trail that leads to the caretaker's cabin, and the red wolf intern directs people to the parking area. People file out of their cars silently and gather around Kim. She waits till everyone is there and then explains that she is going to walk about a quarter of a mile down the trail to Sandy Ridge, where she'll howl at the wolves inside. She tells us that sometimes it takes a few howls to get them interested, but we should hold tight and hope that they'll howl back. Last week, she says, people heard one of the pups howl back. She sets off down the dark path with her flashlight aimed at the ground so as not to spook the wolves. We stand in a pool of weak, wobbly light cast from people's flashlights and head lamps. The forest darkness encircles us. A few minutes later, we hear Kim's call pierce the night air. The buzz and drone of insects create a background of uneven noise that I strain to filter out. I hear Kim howl again, and everyone around me seems to be holding their breath and trying not to move. We listen and wait for an answer.

Nothing.

Kim tries again.

No response.

I wonder what the people in the crowd are thinking. Is this all just a sham? Just another tourist attraction?

Kim makes a fourth howl, and then it starts. A lone howl rises, forlorn and low. It meanders through a few octaves and claws higher and higher. It trails into a thin high-pitched note, and then a second and a third howl pick up at lower pitches. People in the crowd gasp, some lean forward straining to hear. Within thirty seconds, a parade of howls sings loudly from the dark woods. It is hard to believe the wolves are a few hundred yards away. They sound much closer, perhaps less than a hundred feet.

Kim walks back to the crowd, flashlight downturned on the ground. Howls waft from somewhere behind her, persistent but not aggressive. The wolves sing. They sing to each other as much as they sing to us. One pitch stands out from the others, higher, thinner, and much lighter. It must be the pup. I imagine him standing next to his parents, watching them throw their heads back and open their jaws wide, letting loose with a call that says, "Here we are! Where are you? Here we are!" And the pup joins in, calling, "I'm here too! I'm here too!" I don't know exactly what these wolves are saying, of course, but it is difficult to imagine the howling being anything other than a communication to locate other packs or individuals, a way to call out to the night and exclaim: *I am here, and I know how to take care of myself so well that I'm going to let you know that I'm here! And my mate is here, and my kids are here. We are all here together in this place that is ours.*

After a minute of steady howling, the wolves' entwined calls dwindle out to one lone call that seems to pivot between notes before ending in a series of high, broken yips. Kim asks all the kids to come to the front of our bunched group. Children filter forward, wide-eyed in the forested night, clutching flashlights close to their chests. Kim instructs them to howl on the count of three, and they let loose with a careening, loud set of human yowls. A short while later, the wolves answer back again, proclaiming their space and presence in the night. The children grin, entranced by this tenuous connection to a wild and unseen creature. After the kids, it is the adults' turn.

"Dig deep and howl!" Kim instructs gleefully. "Howling is the best stress reliever in the world. If you are on vacation here, you must howl," she jokes. We howl on her count, and the wolves answer a third time. Their howls seem to weave in and out of each other as they change pitch and perhaps meaning. Kim is excited that we got three responses from them and also heard the puppy. "We really rocked it tonight!" she exclaims, pumping her fist in the air. Everyone is smiling.

It is never certain for her that the wolves will answer each Wednesday. I wonder for a moment why they do. Surely they know that these are just a bunch of humans trying to speak wolf. Surely they smell us, a group of sixty people cloaked in lotions, colognes, insecticides, and deodorant—announcing our odiferous presence to an animal whose world is ordered by scent—standing in the woods a mere few hundred yards away. Surely they heard our engines as we arrived. Surely they could hear that our pitch is off, that we are an imitation. Yet they accept this and play along. Why?

Wolves, it turns out, will howl to a variety of stimuli, including the sirens of emergency responder vehicles. In the late 1960s, when researchers discovered that the red wolf was nose-diving into extinction, they played electronic sirens in southeastern Texas coastal marshes and plains to elicit howls from wild canids. From the howls, they made probable identifications of red wolves and possible hybrids. Coyote vocalizations often have a series of broken yips and barks and emanate at a comparatively higher frequency, whereas red wolves will howl at lower frequencies that start "deep and mournful" but may break off into yapping like a coyote, according to a report authored in 1972 by two trappers, Glynn Riley and Roy McBride, who were employed by the federal government. Early surveyors noted, too, that the red wolves were more likely to howl in good weather and less likely to respond in rainy or overcast weather.

Confined to their facility, perhaps the red wolves of Sandy Ridge howl to humans because it gives them a way to communicate with living beings outside their fence. Who knows: maybe they are simply telling us to bugger off and go away. Or, as frightened as they are of seeing a human, perhaps howling to a group of them on a dark night is more palatable since they do not have to look at us or be gawked at in turn. Perhaps howling is a way of reaching out on their own terms, in their own language, through which they can proclaim their space and their place on the land—their way of saying, "Even though I'm in here, behind this fence, I own this place."

Or maybe they just want to remind us that this land had been theirs for millennia before we invaded and claimed it. In the dark of night, I fantasize that their howls are calling out: "All this was ours. This was ours."

## CHAPTER 5
# Tracking and Trapping in the Fall

When the mercury and humidity slide downward at summer's end, it signals the red wolf biologists' return to the field. Trapping is central to their fall fieldwork. Usually they start in late September, but a long summer, a late fall onset, and a host of rain showers put them well behind schedule in 2010. When they finally get going, their first priority is to catch red wolves, and sometimes coyotes, that are wearing failing radio collars. Usually, the culprit is dying batteries. Later in the season, they target the puppies born the previous spring to fit them with radio collars that the wolves will wear their whole lives. To capture a specific wolf, the biologists bury soft-catch leg-hold traps in its territory. State law dictates that they must check their traps every twenty-four hours, so they work seven days a week when they have an active trap line.

Radio collars are a crucial component to managing the wild red wolf population. They are a vital conduit linking the biologists to individual wolves and packs through radio waves and satellites. The need to closely monitor red wolves through their collars differs starkly from other studied wildlife populations. Whereas collaring animals is a common way to gather life-history data, collaring red wolves is an integral part of biologists' strategy for preventing hybridization among the wild canids of the Albemarle. Trapping is not without risks. Sometimes animals are injured, although the red wolf team does everything within their power to prevent this. But even the relative risk of injuring a red wolf in a trap is drastically overshadowed by the deep hazard that hybridization poses to the species' recovery.

The red wolf team is just getting started in mid-October when I drive across North Carolina to the Albemarle Peninsula. In the center of the state, sourwood trees are fierce shades of magenta, and the maples are living watercolors bleeding greens straight to auburn oranges and apple reds. As I drive east, the trees transition to sharper and deeper greens. An hour past Raleigh, the temperate coastal weather pushes back against autumn's arrival. The next morning, the moon is setting to the east and the sun has not yet risen when I meet Ryan at the Red Wolf Recovery Program's headquarters. We set off on an hour's drive to Lake Mattamuskeet. During trapping season, Ryan wakes at half past five to check his traps by 7:00 A.M. If something is caught overnight, he wants to be the first to lay eyes and hands on it, and he wants to reduce the amount of time that it is trapped. Plus, if the animal was injured during the trapping event, he wants to give it medical attention right away.

To whittle away our drive, Ryan tells me about his experiences riding horses through the Badlands of western North Dakota, where he grew up. He was raised on a small ranch seven miles outside of a small, rural town of 2,000 people. His dad taught him how to hunt pheasant and deer, and he taught himself to bow hunt and chase after elk in his late teens. But somewhere along the way, when he was in college at Montana State University, his taste for killing dwindled, and he realized he'd rather take a picture of a wild animal than take its life. His awareness of the natural world grew. Back in high school, he'd throw glass bottles out of car windows and not think twice about it. But as he hiked around Montana's wild areas, he grew angry at seeing other people's Coke bottles littering the trail, and his ideas about litter shifted, too.

"Basically, I just grew up and got a wider view of the world," Ryan says. "I got educated and developed a different perspective of wildlife. I got interested in a career where I could help wildlife." He was working on a seasonal field project in Alaska when he heard about the red wolf internship caretaker position. He applied for it and went from branding Stellar sea lions to feeding red wolves. When the internship was up, he worked construction at the beach to figure out his next steps. Soon, a technician position opened up in the red wolf program, and he landed it.

Our plan for the day is to check the more than two dozen traps Ryan has set in a small area of private land on the northeast side of Lake Mattamuskeet. He has trapped the same area for a week, trying to catch the breeding male of the Waupaupin pack before his GPS collar battery dies. A few days before, he inadvertently caught the Waupaupin breeding female. She is a foster animal that was born in 2006 in the Graham captive breeding facility in Washington State. Her adoptive wild mother had paired with a male coyote. The team pulled the resulting hybrid litter and replaced it with a similarly aged litter of captive-bred red wolves, including her. When she matured, she originally paired with a male red wolf that dispersed from the bombing range south of the Alligator River refuge. In 2009 they had a litter of seven pups. But soon after the litter came, her mate was displaced by a bigger male that had been fostered into the wild from St. Vincent's Island in Florida. (St. Vincent's Island is a small coastal island where a pair of red wolves live free as part of an island-propagation program. Their offspring are caught and then released into the reintroduction site as wild wolves.) The team surmised that the Florida-born wolf kicked out the previous male's litter earlier than a parental wolf would have, which made the pups' future a little more uncertain. It's the Florida-born male wolf that Ryan is trying to catch today.

We exit off of Highway 264, and the truck jerks along potholed dirt roads. The landscape here is flat and carved into a matrix of long rectangular blocks of alternating timber stands and agricultural fields. The blocks are divided by blackwater canals, dikes, and dirt roads. We pass fields where soybean stalks have lost their leaves to fall. Their dry, silt-gray pea pods rustle in the wind. Hundreds of tree swallows swarm the fields. We pass rows of sorghum topped in deep amber seed heads and cotton so swollen with bursting fiber bolls that it looks as if someone splashed the contents of a giant snow globe across the ground. As we round a corner, I watch a yellow-billed cuckoo standing sentinel on a tangle of low brush. The bird is statuesque. Its button eyes track us, and then in a lightning flutter burst, it flees to the refuge of tall trees. A nearby field was cleared in prior weeks, and the owner is burning large brush piles. The charred remains smolder and release clots of light gray smoke.

We arrive at a spot where Ryan has set four traps in pairs at a bend in a dirt road. Raccoon, deer, bear, and bobcat prints litter the velvety, latte-colored dust. Ryan spies the unmistakable oval prints of a wolf. Then another set: the male and female moved through here during the night. Both of the traps are sprung, and bear prints nearby tell us who the culprit is. (Bears can usually slip off the traps that the wolf team uses.) Hidden beneath long blades of sedge grasses, near the traps, flies congregate on a rotten deer thigh. Ryan tucked this hank of roadkill here to attract the wolves, but the bears love the free food. Ryan shows me how to reset the sprung traps.

The land he really wanted to be on to trap the Waupaupin male is nearby, but he has not been able to access it yet. The owner is supportive of the program, but he leases his land to hunters, and he wants Ryan to wait until deer season is over. For now, it's Ryan and the bears. One morning last week, he pulled up to find a bear cub stuck in one of his traps set on the edge of a tree line. He approached the juvenile, which struggled frantically then gave up, sat on its butt, and whimpered. Two dozen yards back in the trees, a smallish mother bear paced. She too emitted a whiney wheezy sound, one Ryan had never heard a black bear utter. He returned to his truck and pulled it up close to the cub, but he left the door open in case the mom got nasty. He used a catchpole to secure the cub's head and then stepped on the lifters to open the trap's jaws. The cub's foot slipped out unharmed. He released it from the noose and it scampered off in a beeline for the she bear.

In past years, Ryan has also found abandoned hunting dogs in his traps, an unfortunate event that all members of the field team have experienced at some point. Many people in the Albemarle hunt deer. Some do it from deer stands, and some spot their prey and stalk it, but others use deer dogs. Because the underbrush is so impenetrable in many areas, the hunters train dogs to flush deer into clearings, where they are more easily targeted. As a rule, the wolf team never traps land when hunters are running dogs, unless they get consent. But sometimes a dog gets lost during a hunt and ends up wandering in the woods for weeks or months. Hunters think their dogs run better if they're motivated by an empty belly. Ryan says many of these dogs are lanky skin and bones. Once, a young hound got stuck in one of Ryan's traps overnight and died. The starved, exhausted dog apparently didn't have the strength left to survive the few hours it was caught. "It looked like the animal just laid down and died," Ryan recounts. "It didn't even pull the drag out of the ground." The biologists spent days looking for the dog's owner. (The phone number on its tag was not current.) When they finally found the owner, he demanded reimbursement for his loss. In the five years he has worked in the area, Ryan has taken more dogs than he can recall to a local animal shelter, though he only does this when they appear to be lost pets or abandoned and in bad shape. He has also found several gunshot hunting dogs in ditches—the sad castoffs of dissatisfied owners unhappy with their animal's hunt performance—and entire puppy litters discarded on the roadside. Two of Ryan's four dogs had been abandoned when he res- cued them from refuge lands after finding them wandering, alone, terrified, and bone-bitingly hungry. I listen to his stories, and though I hope we find something in the traps this morning, I pray it's not a hound.

In order to trick the wolves into treading over one of his traps, Ryan spices them with scent lures. "Sometimes you have to get creative with new setups," he tells me, after we finish resetting the sprung traps. "But I always fall back on the 'two traps and a turd' method." He explains that this method, tried and true, consists of placing two traps around the scat of a red wolf from a different pack. The scent of a faux intruder wolf is usually a good ploy for attracting the target wolf to investigate. Ryan keeps a collection of red wolf scats saved in carefully labeled plastic baggies stashed in his truck bed. With ungloved hands, he squeezes a black-brown gloppy piece of feces out of a bag. It plops onto a pile of twigs near his reburied traps. Next, he dribbles a tarry residue from the bag over the feces and the twigs.

"That looks really fresh," I comment.

He pokes at the twig pile, arranging it just so.

"Let's see what else I got in my box of stinky," he says. He roots around in a tool box, then lifts out a tray loaded with commercially bought scent lures. Glandular aromas and urine scents are bottled in neat little rows. He selects one and squirts it on the arrangement. For good measure, he takes a metal rake and etches scratch marks into the dirt. The marks mimic the scratches wild wolves often leave near their own scats and scent posts. Granted, a real wolf has interdigital scent glands that spread odiferous communications, but Ryan is only trying to craft a scene to lure a wolf in to investigate. Hopefully it will step on one of his two-inch-round pans hidden beneath the dirt. When he is satisfied with the setup, we move on and check the next trap set, where he used a coyote and a deer carcass to tempt the wolves; but again, bears were the only takers.

Since the traps are empty, we spend the rest of the day casing out sites where Ryan might be able to trap once hunting season ends. We creep along miles of farm roads and hang our heads out of the truck's windows to spot for canid tracks. We drive along a road that edges the Alligator River refuge and see three juvenile black bears inhaling paws full of corn kernels around a wildlife feeder. They perk at the sound of our engine and clamber for the safety of a giant tulip poplar tree, which grows on the edge of a wide canal. They glance at us over their shoulders every few seconds. Ryan grabs his camera and snaps pictures. Sensing we won't approach closer, the bears skitter butt first down the trunk. I run to the bank and watch the last one cross the canal. Water splashes between his large paws as he swims to the other side. He snorts water from his nose. Coffee-colored water pours off of his flanks as he heaves his bulk up the opposite side and jogs flat-footed into the trees.

Farther down the road, we stumble upon a spot where hunters dump their deer carcasses. Wolf and coyote tracks weave around deer skulls and rib cages smeared with dried blood. "See how this is a spot they are coming to nightly to scavenge? This is exactly where my traps should be right now,"

Ryan fumes. He has permission to scout this land but can't trap it until deer season concludes. With a carcass pile like this one available, it's easy to see why the wolves ignore his trap line.

At around 3:00 P.M., after eight hours of fieldwork, we head to a facility near Columbia where the team stores equipment. Called the Red Wolf Education and Health Care Facility, it is also where the team brings wolves they've trapped to give them vaccines, put collars on them, and provide veterinary care if needed. Art Beyer, the red wolf field team leader, is assembling traps when we arrive. He has an athletic build, brown hair, and piercing blue eyes. His long gait speaks of someone used to working out of doors. The facility has tall ceilings but a small floor space that includes only a tiny office and a large workshop. The latter has a large workbench, shelves for medicines and supplies, and an exam table. Drains are set in a concrete slab floor. Several empty kennels lie around, and there is enough space left over to park an all-terrain vehicle. Dozens of traps are strewn under the workbench and on the floor. Red wolf, boar, bear, coyote, raccoon, and fox skulls fill rows of shelves along a wall. Art and Ryan swap stories about how their target wolves are either smart regarding traps or just plain disinterested in their bait.

But the day is not a complete bust. Ford calls and announces he's caught a young, uncollared red wolf. It's loaded on his truck, and he's headed our way.

Twenty minutes later, Ford clonks an aluminum kennel on the concrete slab floor. A large animal crouches within and averts his gaze from human eyes.

"You got a wolf?" Ryan asks.

"Yeah, I mean, I'm pretty sure it's a wolf," Ford jokes. He caught it near N.C. Highways 32 and 99 on the western side of the Albemarle Peninsula. It rained before sunup, and when he found the wolf, it was smeared in dark mud. Art sticks his arm inside the kennel with an economy of precision and caution born from decades of experience. He waves the PIT-tag scanner over the wolf's shoulders. It beeps.

"It's a wolf. Number 11755," he confirms. He grabs a "Canid Info" book, which documents all of the collared animals in the program. It lists each wolf's radio-collar frequency, PIT-tag ID, pack name, natal pack, and all the vaccines it has received and when.

"This guy is one of the dispersing pups from Waupaupin," Art announces in surprise. The men pause from their work, glance at the kennel, and share a smile. "Kind of nice to know where he's at." The wolf is one of the pups, now a large juvenile, that the Florida-born male foster pushed out of the Waupaupin pack last summer. The pup traveled from Lake Mattamuskeet to Pocosin Lakes National Wildlife Refuge, where the recovery team caught him last winter and had a vet place an abdominal radio transmitter implant in him; he was too small to wear a radio collar. Since then, his transmitter had quit, and they'd lost contact with him. Now they know that he has traveled about sixty miles as the crow flies from his natal pack to an area nearest to the Pungo pack north of Washington. He has likely made a living by staying within the buffer zones between existing packs. He is about nineteen months old, and today marks the third time in his life that the red wolf team has handled him.

I peer into the kennel. Triangular ears spill from a large head at about a forty-five-degree angle. He is so tall that he must droop his head while sitting upright inside the metal box, a posture that adds to his submissive demeanor. Every ten seconds or so, he flicks his amber eyes until they meet mine, squints, and then looks away. Mud covers his hindquarters, and a tart stench emanates from his fur. His ears twitch at every sound, especially when the men bang rubber mallets against the traps they are fixing. (They are knocking wax from the springs on the drag chains to make sure they will work once set. The traps are boiled and dipped in wax before each seasonal use to cover the scent of the metal.) If the traps do have a scent, this young, impressionable wolf is less than ten feet from about four dozen of them, and he is getting a good whiff. The radio collar they want to use on him is programmed to stay on for twelve hours per day, but starting it requires physically flipping a magnet switch at the time they want the twelve-hour cycle to commence. This means they must switch it on tomorrow at 8:00 A.M., and the wolf must spend the night here.

The following morning, I help Art check his trapline before we meet Chris back at the red wolf health-care facility. He mutters about the Timberlake pack not caring for his buck carcass baits as we drive across wide open fields of soybeans and spot empty trap after empty trap. Art toys with the idea of stuffing a frozen sturgeon he had found at the refuge office in one of the canal banks, though usually fish baits catch only bobcats. He resets a lone sprung trap, and then we rendezvous with Chris back at the workshop.

When the biologists process a wolf after capturing it, they work within parameters laid out in protocols and standard operating procedures developed by licensed veterinarians that clearly delineate what they can and cannot do. It is not practical for a vet to be present at each and every wolf or coyote processing, so the field team works with direction from participating veterinarians. The red wolf biologists have been trained by vets to take limited action on their own, like deciding when to administer vaccines and whether stitches are necessary to close up a wound or more advanced care is called for, and they also know how to withdraw blood.

Chris and Art slip on blue latex gloves and set to work processing wolf 11755. They tip the kennel on end, and Chris slides a catchpole over the young male's head. He slides the pole into my hands and asks me to hold it to relieve pressure on the wolf's neck. I do, and Chris reaches into the kennel with both arms and takes hold of the wolf by the scruff of its neck. I have grown accustomed to the fact that they sometimes handle the red wolves without drugs or sedatives, though at first it was a bit of a shock. Once captured, the animals are typically so docile that they make a mockery of people's fear of them as fierce killers. Their meek nature upon confinement may be one reason they were so easily pushed out of the East. Still, some fight. ("Some wolves will fight you tooth and nail when you try to put your hands on them," Ryan tells me later. "Larger wolves sometimes have to be sedated in order to process them.")

By now, the wolf stinks to high heaven. He peed on himself overnight. Art places a muzzle blindfold over his rostrum. Chris heaves the wolf up, and Art grabs hold of its rear legs to lift it gently out of the metal box. I'm still holding the noose pole awkwardly, and when they shift the animal's weight, I try to help by lifting as well, but my "help" strains his neck and chokes him. As I fumble with the noose, a torrent of pilsner-colored urine flows from the wolf's hindquarters. The men tip him with practiced precision onto his side, and the pee flows into his cage. After his bladder is spent, they place the male on an exam table and hogtie his legs with rope. He submits completely to their maneuverings, but his ears follow their every movement. The wolf's eyelashes flick rapidly against the muzzle fabric, which also covers his eyes. He defecates. Chris scoops the fresh feces up with gloved hands and places it in a manila envelope to save for a graduate student's genetic research. The wolf weighs 55.8 pounds. He is a small male, but he hasn't yet reached his prime.

Chris and Art chat about their kids, like coworkers gathered around a water cooler, as their fingers systematically sift through the wolf's ruff. They untangle dozens of cockle burrs from its fur and pluck gargantuan grape-sized ticks from its skin. Chris pulls back the animal's lips to inspect his teeth. My gaze lingers on the long, sharp fangs that bookend the six incisors of his mandible and maxilla. The fang is the wolf's signature anatomical feature, its canine. This is the sharp tool it uses to puncture and hold onto prey during a chase. Wolves lack the retractable claws that lions, tigers, and panthers have, so they rely on their canines, incisors, and bite strength to drag their prey to the ground. While the canines puncture the prey, the upper and lower incisors interlock to form a wriggle- and buck-proof bite that allow the wolf to hang on, even when the prey slings its attacker airborne. This wolf's incisors reveal his young age, because where the base of each tooth meets the gum line, small cusps are visible. Only puppies and juveniles retain these cusps, which will wear away by the time the animal reaches sexual maturity.

Chris and Art measure the wolf's upper canine length, zygomatic breadth (the distance between its cheek bones), and the length of his skull. They measure his ears, tail, front and rear paw pads, shoulder height, body length, and hind foot. They give him a dose of Revolution. Then Art jabs him in the thigh with an eight-way vaccine shot to protect against things like parvovirus and rabies, and he flinches from the injection. They find a gash on his knee.

"Think we oughta take him to get stitches?" Chris fingers the edge of the laceration where the tissue has begun to granulate.

"It's in a bad place for stitches, right on the front of the knee like that. I don't know that it can be stitched," Art says. "Even if we have him stitched up, he'll probably just tear them out. I think it'll close on its own."

"It may close on its own, but maybe we ought to keep him at Sandy Ridge for a few days to make sure it doesn't get infected, keep him on some antibiotics," Chris says.

"Yeah, alright," Art replies.

The last order of business is to fit the young wolf with his jewelry: the radio collar he'll wear the rest of his life. They comb his ruff with their fingers, streaking it smooth before wrapping the resin-coated leather around his neck. The male stiffens but does not resist when they bolt the collar in place with just enough looseness for him to grow into it. They unrope his legs and carry him back to the kennel.

Chris invites me to ride with him to Sandy Ridge and help move the male into a pen. He and Art load the kennel into the truck bed and we take off. We stop at a gas station in Columbia, where Chris buys lunch. I can't help but find it absurd that an endangered red wolf is stuffed in a kennel in the pickup bed like a deer hound, while a half dozen Columbia locals pump gas and buy sodas. Such novelty, I suppose, had long ago worn off for the biologists.

Chris doesn't like to pen a wild wolf unless he knows he can do something to help it. When we get back on the road, he tells a story about a wolf that was injured in a trap in the mid-1990s when the red wolf program had a second reintroduction site active in Great Smoky Mountains National Park. They couldn't find the animal right away, and when they finally did, its toes were so torn up that several needed to be removed. Its skin hung off of exposed bones. They took it to the University of Tennessee in Knoxville, and skin grafts were done and redone three times to spark the epidermis to grow back over the amputation site. It took months to heal. Though it was an extreme case, his point is that sometimes animals that are held in captivity don't heal as well as ones that are simply released. He also tells me about a wolf in the wild that lost its foot but regrew skin over the stump in about two weeks. Chris questions whether wolves that are held experience suppressed immune systems due to stress. He prefers to let them heal naturally. But in this case, he felt there was something they could do for the male's laceration to prevent infection.

We arrive at Sandy Ridge, and Chris drives the truck through the gate of the double-fenced perimeter. We meet the caretaker, a new intern named Janet. She's just received a degree from the University of California, Davis. She carts a wheelbarrow to the truck, and Chris hauls the kennel, wolf and all, into it. They tuck a large five-gallon water jug next to the kennel, and then we set off pulling the male down the main thoroughfare that divides the pens of Sandy Ridge. It has rained heavily this fall, and everything from mushrooms to few-days-old kibbles is coated in mold. Chris pauses for a moment and points into the trees at regularly spaced depressions in the ground.

"Did you know that this used to be a cemetery?" he asks.

We shake our heads.

"This is the highest land around," he says. "It's a natural ridge, so it was used for graves. There are a few unmarked ones right there." He points at the depressions where soil has settled and compacted lower than the surrounding areas. "That's why we don't have any wolf pens right there." High land, in the peninsula, usually means an elevation of a few feet above sea level. The unmarked depressions seem a poignant reminder of how man and wolf share the same spaces in this area, whether knowingly or not.

We place the kennel inside a naturally vegetated pen just past the graves. Light filters through a canopy of sweet gum leaves above, and wind ruffles long grass blades on the forest floor. Janet fills the wolf's water tank. Chris walks the perimeter fence and checks for holes. He tells Janet how to medicate the wolf: slip the medicine in small meatballs pulled from a carnivore log and feed them to him in advance of the main meal. "That way, you know he's eating it," Chris says. We leave the kennel door open, lock the pen gate, and depart.

One wolf at a time, the team whittles down their fall trapping to-do list. They catch as many of their target animals as possible, with the greatest emphasis placed on finding the uncollared young wolves born in the spring or—like the young Waupaupin male—the previous year's uncollared pups. They also turn their eye to trapping the coyotes in newly formed wolf-coyote pairs to prevent hybridization by sterilizing and collaring the coyote. Later in the winter, they will trap specific wolves that are single to try and pair them with other single wolves that are holding a territory in the hope that the animals will bond and mate. About 50 percent of their attempts to create bonded pairs actually work.

Collaring the wolves, and finding the ones with dying collar batteries, is perhaps the most important aspect of their fieldwork. Scientists call noninvasive methods like this "remote sensing" because it allows them to gather information about the animal remotely, without having to disturb it. Most of the collars the red wolf biologists use are VHF collars, named after the very-high-frequency radio waves they emit. When the batteries are old, they begin transmitting a double-beep signal (instead of a normal single beep) that the biologists call "recovery mode." This double beep may last for a month or several months, but it's a clear prompt that the animal needs to be found quickly.

They also use a few GPS collars that mark a wolf's global positioning system coordinates every few hours. The team downloads the stored data remotely via a satellite connection. This technology gives them access to fine-scale spatial data. This means they have a lot of data points locating the animal at closely spaced time points over weeks, months, or years. The data give a detailed picture of where and when the red wolves travel and rest. GPS-collar data has revealed that the wolves use heavy forest cover and rest more often during the day, and that they use roads and open fields more often when they are active at night.

GPS collars also help scientists understand how the wolves use different kinds of habitat in different seasons. John Chadwick, a professor at the University of North Carolina at Charlotte, gathered GPS-collar information from four red wolves to study their home range sizes and their use of agricultural and natural land cover across seasons. He and his then-doctoral student, Melissa Karlin, found that the wolves' home range shrinks in the late winter and early spring, when the breeding animals are busy mating and raising puppies. In late summer, the home range expands, and it grows larger throughout the fall and early winter. This may be because the wolves and their growing puppies use more of their territory, presumably to hunt, once the puppies are older and large enough to participate in hunting forays. Chadwick and Karlin obtained four locations per day from GPS-collared wolves for eleven to eighteen months. The data revealed that when the tall row crops—like corn, cotton, and soybean—are more than three meters high in the summer and autumn, the wolves spend more time resting in the agriculture fields than in the timber blocks, though they still use both types of cover. When the harvests begin in late autumn, the red wolves shift the bulk of their time to using tall grass, brush, and forested areas and continue to do so throughout the winter and spring. Though the sample size was small, the results match well with what the red wolf field team has observed over the years. These results were published in *Southeastern Naturalist* in 2010.

One reason the wolves move into the agricultural fields in the summer may be because when the heat sets in, the timber blocks and swampier hardwood forests become thick with bugs. The open fields, many of which are sprayed with pesticides, are a welcome respite. Perhaps the juiciest nugget of this study was the novel idea that when red wolf home ranges are smallest, coyotes further infiltrate the recovery area by taking advantage of interstitial spaces between the pack's territories that are poorly patrolled—or not patrolled at all—because the wolves are busy sticking to their den sites and caring for their young.

Previous research on western gray wolves shows that prey species and even coyotes take advantage of the interstitial spaces between wolf territories. Imagine it like this: a single wolf territory is an irregularly shaped polygon, and a population of wolves is made up of a lot of these polygons arranged next to each other. Because the odd angles don't always fit snugly like puzzle pieces, there will be some pockets of unused space that occur between the territories. Chadwick and Karlin's study suggests that these cracks grow larger when the red wolf home range shrinks seasonally, allowing a semisafe haven for animals like coyotes to move farther into occupied wolf territory. Though wolves mark and defend their range from other wolves and canids, some studies show that they spend little time hanging out along their territory borders. This decreases their chances of being attacked by a neighboring wolf pack. As a result, prey species and coyotes spend more time in these same buffer zones resting, traveling, or feeding because they seem to know the wolves are less likely to be there.

Karlin did an additional study using data collected from VHF collars to assess the suitability of habitat within the Albemarle for red wolves, wolf-coyote hybrids, and coyotes. She first created maps of the peninsula that incorporated land cover and land use characteristics, such as the presence of primary and secondary roads, urban development, wetlands, forest, shrub-scrub habitat, and farmland. She then overlaid this map with more than 6,000 data points from VHF telemetry readings of about 500 red wolves, forty wolf-coyote hybrids, and eighty coyotes that had been collected between 1999 and 2008 by the Fish and Wildlife Service. This allowed her to analyze where these three groups of canids tended to establish territories and settle. Her results confirmed what the red wolf biologists had long observed: all the canids preferred agricultural lands. Because both coyotes and red wolves prefer farms, Karlin identified agricultural lands as the type of habitat were hybridization was most likely to occur. She also found that red wolves used wetlands, whereas coyotes and hybrids more often avoided these areas. The wolves showed a clear pattern of avoiding primary roads and areas of high human population density. In contrast, coyotes and wolf-coyote hybrids showed a higher tolerance for the presence of people and exhibited a more general use of the landscape. This may explain the current pattern of how coyotes and red wolves have come to be living side by side in the Albemarle: coyotes can simply live in the places where red wolves choose not to.

In a separate study, published in the *Journal of Zoology*, Karlin and Chadwick used telemetry data to analyze characteristics of red wolf dispersals. Using data spanning from 1990 to 2007, they found that the majority of red wolves dispersed their second winter at around twenty to twenty-one months of age, while a lesser number of pups dispersed their first fall or winter at around six to nine months of age. Pups also tended to disperse greater distances—on average, 26.4 miles—while the yearlings and young adults dispersed shorter average distances of about 18.3 miles. There was no difference between the distances traveled by males and females.

None of Karlin's studies would have been possible without the cumulative and consistent data gathered from VHF and GPS collars—data that would not exist were it not for the consistent trapping efforts of the red wolf field team. Though the VHF collars have been used reliably on the red wolves for several decades, the GPS collars have proved a little more temperamental. One of their major drawbacks is their comparatively shorter battery life. Whereas the VHF radio collars can theoretically last eight to ten years when programmed to emit a signal for only twelve hours per day, the GPS collars are supposed to last two or three years; yet many that the red wolf team deployed failed after one. While they provide a rich resource of data and insight, they demand the wolves wearing them to be trapped more frequently. This not only eats up the field team's time, but it is hard on the red wolves, too. In the fall of 2010, Art was close to calling it quits with the GPS collars after deploying them forty-four times.

## CHAPTER 6
## Winter's Bite

In mid-November, I receive a text message from Ryan: "Another day, another dead wolf—actually, make that two. This has got to stop."

Since the start of deer-hunting season, everyone has been on edge waiting to see which wolves will survive and which will succumb to hunters' bullets. Ryan takes the deaths especially hard. It has become difficult for him to keep his heart in his work because this time of year, there is just so much heartache. "We need some changes in the regulations to help red wolves survive," he says when I call him that night. "They start dropping like flies as soon as deer season opens." Throughout the year, red wolves are at risk of being shot in cases of mistaken identity when hunters believe they are shooting coyotes, which can be shot legally any day of the year. But according to the field team, the number of red wolves that die from gunshot wounds increases significantly during the deer- and bear-hunting seasons. Without a policy change, no amount of fieldwork would alter the fact that anyone can take a bead on a red wolf and shoot it. The team believes that the current rate of illegal killings is harming the restoration program, but they stop short of saying it might cause the program to fail.

The image of someone blasting away endangered red wolves makes my stomach churn. I still don't grasp why it happens. It isn't like the area is full of livestock operators, as much of the gray wolf range is in the West. Most of the farmers in the Albemarle raise fiber and food crops; if anything, they should want wolves around to deter the deer from hammering their field corn and beans. Hunters, on the other hand, might see wolves as competition for the deer.

"I still don't know if people are shooting them by accident, or if they are targeting them," I say.

"Yeah, we're not too sure, either," Ryan says. "I think it's maybe that the majority of people think they're coyotes, and it's customary with some hunters to shoot any coyote that you see when you're out hunting because they're considered varmints. But I think there's maybe a small percentage that are doing it on purpose."

"So why not shut down the open season on coyotes throughout the peninsula? Put some kind of moratorium on it until the wolf population can get larger?" North Carolina had declared an open season on coyotes in the summer of 1993. The state Wildlife Resources Commission went straight from no season to an open season.

"We've talked about that before. There might be some backlash among the local people if we pursued that, but really only the state of North Carolina could do it. We're a federal agency, so we don't have any say in how the state manages its hunting regulations."

After talking about the possibilities, we say goodnight, and I hang up the phone feeling helpless. People are shooting one of the world's rarest canids and nobody seems to care. It sounds absurd, but the person pulling the trigger might not even know they are shooting an endangered animal. The killings are barely news to the state's regional newspapers anymore. They just run short blurbs stating that another red wolf has died unnaturally and that the Fish and Wildlife Service law enforcement is investigating it. The worst part of the succession of deaths is that no one has been prosecuted, and the locals are wise to the fact that all they have to say is they *thought* they'd shot a coyote and there will be few repercussions. That fall, a local talking to Chris had smirked and said, "Yeah, but if I *say* I thought it was a coyote, it's okay, right?" It was a deeply cynical perversion of federal law. I knew from talking with David Rabon, the red wolf program coordinator, that the program was working to eliminate misperceptions such as these. Specifically, they were collaborating with law enforcement to revise their regulations and open investigations in all cases where red wolves were found shot or poisoned or had disappeared in suspicious circumstances.

The red wolf biologists are hamstrung. They can't come down too hard on the local people for the killings, or their access to private land for population monitoring and management could dry up. But if they do nothing, they are tacitly allowing the killings to occur.

David shared with me that by the end of 2010, eight red wolves had died unnaturally, and two more were found dead under what they considered suspicious circumstances. David said that in February 2010, one female red wolf yearling was found shot in Tyrrell County. In April, two male wolves were found shot in different locations within Hyde County. On October 4, one female red wolf was found shot in Dare County in Alligator River National Wildlife Refuge; she likely had died two days earlier on the opening day of muzzle-loader season for deer. On October 29, another female red wolf was found dead north of Washington. She was suspected to have been shot, but her body was too decomposed to be sure. The fact that her carcass appeared to have been moved by a person from the location where she died, along with other factors, made the biologists highly suspicious that she'd met her end by way of someone's bullet. Also in October, a third red wolf disappeared under extremely suspicious circumstances. She had a new collar and had birthed pups in the spring; and at the young age of three and a half, she was strong and not likely to have been kicked out of her territory. One day, she was present in aerial telemetry surveys, and then, poof! She was gone. The biologists never found her body or her collar. Because the area where she disappeared had seen multiple gunshot wolves in years prior, in addition to other factors, the biologists strongly suspected she had been shot and disposed of. Then on November 16, the night Ryan texted me, there was a double whammy of one red wolf found dead in Beaufort County and one found dead within its home range in Hyde County. The first case was a gunshot male wolf, but the second was determined to be mauling by other canids. Deer hunters present in the area were reported to have been running dogs earlier in the day. The incident occurred on private land where using dogs to hunt deer is legal. Two more gunshot female red wolves were found by the month's end. (By the end of the year, a wolf that Ryan nicknamed Wolfzilla, due to his eighty-two-pound size, was thought to be missing for several weeks, but he later turned up again with a malfunctioning radio collar. It was the second time he'd been presumed dead, only to reappear. Art told me Wolfzilla is one of the biggest red wolves he's seen in his two decades with the program.)

Since 2004, an average of 6.5 red wolves have died each year from gunshot wounds. Studying years past, it is easy to see an emerging trend: between 1987 and 2003, twenty-eight red wolves were shot. But between 2004 and 2010, the number of gunshot red wolves rose to forty-five confirmed cases. By the end of 2011, the total number of gunshot wolves increased to fifty-two. In other words, 65 percent of the known gunshot red wolves occurred in the most recent eight years of the twenty-five-year-old program. Six were shot in 2004; five were shot in 2005; four were shot in 2006; nine were shot in 2007; six were shot in 2008 (plus two confirmed poisonings); seven were shot in 2009; eight were shot in 2010; and another seven were shot in 2011. The killings are akin to death by a thousand slices to the population as a whole.

Unfortunately, the breeders are hit disproportionately, according to the red wolf team. Since 2004, the biologists calculate that breeding individuals compose 73 percent of the wolves shot illegally. Losing a breeder busts up packs, which in turn leads to single wolves becoming vulnerable to intra-specific aggression. The loss of a breeder can also equate to pups or pre-dispersing age juveniles losing parental protection. Most worrisome to the red wolf field team is the fact that losing a breeder puts that pack's territory at risk: they have too often observed fertile coyotes move into territories shortly after the disruption of a breeding pair. The reason breeders are shot more often is unclear. One would think that if hunters were mistaking the red wolves for coyotes, it would be the young juveniles, which look the most coyote-like, that would be taken. However, this is not the case. Ryan mused to me that perhaps the mature breeders were simply bolder and more visible on the landscape, which in turn increased the probability of their exposure to hunters during gun seasons.

A study published in 2011 in PLoS-ONE by Dennis Murray and Amanda Sparkman from Trent University and Lisette Waits from the University of Idaho was the first to address the issue of how anthropogenic killings affect the red wolf population. The researchers tested two ecological theories. One proposed that human-caused killings have an "additive" effect that reduces a population's overall survival rate; the second proposed that human-caused killings trigger a "compensatory" effect that makes up for unnatural losses, possibly by reducing the natural mortality rate, which then balances the overall survival rate.

The researchers divided the red wolf population growth into two major time periods—from 1990 to 1998 and from 1999 to 2006—and classified the first time frame as having a low population density (when the reintroduced population was still growing) and the second as having a high population density (when the recovery area began to approach being full). They found that at low population densities, the red wolf population experienced a strong additive effect from human-caused killings. But they found evidence for both additive and compensatory effects at higher densities. They hypothesized that as stable red wolf packs dissolved due to human-caused killings, it freed the surplus breeding-age red wolves to either begin breeding with the surviving mate or to take over the territory of a dissolved pack and form an entirely new breeding pair.

During the time frame examined within the study, the rate of pack dissolution and new breeding-pair formations compared to the rate of human-caused killing was essentially a wash, according to North Carolina State University veterinary medicine professor Michael Stoskopf. "What they reported is that it's not a good thing to have people shooting wolves, but it's also not going to be the thing that takes the population down," Stoskopf told me. He chairs the Red Wolf Recovery Implementation Team, a group of academics who have advised the recovery effort in the past. Stoskopf said the study findings were highly dependent upon the specific population densities recorded at specific points in time and the rate of human-caused killings tied to those densities. In other words, while it described past scenarios, the authors did not detail at what threshold of density the compensatory effects might be diminished by the additive effects and lead to population stagnation or decline.

Stoskopf added that the study was as robust as can possibly be done because the researchers had access to the red wolf database, which includes a complete pedigree of every wild red wolf that has inhabited the recovery area. "It's as complete a database as has ever been available for any wild population," he told me.

A second study with insight into how anthropogenic killings affect red wolves took the form of a dissertation under the tutelage of Lisette Waits, a wildlife conservation geneticist. (Waits is also the person responsible for analyzing the blood samples of the red wolves for the genetic markers that qualify them as true red wolves.) Waits and her then-student Justin Bohling examined characteristics of individual red wolves that were involved in hybridization events verified to have occurred. They discovered that the majority of the red wolves that crossed with coyotes did so under similar circumstances.

"A high proportion of these hybridization events were occurring after the disruption of a stable breeding pair," Waits said. "Particularly, it's been a problem associated with gunshot mortality during the hunting season, and the hunting season precedes the breeding season."

Waits and Bohling pored over breeding records and the individual life histories of red wolves known to have been involved in hybridization events between 2001 and 2009. They studied twenty-one hybrid litters and ninety-one red wolf litters and examined them in an attempt to establish correlations between age and breeding experience, whether an animal had a mixed red wolf/coyote ancestry, birthing locations within the red wolf recovery area, and whether pack disruption was a factor leading to future interspecies crosses. They found that the hybrid litters were clustered toward the western side of the Albemarle Peninsula, and that the average age of female breeders who birthed hybrid litters (4.2 years old) was slightly less than the average age of female breeders who birthed red wolf litters (about 5.4 years old). But perhaps the most interesting result was that thirteen of the twenty-one hybrid litters were produced after a stable breeding pair of red wolves were broken apart. Seven of these dissolutions occurred because a breeder had been shot and killed, while two more involved the death of a breeder from poison or trap injuries; in all, nine of the thirteen broken pairs were attributed to human actions.

In the eyes of the red wolf field team, Murray's study described the past, but they felt the spike in gunshot mortality they had observed since 2004 significantly altered the possibility that the compensatory effects would continue to balance the additive effects. They also countered that the study failed to capture the level of management efforts that the team had to invest in fostering new red wolf pairs each time a pair dissolved—not to mention their efforts to trap, sterilize, and monitor new coyotes that moved into a former pack's territory. They had increased their management efforts in step with the uptick in illegal killings since 2004, and they felt that Murray's conclusions—that the additive and compensatory effects balance each other out at high population densities—omitted how an increased rate of killings stretched their management workload to the point of bursting. They believed Waits and Bohling's study accurately described the scenarios they had witnessed time and time again when a pack dissolved largely due to human-caused reasons and hybridization often followed.

The Red Wolf Recovery Program hinges upon successful fieldwork, and in order to grow the population, the biologists believe their breeders need to maintain stable territories and stable packs that regularly produce puppies each spring. But the illegal killings, whether accidental or not, are possibly curtailing the program's success, including the field staff's ability to control hybridization issues by using coyote sterilization as a management tool. According to David, if you slice the red wolf's population data certain ways, it actually looks like the program is failing because there are fewer breeding pairs now than in the past due to the disproportionate number of breeders becoming gunshot victims. In mid-October 2010, he told a reporter for the *Virginian-Pilot* that the illegal killings had "arrested" the wolves' population growth.

Art and Chris attribute a large part of the problem to hunters coming in from other areas. The Albemarle has one of the densest black bear populations in the East. In some areas of Pocosin Lakes National Wildlife Refuge, they number 3.5 bears per square mile. The bear season in the eastern part of the state runs in two short seasons embedded within the regular deer season. In 2010 deer hunting opened on October 2 and closed on New Year's Day. The bear season ran from November 8 to November 13 and again from

December 13 through Christmas Day. Art suspects that gunshot incidences spike during bear season, but he has not analyzed the population data to definitively answer this question. "We do know for sure that hunters come from other states just to hunt the bear population here," he says. Perhaps their ignorance of the differences between coyotes and red wolves leads to more wolves being shot.

Or perhaps some people conveniently forget what a red wolf looks like. This may have been what happened one morning three years back in Beaufort County, when Ford drove up to check his traps on private property and discovered the two-year-old wolf he'd been trying to catch lying in a soybean field with two traps on his feet and a bullet in his head. "I just immediately got out of my truck and started looking around," Ford recalled. "I could tell where the guy had shot from. It was about thirty yards away. It looked like he was out there at night spotlighting for coyotes, and he pulled up and saw this thing in the traps and just leveled it. His story is he thought it was a coyote, and so he shot it. When they say that, that's the end of the story." (At the time, spotlighting for coyotes was illegal.)

But one hunter I spoke with disagreed with the biologists' perception that mistaken identity was a key factor in why red wolves are shot.

"I can tell the difference between a red wolf and a coyote from a half mile away, from behavior more than anything," Troy Respess said. "They are two different animals. The red wolf, when he runs away from you, he's going to run kind of sideways and keep his eye on you the whole time. A coyote, when he takes off, he's going to bounce left and right the first hundred yards, and he won't look back till he's put some good distance between himself and you. It's just apples to oranges." In addition to hunting deer and bear, Troy said he'd hunted coyotes and other predators for the past ten years and that he never pulled the trigger without being sure that what he was shooting was a coyote. A few times when doubt set in, he'd taken his carcasses to the red wolf program biologists just to double-check. But so far, he'd shot straight. He said he most often hunts with his cousins, who still live near to where he grew up, in the community of Pungo. For him, predator hunting was a recreational and a social activity. He wasn't trying to manage land to thin coyotes out. And while he loved wild deer meat, he didn't hunt solely for protein, either. It was simply a way to escape the pressures of work life, to be outside with family and friends, and to interact with wildlife in a way that he enjoyed.

When I asked Troy if mistaken identity was ever a problem among the other hunters he knew, he huffed a little and said he was pretty sure that if someone shot a full-grown red wolf, they knew good and well what they were doing.

"If they weren't sure of the difference between the two, don't you think they'd be shooting the young red wolves?" he asked. It was an excellent point, and it exposed a mismatch between the logic of mistaken identity and the reality that the mature breeding wolves are shot more often.

"But what about hunters that come to the area from elsewhere," I asked. "Do you think they are aware of the red wolf program?"

"I think so," he replied. "The ones I know that visit from elsewhere have been doing so for a long time, and they know about it. Personally, I just think the red wolf has a target on it. I feel that they're targeted, they're not mistaken, more often than not."

Troy's candid responses made me wonder if perhaps the red wolf program was being too forgiving in offering the possibility that mistaken identity was the main problem. A more cynical reading of the situation might indicate that some folks were targeting red wolves knowingly. If this was true, then the issue would not be solved with measures like increased hunter-education opportunities.

The Humane Society of the United States, the Humane Society Wildlife Land Trust, and the Red Wolf Coalition offered a reward of $2,500 for any information that led to a prosecution in each of the six red wolf deaths in 2010. By the following spring, additional funders swelled the reward to $15,000. And by the summer of 2011, the FWS suspended indefinitely publishing updates on red wolf packs in the program's quarterly report because they believed some people used the information to locate and kill red wolves.

Under the law, the maximum criminal punishment the government could mete out was $100,000 in fines and one year of imprisonment per each illegally killed wolf. Yet there were few leads for the new FWS law-enforcement agent to follow. She helped the biologists to establish new protocols for when they find a wolf that has died suspiciously. Previously, if the wolf had an active radio collar, the biologists might have driven right up to the carcass in their trucks or all-terrain vehicles, picked up the dead wolf, and brought it back to a refuge facility, where they stored it in a walk-in freezer. But this procedure wiped out potential evidence like footprints or bullet casings and generally disturbed the crime scene. When the new agent assumed responsibility for the red wolf area in early 2010, she asked the field biologists to photograph the scenes where the wolves died and to park farther away and walk up to the carcasses in order to preserve evidence. They learned not to move a carcass until all the evidence was properly documented, even if it meant leaving the dead wolf to decompose further while she drove three hours to the site from her office in Raleigh. They ran metal detectors over the wolves' bodies to determine if buckshot or bullets were still inside, and they noted any holes in the carcasses. Bullet holes can be difficult to distinguish from postmortem scavenging activity by other animals. David hoped that her work would bring some resolution to the issues his program is having, and he expressed optimism that she will bring a fresh set of eyes to the issues. Only time will tell.

In addition to the problem of illegal killings, the program loses wolves in myriad other ways. The team tracks their wolf mortalities in five categories: natural, unknown, incidental, management, and foul play. "Natural" is self-explanatory, and "unknowns" include animals for which they can't determine a cause of death. "Incidental" includes cases where someone is doing a lawful activity, such as deer hunting with dogs or driving a car, and a wolf is killed accidentally. "Management" includes wolves that die from the biologists' actions, such as when a diseased wolf is euthanized. And "foul play" includes cases where something is definitely fishy. Between 1987 and 2010, the program documented the loss of 312 red wolves. Of these, 22.4 percent were deemed natural, 19.2 percent were unknowns, 25.3 percent were incidental, 6.4 percent were management, and 26.6 percent were foul play. If you group the incidental and foul play categories together, it means that 51.9 percent of red wolf deaths are directly related to human activities, whether lawful or not. Gunshot and vehicular collisions alone tally up to about 44 percent of red wolf deaths, according to a five-year report issued in 2007. If authorities could find a way to reduce the number of red wolves shot and run down by vehicles, that boost in number alone could lift the population out of its decade-long plateau.

When I return to the Albemarle in early January, winter grips the peninsula. Deer- and bear-hunting seasons are freshly concluded, and the biologists are up to their necks in trapping. Their targets are red wolves born only eight or nine months ago, which they want to collar. No longer wriggling pups that can fit in your palm, wolves at this age have nearly full-grown frames and are larger than a coyote. Ryan is after the pups of the Milltail pack in Alligator River National Wildlife Refuge. His trap line is hot: he caught four animals in the four days before I arrive. He still hasn't caught the breeding Waupaupin male with the dying GPS collar, though. The black bears that plagued him in October have slipped into their winter stupor, and bear-sprung traps are a thing of the past, at least until next fall. Ryan has trapped straight through the Christmas and New Year's Day holidays, but he doesn't seem at all tired when I catch up with him at 7:00 A.M. on the first Tuesday of 2011. "We ought to have a little more wolf action for you this time," he says as he greets me outside the red wolf headquarters. I hop into his truck. He briefs me on the pack he's after as we drive.

The Milltail breeding female birthed seven pups in the spring of 2010 and three in 2009. Of the three from 2009, one was hit by a car, one collared female juvenile was still with the pack, and Ryan had caught her brother over the weekend. Of the seven puppies born in 2010, Ryan has caught three since Friday. He is after the remaining four. Trapping puppies tends to be easier, he says, because they are more naive than their older siblings and parents. You just have to set a baited carcass out in their territory and wait.

On this morning, hoar frost coats blades of grass in the salt marsh. It renders their straw-colored shoots a translucent, washed-out blonde. A pair of tundra swans, visitors from the far North, flap slowly overhead. Skins of ice smother the canals across the refuge; everywhere, it contrasts with patches of exposed coffee-colored water. This sort of weather is borderline for trapping. Ryan reasons that the overnight low of thirty-four degrees Fahrenheit is just above the freezing temperatures that cause frostbite or exposure problems for the wolves (if they are trapped). Plus, there is just too much left on his trapping to-do list to close his line entirely because of one cold night. If it dips any lower, or if the coldest parts of the next few nights were forecast to last longer, then he'll pull his four dozen traps out of the ground.

We drive south and east a few miles from the Creef Cut Wildlife Trail off Highway 64 and pull up to a yellow metal swing-arm gate, which is closed. It sparkles with a sheen of ice crystals. About fifty feet past the gate, canes poke up in the underbrush of the forest's edge. Suddenly, they begin to shake. Twenty yards from this disturbance, a second patch of forest understory vibrates. Leaves, saplings, and grass quiver and tremble.

"We've got two animals!" Ryan exclaims. We hop out of the truck, and he unpacks two kennels and a catchpole. He pulls on leather work gloves as we trot to the first trap site. There is no need to track the trap's drag marks. The wolf had not moved far before the drag was caught in stiff brush.

"It's down on the bank," I say, and point to the base of a sweet gum tree where the land slips down into one of the refuge's ubiquitous canals. The young, lithe wolf hops around on three legs while the fourth stretches akimbo, stuck in an unmovable trap. The wolf struggles. It thrusts and heaves against the chain. It looks at us over its shoulder, whites of the eyes exposed, and jerks and strains. Ryan loops the catchpole expertly over the young wolf's head. Pinned, it lies on its side and curls its tail under. Amber-colored eyes fly this way and that. With the head immobilized, Ryan inches up on it and springs the trap.

"It's a female," he notes. "I think this is one of the pups from last spring." If she is a pup, then she is one of the target animals that Ryan had been trying to catch. We'd need to scan her PIT tag to know for sure.

Overnight, she had flattened the surrounding area. She snapped small saplings no bigger than my wrist and stomped the grasses flat. One sapling is reduced to an eighteen-inch-tall splintered spike that juts from the leaf litter. It glimmers with red.

"There's some blood over here," I say. "Is she bleeding anywhere?"

Ryan checks her over.

"She's got some small cuts, but not bad."

The wolves often struggle violently when they first get stuck in the trap, he explains. They may thrash about and stomp around. They chew down the stems of canes and saplings. Their panicked gnawing tatters their tongues and sometimes leaves bloody mouth prints. I lug the kennel down the embankment. He grabs the red wolf by the back of her neck, behind her ears, and she curls into a submissive ball, with her forelegs bent as if begging. He tugs her off the ground, noose still around her neck, and pushes her into the kennel. A touch of red streaks her trapped foot. She makes no sound. No growl. No whimper. She doesn't even snap. But our movements spook a flock of a hundred or more red-winged blackbirds. They alight from the crown of an oak tree, where they were cackling overhead moments before. The flock knots itself into a throbbing swarm and careens southwest.

With the first wolf in a locked kennel, we jog to the second animal. The bushes thrash and sway at our approach. Not far beyond the brush line, a wolf larger than the pup Ryan has just caught lunges in a blind panic. A radio collar hangs on its neck, an indication that this is probably the female yearling born in 2009. Ryan wades into the brush and angles the noose around her neck. The wolf collapses on her side, pushing her head against the ground.

"Aw jeez, she got into two traps," Ryan says. One hind foot and one forefoot are tangled in metal. Then he stiffens. I'd ridden with him long enough to read his scrunched shoulders and pursed lips as a warning sign. Something is wrong. He cusses, leans closer, and then thrusts the catchpole, secured around her neck, into my hands so he can examine her foot. "She bit off two of her toes," he says. His voice is flat and emotionless, a clue as to how upset he is. I peek over his shoulder. The female wolf's paw is mangled in the middle. Bits of tissue hang off the soft-sided trap jaw where she'd gnawed her own flesh during the night. Blood rings her muzzle, dyeing the white fur around her lips a garish rose. I clinch my teeth and grimace. While I was tucked in bed in my warm, heated hotel room the night before, this two-year-old red wolf had likely been caught, and then her feet had frozen when the temperatures dipped. Numb from the cold, she may not have realized that her razor-sharp incisors nibbled away on her own digits. Ryan removes the traps from her feet and then loads her into the kennel. Gently.

"Maybe I ought to have come out in the middle of the night to check this line." Ryan barely conceals his frustration. He is angry at himself for her loss. Each wolf, and their well-being, is extremely valuable to the recovery program.

"It doesn't seem feasible for you guys to check the traps at midnight, and still get up at dawn to check them. Not unless your staff was doubled and you ran it in shifts," I offer.

"Shifts, yeah I wish we could do that." He shakes his head and glares at the ground. "This sucks. We've only had this happen once in the past three or four years. She's going to have to go to the vet." The fact that she was already collared, that she is an unnecessary capture, compounds his dark mood.

With the wolves secure, he resets the triggered traps. There are still potentially three more pups to catch from this pack. He digs the traps back in and recounts trap injuries he's seen in the past that healed well with time. I am unsure if he's trying to reassure me or himself. He enjoys the challenge of trapping, he says, but hates it when the animals get hurt. When he's done, he walks back to fetch the truck closer. I wait with the wolves and drop to my knees to peer into the yearling's kennel. She sits awkwardly in the carrier, half-crouched with her injured legs askew. Her mangled hind foot juts out. Blood drips steadily from her fur onto the kennel bottom like a leaky tap. It pools. She smells of moist earth.

We drive the captured animals to the red wolf health-care facility for processing and treatment. Inside, a large cage with metal bars holds a seventy-pound male red wolf in the workshop area. He lies stretched out against the back wall, his head resting on straw. No matter how nonchalant he poses, no matter the disinterest he feigns, he keeps tabs on the exact movement of each person in the room. He's easily the largest red wolf I've yet seen, and if I happened upon him in the woods, there is no chance I'd mistake him for a needle-nosed coyote. When trapping specific animals in a pack, the team will often hold onto nontargeted animals for a few days if they happen to trap them. Such was this wolf's fate. The idea is that with nontargeted animals out of the picture for forty-eight to seventy-two hours, it ups the odds that the target wolf will tread across the two-inch pan of the trap laid for it. At first, the team thought this big wolf was the breeding male of the Northern pack because Ford had caught him within their range, so they didn't bother to scan his chip. But after they weighed him and he came in at a good seventy pounds, they realized it was a different animal. The male of the Northern pack only weighed sixty pounds; they'd caught him a few weeks prior, and it wasn't likely that he had gained so much weight so quickly. They finally figured out, from the PIT tag buried under his skin, that this wolf is a dispersing pup from the Newlands pack. This pack lived in proximity to a large hog farm, and they had learned to feed on carcass piles of piglets and adult pigs left out by the farm operators. The biologists suspect that the supplemental food helped the wolves grow larger, as their offspring always seemed comparatively burlier than those from other packs. (They also wondered if perhaps, by eating these carcasses, the wolves ingested some of the hormones given to the hogs while alive to make them grow faster and larger.)

Ford and Michael Morse, another red wolf biologist, uncrate the Milltail puppy Ryan has caught this morning. She has balled herself up in the back of the kennel and refuses to move. They upend her box. She topples out ungracefully, like a frozen statue. Paralyzed with fear, someone says. They blindfold her and place her on the exam table. The eight-month-old wolf weighs 35.2 pounds and measures fifty-nine centimeters tall at her shoulder. They jab her with vaccines and inspect her cuts. They pull back her gums and scrutinize her teeth. Her front incisors still have small bilateral cusps. By the time she's two, these will have worn away—perhaps faster if she chews on a lot of bones, fences, beer cans, or scrap metal. Michael finds an inch-and-a-half-long slice on her hind flank. He fishes in his pocket for his bifocal glasses.

"Stitch it," Chris offers.

"No, she'll chew them," Michael says.

"Yeah, she'll just lick at 'em," Ford agrees.

"The tissue is granulating. It'll close on its own," Michael says.

"Well, you could put one stitch here, where it's more open," Chris suggests.

"Nah, just leave it," Ford says.

They place a radio collar on her neck, careful to leave room for her to grow. Not once does the wolf struggle. They place her back in the kennel.

Her older sister, the yearling, weighs in at 45.8 pounds and measures 67.3 centimeters tall at the shoulder. Her tail has acted like a paint brush, smearing the kennel floor and other interior surfaces with her blood. Clots cling to her guard hairs. Blood cakes her hind foot.

"Something tells me you are going to lose those two toes," Chris says, leaning in for a closer look. "Yep, that's the knuckle." He points to an exposed, gray, gristly looking joint. Michael and Ford each take turns examining her mangled paw. The men sigh and frown. They abhor trap injuries. By the time they finish their examination, their blue latex gloves are streaked with her blood. Ryan records notes on her data sheet with extra care to avoid staining them with his blood-smeared hands. Again, the biologists discuss treatment. But this time, they all agree: she'll go to their veterinarian in Manteo.

The next day, the team gets a morale boost. The Northern pack is ready to be released back into their home range. When Ryan calls to tell me the news, excitement colors his voice. For as upset as he was over the lost toes, he is ecstatic about releasing these wolves. They never found the den of the Northern pack last breeding season, he tells me, because the breeding female's collar had quit. But the day before, Chris caught and recollared the Northern breeding female, and her four pups were captured during the past three weeks. (Earlier, a fifth pup was found dead in a farm field near to their den site. The pup tackled by Justin Dellinger was also from this pack.) It was the first evidence they had of the breadth of her litter. The family was being held at Sandy Ridge while the biologists tried to determine if there were any more puppies in their territory. Unfortunately, the morning the biologists try to kennel the Northern pups to transport them for release, they discover that one of the pups has severely damaged a toe. (All of the puppies gained ten pounds in their three-week-long captivity at Sandy Ridge.) Perhaps he'd tried to dig his way out, they surmise. They send him to the vet for stitches, but he'll need to be held for at least another week for a course of antibiotics. The field team is frustrated, because if the pup hadn't tried to escape, he would have gone home today.

Ryan and graduate student Joey Hinton load the Northern pack's kennels into their truck beds. Joey is a student at Louisiana State University, and he is working on a coyote–red wolf interaction study in the red wolf area. He sometimes lends a hand with fieldwork. We race a setting sun to the release site, some ten minutes from the workshop facility. Once there,

Ryan opens one of the pervasive metal swing-arm gates that blocks a gravel refuge road. He pulls out some binoculars to study a black speck several hundred yards away. A small bear stares back at him and sniffs the wind. We unload the kennels in a line along the dirt access road. Ryan springs the breeding female's door first. I half expect her to leap out and run into the nearest brush, but she doesn't. She sits stooped in the kennel. The door creaks in the wind. Ryan walks behind the kennel and gives it a sharp whack with his foot. She springs out and sprints a few yards. Her head strains forward and rear legs charge past her ears. Then she slows, stops, and looks back at us with her body exposed broadside.

"I wish they wouldn't do that." Ryan shakes his head. "They stop in the middle of the road, fully exposed and show their whole flank. I wish she'd find some cover."

He stomps and raises his arms, challenging her to run off.

She stands on her long legs, staring at us with amber eyes. She turns and trots slowly, looking back frequently. We still have her babies.

One by one, Ryan opens the doors of the pups' kennels, then kicks the back ends to encourage them out. It is like watching track stars leap out of their starting blocks—except the wolf pups are not as coordinated as track stars as they rev up to full speed from a sitting position. They scramble out so fast that they trip. Paws and legs shoot out in all directions before they corral all their limbs into a back-legs-to-ears gait that swallows up yard after yard. One lands nose first in the dust a yard past his kennel. He picks himself up and takes off again. The pups are gifted but ungainly athletes who haven't yet harnessed their full potential.

The sun is at the horizon line, and a cold wind picks up. The four wolves nose into the woods and out of sight. Ryan watches them with binoculars to make sure they stay out of the road.

"It is a nice feeling," he says to no one in particular, "to know that you are helping them."

I reflect on the fact that in roughly three weeks, the red wolves will breed. About sixty days later, the females will birth new litters. Between now and then, the red wolf team will work long days to trap as many animals as they can right up to breeding season. Then they'll back off, increase their telemetry surveys, let the wolves have their privacy, and hope for a groundswell of pregnancies.

Each season of work holds a different purpose, a different goal. In the year and a half I have spent visiting, I learned that nearly every day in the field brings unexpected situations, surprises, disappointments, and achievements. Rarely have things proceeded exactly as planned. Improvisation is one of the field biologists' best assets. Perhaps what has made the red wolf program so successful to date is its ability to adapt its management of the wolves as circumstances, and our scientific understanding of red wolves, change.

But I also know that Ryan, Chris, Art, Ford, Michael, and David can work long hours and manage the wolves until they are blue in the face, and it will be for naught if the local citizens don't tolerate *Canis rufus*. For this program to work, the local people must be on board.

## CHAPTER 7
# People of the Albemarle Peninsula

Today, the Albemarle Peninsula contains some of the poorer and more sparsely populated counties in the state. But this does not mean that the people here are without resources or a strong sense of community. Kelly Davis is a farmer's wife in her early fifties who lives on the southern shores of Lake Mattamuskeet. Her husband, Blythe, is one of the many farmers in the area who grow field corn, soybeans, and winter wheat. In his fields, he fosters wild quail for hunting. Other crops in the region include cotton, cucumbers, string beans, cabbage, and sweet corn. Kelly is in the 11 percent of people in Hyde County who hold a master's degree or higher. A former biologist at Mattamuskeet National Wildlife Refuge, Kelly creates every opportunity possible to teach her two young children about the natural wonders in their area. Her family takes a footpath directly from their farm onto the refuge, where her older daughter dabbles in nature photography. During waterfowl-hunting season, they hear the pop-pop-pop of shotguns fired on the giant lake where ducks, geese, and swans roost and feed. She homeschools her children, teaching them such things as how night-sky brightness and water temperatures affect breeding frog calls. During waterfowl season, she helps them cut the wings from ducks that the hunters have shot to make interpretative displays for the refuge. At night, she shows her children the Andromeda Galaxy and Jupiter's moons with a telescope. Hyde County's sparse density of ten people per square mile translates to an uncommon clarity in the night skies. When an enormous male black bear (she claims it was 800 pounds) was road killed near her house, Kelly got an education permit from the state to collect its bones for rearticulation. Blythe used their combine and a chain to pull the bear off the road and into the brush. She and her kids documented the animals that scavenged its carcass until it was nothing more than bones resting on a giant grease stain.

"When you live somewhere like this, you have to squeeze the juice out of it," Kelly says. "So I squeeze, and I squeeze, and I squeeze." Lines on her youthful face speak of someone who has spent the better part of her life out-of-doors. As a resident of Hyde County since 1980, she remembers when the red wolves were reintroduced in 1987. The first time she found a larger-than-normal canid scat, she tucked it in an envelope and sent it to the program biologists for identification. She hoped it was from a wolf, and it was. But not everyone was as curious as Kelly. Some people were anxious and others angry at the wolves' arrival. "I think initially it was a perception thing, that there would be wolves all over the place, that they'd be eating your house cats and your geese in your backyard," Kelly says. "But you know, I have heard so little in the past five or ten years. So few complaints. I think it's just sort of settled out."

In the early days of red wolf reintroduction, some community members were concerned for their safety, but it was the deer hunters who complained, she says. In the beginning, the Fish and Wildlife Service told people that the wolves would not eat deer. It was a partial truth—but also a partial lie. The last wild red wolves in southeastern Texas and southwestern Louisiana ate mostly rodents and rabbits. But they were also living in coastal prairies where, at the time, deer were absent or thinly distributed. No one performed a dietary study on the last remaining red wolves. So in reality, the FWS didn't know for sure if the reintroduced wolves would eat deer. But they did, and when the deer herds began to be affected by the reintroduced wolves, it only served to heighten the distrust between deer hunters and the red wolf program. "It probably ticked them off because they were paying to hunt those deer," Kelly says. "They were competing with another predator. Isn't that what we get mad at? The ones that get to the meat before we do?" The issue became less pointed when years passed and the deer-hunting clubs still had successful hunts, she says.

One thing that changed people's minds was when they encountered the program biologists. People in Kelly's community talked among themselves that the biologists were "really nice people." And in Hyde County, treating someone right goes a long way. Even if the community did not agree with having wolves on the landscape, their attitudes sometimes softened once they interacted with the wolf crew. People liked Michael Morse especially and felt he treated them fairly. Usually, these encounters came about when residents called with complaints about missing chickens or goats or requested to have a wolf removed from their property.

In general, the wolves are more thinly distributed south of Lake Mattamuskeet than north of it near Fairfield. Kelly doesn't have any red wolves living on her farm, but her family finds prints and scat on occasion that lead her to believe they pass through. (When her kids want to sleep outside in their tent, she checks the yard for signs of wolves and bears; if there are any, the kids must slumber indoors.) Blythe wants wolves on their land to curtail the herbivory damage their crop suffers from deer each year and to keep the number of foxes lower, which enhances his quail hunting. "To me, the wolves add a lovely dimension to Hyde County," Kelly says. "It's one more way to say, 'How cool is it that this place can sustain an animal as wild as a wolf?' There aren't many places like this left. We're proud of our dark skies, bears, rattlesnakes, and wolves."

But not everyone is as open-minded as Kelly and Blythe. Some local people have toed the neutral line on red wolves for years, or remained tepid supporters afraid to speak out to others in their community. Jamin Simmons might fall into this category. Jamin was born and raised in Fairfield on the north side of Lake Mattamuskeet, where there are more red wolves than on the lake's south side. He's the fourth generation of his family to live in this small farming community of a little more than a thousand people. The largest employer here is the state forest service. His father was a district forest ranger and scheduled all of his vacation time during hunting seasons so he could work as a guide in the business that Jamin's grandfather started in the 1930s. Jamin works in this same business today.

Jamin also created a job for himself as a land manager, and he offers technical services in wildlife resources and conservation. After managing Mattamuskeet Ventures, a 15,000-acre farm (the one where Ryan and I spotted the black bears at the corn feeder) for ten years, he received consulting requests from other farms across the state and soon the Southeast. His work grew into Mattamuskeet Management and Consulting, a company that manages farmland in three states and consults in seven. He's worked with researchers from N.C. State University on bear studies and cooperated with Ducks Unlimited and the Wild Turkey Federation on conservation projects. He's also long cooperated with the red wolf program by allowing them access to land he manages and owns. The first red wolf born in the wild after reintroduction came into the world on his farm in 1988.

"The thing you got to understand about Hyde County," he tells visitors, "is that we got the 'three twos.' We are the second-largest county by land area, the second-least-populated, and the second-poorest in the state." The per capita income in Hyde County is about $16,000. Portions of the county that lie on the mainland exhibit a palpably more conservative culture than areas that lie in the Outer Banks. The second thing to understand is that most people in mainland Fairfield have what Jamin calls an "anti-bureaucracy attitude." He says they are dead set against the FWS and the state Wildlife Resources Commission managing the natural resources in their county. So when the FWS announced its plans to release wolves in the late 1980s, the animals became four-legged symbols of the bureaucratic overlords that some people perceived as controlling the local natural resources. This is not an entirely new phenomenon: wolves have long been been receptacles of meaning attached to them by others. Some people see them as symbols of wilderness, others see them as symbols of government control, and still others see these animals as evidence of someone else's dictatorial value system.

In the beginning, Jamin told folks he was "cautiously optimistic" about the program. But later he felt that the red wolf program made a large misstep by telling people that the reintroduced wolves would not eat deer. "As soon as the first wolves were out, people found skeletons or partially eaten ones, and we knew they were eating deer, especially the young ones," he says. Folks in his community were upset and anxious about the deer herds. An average landowner here can lease his or her property to deer hunters for $5 or more per acre, and an average lease might range from 50 to 300 acres. While that may not seem like a lot of money, it could help pay for necessities for a cash-strapped family. Some people felt that their income, as well as their protein supply, were threatened. It added fodder to the government stigma that the wolves bore and widened the gulf of mistrust. (As a biologist working at Lake Mattamuskeet, Kelly says her supervisors told her, "Don't tell the people the wolves eat deer.")

Before Alligator River and Mattamuskeet National Wildlife Refuges were formed, many of the local people hunted these lands, some of which were owned by absentee landlords. After the wolves came, they felt that their "rights" to the land were snatched out from under them. When wolves were placed in the Alligator River refuge and the canids came out of the refuge and ate deer elsewhere, it pushed people's buttons. The passage of time has softened the intensity of some people's anger. Others have noticed small favorable changes in the land around them that is possibly due to the wolves, such as more quail and less nutria in their fields, Jamin says.

Like Blythe, Jamin maintains habitat for quail, and he manages his land to minimize the presence of small predators that eat quail and their eggs. This means trapping bobcats, foxes, raccoons, and possums and killing black snakes. His management actions mimic what the presence of a large predator in the area, like a red wolf, is predicted to do under the ecological theory of mesopredator release. The theory, first proposed by ecologist Dave Wilcove in 1985, states that when larger predators are in a given ecosystem, they limit the smaller predators, called mesopredators, to a certain threshold of abundance. When the larger predators are removed from the ecosystem, the mesopredator populations swell unchecked. This translates to widespread changes within food webs because there are more mesopredators eating more prey.

A study published in the science journal *Nature* by Michel Soulé and Kevin Crooks in 1999 further refined Wilcove's idea and showed that the presence of coyotes had the effect of protecting birds in certain landscapes. This is because the coyotes kept smaller bird-eating predators like raccoons, possums, foxes, and house cats at bay. Soulé's paper focused on the local extinctions of scrub-breeding birds in study sites fragmented by urban development. Nearly half of these fragments were visited by coyotes, but the other half were not. (Coyotes were the largest predator in this ecosystem; next were gray foxes, raccoons, possums, and house cats.) He found that the coyote-patrolled scrub fragments contained higher numbers of birds and more diverse bird species, whereas the scrub fragments that lacked coyotes had fewer overall birds and species present. The paper is considered a landmark ecological study demonstrating mesopredator release.

Five years ago, Jamin saw similar cascades through the food web on his land, where his quail population was healthy. But since then, the number of quail he's seen each season fluctuates. "It's hard to know if it's our management, or the wolves," he concedes. "But I'll tell you this, before the wolves were reintroduced, we had a real bad nutria and muskrat problem. They were ruining our roads. Now, we don't have a problem at all. Plus, our bucks are getting bigger, and their racks are getting bigger. Now, it's hard to say if that's the wolves or our management, but our deer herd is steady. We take between 200 and 300 every year, and our deer herd is in really good condition." Jamin's observation of fewer muskrats in the area since the red wolves were reintroduced to the land also fits with the mesopredator release theory. The controlling effect that red wolves may have on nutria could be attributed to what ecologists call the top-down controlling effect that apex predators—those predators that sit at the top of a food web—have upon the prey that occupy niches in the food-web levels below.

But landowners may see these effects of the wolves more often than they see the animals themselves. Jamin has had a few run-ins with red wolves. He sees the long-limbed, reddish canids on the Mattamuskeet Ventures farm, usually around breeding season, and he sees both wolves and coyotes on another farm where he hunts. The property is half in Hyde County and half in Tyrrell County. He thinks there are more coyotes there than on his own nearby farm because an intracoastal waterway separates the two properties and may be a barrier to the smaller canids crossing further east. Twice when hunting bears, Jamin encountered wolves in recent years. Once, his dogs ran a wolf, but he was able to stop them. Another time, eight bear dogs he was hunting with bayed a wolf, but he and his hunting party were able to "catch the dogs off the wolf" before any of the creatures were harmed.

Hunters rarely worry about run-ins with wolves, he says. Rather, it is people in the community who feel vulnerable. His son's kids were playing in the yard one day when a red wolf wandered in. No one was hurt, and Jamin says the wolf approached in a nonthreatening way. But it was the sort of incident that makes folks jittery—kids and a sizable predator in close proximity. People in Fairfield see the red wolves occasionally, and they hear them howling at night because a travel corridor exists south of town where wolves cross east to west on the north side of the lake.

While it would be foolhardy to pledge that a red wolf would never attack a person unprovoked, there are also no valid records that one ever has. The thought of being attacked and eaten by a wolf dredges up humanity's worst fears about becoming prey to wild animals. What fate could be worse than to be devoured as meat? But it's important to keep in mind that some animals we view as safe also inflict injury on a regular basis. More than 800,000 people in the United States seek treatment for domestic dog bites each year, and of these, about sixteen die, according to the Centers for Disease Control and Prevention. The only reported human injuries sustained from red wolves are the result of people who handle them for management reasons. But facts don't always appease the anxious mind of someone who lives in the same landscape where wolves roam. The lessons we absorbed as children from Little Red Riding Hood and The Three Little Pigs cast a long shadow, one that obscures our perception of fact and fiction as adults.

Jamin estimates that of the people in his area today, about 15 percent support the program, 40 percent are neutral, and the rest are opposed to it. "But those that are against it, it's not because they understand the program, or any of that," he says. "It's just the stigma of the bureaucracy. You aren't gonna change their minds." Because he is tolerant of wolves, even supportive behind closed doors, Jamin does not openly share his views with others in the red wolf recovery area. This is not unusual for people who are supportive (or outwardly neutral but inwardly supportive) and who live in rural areas where people generally hold antipredator views. By obscuring their opinions, people like Jamin maintain their place in their community by not rocking the boat.

A study by sociologists Ketil Skogen and Olve Krange in southeastern

Norway found that the rural community of Stor-Eldval used anticarnivore attitudes against native predators—brown bears, wolves, wolverines, and lynx—as a way to unite their community and even perpetuate its identity. Skogen and Krange found that anticarnivore sentiments in Stor-Eldval clustered around a cultural and an economic axis. These two axes converged within the community and had the effect of linking social groups that historically did not get along. While landowners, hunters, and sheep farmers differed in opinions of land use and in their perception of their relationship to the land, they all banded together in an anticarnivore alliance that helped them to symbolically construct their community identity and what constituted threats against it. This alliance improved and strengthened trust between disparate community members by giving them common ground. Wolves, especially, were viewed as symbolic, but not of wilderness or nature; rather, wolves were perceived as symbols of *cities*, because in recent years, it has been advocates from urban areas who push for wolf and carnivore conservation, which typically occurs in rural areas. The reappearance of wolves in their landscape, after a decades-long absence, was widely viewed as an attack by urbanites upon the community's rural life. Though this study was done halfway around the world, the conditions closely mimic the Albemarle, where wolves have been absent for generations and then were brought back, largely with the support of urban advocates from places distant to the recovery area.

Troy Respess is a local who was born and raised in the community of Pungo and has family ties to that area. Though he now lives in Winterville, just inland from the peninsula, he returns to the Pungo area four or five times a week. He's not fond of the red wolf. Troy hunts with his cousins, mostly deer and bear, but he also goes after predators on a regular basis. Troy also belongs to the Albemarle Hunting Club, which leases 12,000 acres from the Weyerhaeuser timber company. The land spans between Hyde and Washington Counties west of Pocosin Lakes National Wildlife Refuge. Most of the deer and bear hunting on the Weyerhaeuser land is done with dogs. Unlike Jamin, Troy says he's noticed a definite decline in deer over the past few years, and he attributes this in part to the red wolves.

"Before the red wolf was introduced, we could run dogs, and we'd see twenty to thirty deer a day," he says. "And not all of those were ones the dogs were actively running, lots were just flushed out because they were scared of the dogs. But in the last six or seven years, a lot of days, the only deer you'll see now is the ones the dogs are on." However, Troy is careful to point out that chronic wasting disease affected the deer in his area at about the same time the red wolf was introduced. He also allows that bear and coyotes likely work the fawns over each spring, too. "To be fair, I don't know that we can blame just the red wolf," he concludes. "But, I do think they've done their part to keep our deer from coming back."

Troy says he often spots red wolves when he's simply driving down the highway, as well as when he's out hunting. His cousins see them when they plow and plant their farmland near the refuge. He figures he spots the wolves around eight or ten times per year. The sightings "come in spells," but he attributes the frequency mostly to the amount of time he spends in the area.

Troy also sees them when he hunts predators. He uses a mouth call that mimics an injured rabbit and then waits to see what shows up. "It's always a surprise, that's what I like about it," he says. "Some days, you might call in a bobcat, other days it's a fox, sometimes it's a coyote or a red wolf. You just never know what's going to come around."

Even though some folks would pay $100 or more for just one chance to see the red wolves he sees fairly regularly, Troy's not at all keen on the creatures. He doesn't believe they are "true wolves" because they have hybridized and likely aren't the exact same animal as what used to be here. The vast majority of the hunters in his club see things similarly and are opposed to the red wolf program, he says. But whereas people used to be more vocal about their opposition, he says it's not really a topic of conversation anymore. "We don't like it any better than we used to, but now we just find other things to talk about," he says.

Troy's stance reflects the fact that, although some locals are still opposed to the program, the length of time they've endured it has perhaps silenced their dissent. While it may be easy to interpret silence as tolerance, the two dispositions really are not at all alike. Perhaps the red wolves that have been shot or poisoned or have disappeared are some people's way of expressing how they really feel.

In the minds of some residents, not only are red wolves not true wolves, but they also never inhabited the peninsula to begin with. One outspoken dissident who embraces this idea is Mike Johnson, a private wildlife manager who works in Hyde County and lives in Dare County, where he serves as a county commissioner. Hyde and parts of Dare are very different due to tourism in the portion of Dare that lies in the Outer Banks. Per capita income in Dare is about $27,000. Dare also has nearly eight times the density of people that Hyde has. As a wildlife manager, Mike's clients are wealthy landowners from the Triangle—a cosmopolitan, well-educated region in the center of North Carolina. (It is bounded by Duke University, the University of North Carolina at Chapel Hill, and North Carolina State University.) His clients want to visit their getaways near the coast for recreational hunting and fishing, so he manages their land for game animals.

Mike grew up in Plymouth, a small town on the northwestern side of the red wolf recovery area in Washington County, and moved east to the beach two decades ago. Around the same time, he began working in Hyde County and immediately felt at home. Mike says that a lack of folklore about red wolves among local families that descend from some of the first European settlers to the area in the mid-1700s and early 1800s leads him to disbelieve that red wolves were ever present here historically. "I found the folklore for things like bears and large cats with long tails, but I just can't find the folklore on the wolf," he says. "I might be missing it, but I have not found it. The only thing we have to go on when we decide whatever happened in an area is local history, local knowledge, local whatever, and there are no written wolf stories in Hyde County or Dare County lore." He also disbelieves that wolves were ever in the whole of North Carolina, or that red wolves are a species. He thinks they are, at best, hybrids. "People here just don't like them, and they don't like the wolf program," Mike says. "You won't find hardly anybody here other than the U.S. government that feels a lot different than me."

While folks like Mike may have searched for wolf folklore and not uncovered it, that doesn't mean it doesn't exist regionally. There are records and diaries of early European explorers and settlers who saw and heard wolves in the swamps of eastern North Carolina. Historic Tyrrell County court records document eight wolf-scalp bounties paid out to different individuals between 1768 and 1789. Other regional records are lacking, likely destroyed in the Civil War; but if wolves were in Tyrrell County, it becomes hard to argue that they were absent from the rest of the peninsula.

Despite his stance against red wolves, Mike says that with time, he's starting to see that the wolves are not as destructive or as ferocious as he once thought they might be. "They're actually kind of docile," he admits. He sees other people in his community who oppose wolves and who have lost the sharpness of their anger, but not because they've come to like the animal. "It's like three-dollars-and-a-half gas. We've seen three-dollar gas before, and we got used to it," he says. "We don't like it, it's an inconvenience, but now we just don't bitch about it." As for the once-contentious debate about whether red wolf restoration should take place here, he chuckles and says, "It's done. It's over. There's no debate anymore. Even for an old hard head like me."

Despite the differences between the views of Kelly Davis, Jamin Simmons, Troy Respess, and Mike Johnson, there are some similarities. For one thing, they each find a certain meaning in the phenomenon of red wolf reintroduction, though the meaning itself may differ. The diversity of their views is reminiscent of a passage written by Dr. Stephen Fritts, a scientist in the FWS: "Ultimately, the wolf exists in the eye of the beholder. There is the wolf as science can describe it, but there is also the wolf that is the product of the human mind, a cultural construct—sometimes called the 'symbolic wolf'—colored by our individual, cultural, or social conditioning."

Perhaps this conception of the red wolf as a product of the human mind can explain the results of a 2009 survey of farm operators in the restoration area that uncovered a strong bias against the animal. The survey was designed by Randall Kramer, a professor of environmental economics at Duke University. It asked questions that probed farmers' interest in compensation for conserving wildlife habitat and ecosystem services on their land, but Kramer was primarily interested in the farmers' willingness to accept payment to conserve the red wolf. The survey asked farmers to place a dollar value upon a program that would enlist their help to conserve red wolf habitat. It then asked the same question of farmers in Bertie County, abutting but outside of the red wolf recovery area, but for Bertie residents it substituted the word "wildlife" for "red wolf." The results showed that within the recovery area, participants demanded an average of $202 per acre to conserve red wolves; whereas outside the recovery area, participants asked for $36 per acre to conserve wildlife. To put it another way, you would need to pay five and a half times more money to farmers in the red wolf recovery area to conserve their land for red wolves than you would to farmers outside the recovery area to conserve their land for wildlife in general. Despite the high value that the farmers in the recovery area placed on conservation payments for wolves, only 13 percent of respondents from the recovery area said they would participate in such a program, while 45 percent of respondents from Bertie County expressed interest for what would be vastly less income. In the wolf recovery area, around half of those who said they would not participant listed their main reason as "do not wish to help [the] red wolf population." The other half cited their main reasons as "concern about government restriction on private property" and "do not want to change the way I manage my land." Perhaps with the cleansing power of many decades, the negative attitude farmers in the wolf recovery area hold toward conserving Canis rufus will soften or even fade, just as it has among some rural citizens.

Most people on the Peninsula live in a closer relationship to the land than the majority of modern Americans, more than half of whom now live in or near cities. Whether the citizens of the Albemarle Peninsula hunt, farm, or fish, their fortunes are closely tied to the health of the land and its wildlife bounty. Trapping animals is another tradition in this area. Settlers trapped for food and fur; today, people trap to rid their land of animals they consider nuisances, such as otters, beavers, nutria, and muskrats. Some also trap red and gray foxes to sell to fox pens. These pens are large areas encircled by dog-proof fences; they may encompass forested woods, swamps, and open fields. Some are a few dozen acres, while others are hundreds of acres. Live foxes are placed in the pens, where hunting dogs are trained to bay them. Often the foxes are injured or killed after several rounds of having dogs set upon them. While state law requires these pens to contain an escape route for a cornered fox to lunge into for refuge from the dogs, opponents to the pens claim that operators barricade these off during competitions in which dogs are scored on how fast they track or corner the foxes. The operations are supposed to be licensed, but opponents say the state lacks the resources to regularly inspect the licensed facilities. Several states, such as Florida, have passed laws making fox pens illegal. But they are legal in North Carolina, where fox hunting and running foxes have deep cultural roots.

In 2003 North Carolina changed its wildlife laws to allow the trapping and transport of coyotes within its state lines, specifically at the behest of fox-hunt lobbyists. The operators discovered that coyotes hold up better in the pens than foxes. As a result, a new market for the purchase of live coyotes opened in eastern North Carolina. (Rumor has it that the allure of fox pens here was so strong that a tractor-trailer full of coyotes for sale came to the state from Florida, even though it is illegal to transport coyotes across state lines.) Today, there are about 140 licensed fox pens in North Carolina, with the majority concentrated east of Raleigh. A nonprofit group called Project Coyote that advocates against fox pens claims some operations are nothing more than legalized dogfighting, since foxes and coyotes are both within the Canidae family.

In the fall of 2010, the red wolf program began tapping a local resource: skilled trappers, many of whom were trapping coyotes to sell to fox pens. The program wanted to get a first look at any canid the trappers caught and to offer them money for their trouble. It all started with the biologists' concern that perhaps some of their juvenile red wolves were getting trapped, being mistaken for coyotes, and being sold to fox-pen operators. (When fall trapping commences, red wolf pups may be coyote sized.) They'd gotten more than one report, which they considered to be highly reliable, of "extra large" coyotes in fox pens that were "good fighters" against the foxhounds. While the red wolf team had only circumstantial evidence that some of their red wolves might be ending up in the fox pens, it was a scary enough prospect that they worked out agreements with the area's best trappers.

Technically, the trappers can sell their quarry only to a state-licensed fox pen. Because the wolf program is not licensed, this initially meant they could not pay the trappers for their coyotes. They worked with the state to authorize private trappers to work under the red wolf program's trapping permit, which allows for the capture and transport of red wolves and coyotes. The program also worked with the state to allow private trappers working under their permit to be compensated for their time and effort at a rate comparable to the per-coyote sales to fox pens. As part of this agreement, the program got a first look at all the canids larger than a fox that the trappers caught. While none of the red wolf biologists like the fact that fox pens are legal, they hope the agreements with private trappers will minimize the risk that immature red wolves are being siphoned off as unwitting foxhound trainers. Plus, they hope it will increase the trust of local residents, which in turn might increase tolerance for the red wolves within local communities.

One winter morning in 2011, while I am riding with Ryan, a private fur trapper working with the red wolf program calls. He has caught a coyote and wants someone to fetch it. The trapper is south of Englehard between Scourge Town and Green Hill Roads. We make the forty-minute drive south on Highway 264 and bounce along a ridged, potholed dirt road near a flooded corn field. We arrive as the trapper is strangling two foxes. He stands next to his pickup truck bed and holds a red fox by a wire wound around its neck. Satisfied that the noose is tight enough, he lays it next to a gray fox suffering a similar fate. Blood and saliva leak from the gray fox's mouth. Its teeth are bright red. Ryan gives me a look. I figure he's unsure how I'll react to someone killing an animal right before my eyes.

"Hey there," the trapper smiles. "Mornin'."

"Good morning," I say. We shake hands.

A death convulsion grips the red fox. Its back arches and its tail straightens. The corneas take on a filmy, dull sheen. It dies as the three of us exchange pleasantries.

"She's in there." He points at a kennel next to the foxes. The gray fox hacks and gurgles. Its chest heaves for oxygen. The trapper doesn't seem to notice, but I can't take my eyes off the animal. Blood and drool intermingle on the metal beneath its head. The men begin to transfer the coyote. The trapper, who wears waders and is about six feet tall, jabs a catchpole into the kennel. He pokes at the coyote but can't slip the noose over her ears. Ryan shoos the trapper aside and plunges his arms shoulder-deep into the kennel, grasps the coyote firmly behind her ears and lifts her out. She dangles limp, submissive, and tiny. She is built more lightly than a red wolf and weighs roughly twenty pounds.

"You just reached right in there!" The trapper laughs and watches Ryan maneuver the coyote. Ryan tucks her into the new kennel.

"She didn't have much fight in her," he says. He nods at the dead foxes. "You're not working in the live market anymore?"

"No. Got to be too much of a pain," the trapper says. "It's gotten to where I have to keep them for ten or twelve days, and feed them the whole time, because the owners don't want to come down and buy till you got about a dozen. For me to get that many, I have to hold on to them too long. I don't like selling to them anyways. I'm going to try the fur markets this year."

The live market might command $30 to $40 per gray fox and $50 to $80 per red fox, whereas the fur markets would garner $10 more per gray fox and about the same amount per red fox. Even though it meant skinning the animals, this trapper has chosen to go with the fur markets because it was simply easier. Plus, with no fox pens in Hyde County, it was often logistically difficult to get the animals to a buyer. It heartens me that he doesn't like selling to the fox-pen operators.

We chat with the trapper for a few more minutes. He peppers Ryan with questions about red wolves and wants to know about their relationship to gray wolves. His questions show a genuine desire to learn about the red wolf's natural history. He says he likes to read wildlife books to pass the hours in his deer blind, waiting for the right buck to wander by. We drive the coyote back to Sandy Ridge. Ryan expresses hope that working with trappers like this one will help reduce the chance that red wolves will be accidentally sold to fox pens. He also hopes that the arrangement will help build community trust with the program and tolerance for the wolves. History shows that it is only through the tolerance and social acceptance of the local population that the red wolf's future can be assured.

But that is not all the red wolf needs. We must also thoroughly understand its biological past and its natural history as a species on an evolutionary trajectory. So few red wolves remained when scientists began studying them that untangling their evolutionary origins proved a difficult feat. But science's inquiry into what a red wolf is today led to a controversy as to whether the red wolf ever existed at all.

A male red wolf gnaws on a sapling at Sandy Ridge, a captive facility, within Alligator River National Wildlife Refuge. (Ryan Nordsven/U.S. Fish and Wildlife Service)

Red wolves have wider skulls and snouts in comparison to coyotes. This captive male was photographed at Sandy Ridge. (Ryan Nordsven/U.S. Fish and Wildlife Service)

Captive red wolves like this one may live to be ten or fifteen years old. In contrast, a wild red wolf may only live four to eight years. (Ryan Nordsven/U.S. Fish and Wildlife Service)

(top) Red wolves may birth between one to nine pups, but the average captive litter size is 3.4 pups. This captive red wolf litter of eight or more, born in 2008 at Sandy Ridge, is above average. (Ryan Nordsven/U.S. Fish and Wildlife Service)

(bottom) Captive red wolf pups are sometimes "fostered" into the wild if they are born within one to two days of a wild litter. This practice ensures a small level of gene flow from the captive to the wild populations. (Ryan Nordsven/U.S. Fish and Wildlife Service)

(top) Ryan Nordsven holds two red wolf pups that had radio transmitters surgically placed within their abdomens. These transmitters can be tracked with telemetry gear just like a radio collar, though their signal is weaker. (U.S. Fish and Wildlife Service)

(bottom) During puppy season, the field team tracks down all breeding pairs thought to have birthed a litter and finds their dens. A tiny amount of blood is drawn from each puppy. Each is also injected with a chip about the size of a grain of rice that will help identify the wolf later in its life. (Ryan Nordsven/U.S. Fish and Wildlife Service)

(top) Chris Lucash (left) bolts a radio collar onto an 82-pound red wolf. Wild red wolves are often processed in the Red Wolf Education and Health Care Facility in Columbia, North Carolina. There they are fitted with radio collars, given vaccines, weighed, and thoroughly checked over. The wolves are not always sedated during these workups. (Debbie Mauney)

(bottom) A red wolf's wild den is never easy to find. Ford Mauney crawled through dense underbrush in a timber stand before finding this hidden entrance, dug at an angle into a slope. (Ryan Nordsven/U.S. Fish and Wildlife Service)

(top) Fieldwork can often change in an instant. After a successful day locating two dens, Ford Mauney (pictured) and Ryan Nordsven found this gut-shot female. Based on her limited movements as interpreted from her telemetry readings, they had anticipated finding her with a litter of pups. She was later euthanized due to the extent of her abdominal injury. (Ryan Nordsven/U.S. Fish and Wildlife Service)

(bottom) Most of the time, a red wolf will flush from its den when the biologists get very close. But sometimes flushing them means getting creative. This enterprising female had dug a den deeply into a canal embankment in an open agricultural field, but Ford Mauney and Ryan Nordsven wanted to capture her to replace her radio collar batteries. Salmon nets turned out to be the perfect trap. (Amy E. M. Johnson)

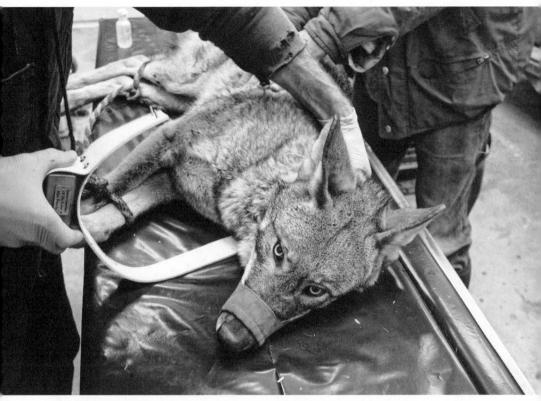

The red wolf field team estimates that they have radio collars on approximately 70 percent of the wild red wolf population. While many conservation programs rely on radio collars to remotely monitor animals, the red wolf program may be unique in employing them to help manage against hybridization. By keeping most of their wolves and many coyotes on the peninsula collared, they are able to assess which wolves are paired with other wolves or with coyotes. They routinely sterilize, and sometimes euthanize, coyotes to prevent hybrid litters. (Ryan Nordsven/U.S. Fish and Wildlife Service)

# PART II

# The Red Wolf Yesterday

When we first started working with this wolf, he was ninety-nine miles down a one-hundred-mile-long road to extinction. We now have him identified, and we feel we have him turned around the other way. It will be a long uphill push to save him; I don't know if we can do it. If we do decide that it is feasible, we need you to help pull; we are sure going to push.

**CURTIS J. CARLEY,** first Red Wolf Recovery Project field coordinator, Fish and Wildlife Service, at a public outreach presentation (1977)

## CHAPTER 8
# Tracing the Origins of Red Wolves

Three theories, each very different, have attempted to peg red wolves' elusive origins. The first theory asserts that a prototype of the red wolf arose in Eurasia from a common ancestor shared with gray wolves. In this scenario, these proto–red wolves were early biological invaders into North America that then completed their speciation into what we now know as the red wolf in the Southeast's forests. The originator of this theory is mammalogist Ronald Nowak. His concept is dubbed the unique-origin theory.

In marked contrast, a second theory states that red wolves are a relatively recent product of hybridization between coyotes and gray wolves, possibly as recent as the last several hundred years. The principal scientist behind this idea is Robert Wayne, a population geneticist; here, this concept is dubbed the hybrid-origin theory.

The third theory posits that red wolves and eastern wolves share an evolutionary history and that they both evolved in North America independently from gray wolves. Eastern wolves (*Canis lupus lycaon* or *Canis lycaon*) exist today in a small population on the northeastern side of the Great Lakes. Although eastern wolves are classified as a gray wolf subspecies, some scientists think they are not gray wolves at all and ought to be given their own species designation. In this scenario, eastern wolves and red wolves are more closely related to each other than to any other canid, and they arose from a lineage shared with the coyote. This idea, like the unique-origin theory, places red wolves' origins as independent from those of gray wolves, but it differs from Nowak's theory in that it posits that red wolves share an evolutionary history with the coyote lineage and not the gray wolf lineage. Here, this concept is dubbed the shared-ancestry theory, and it was conceived by wildlife geneticists Paul J. Wilson and Brad White. The evidence for all three origin theories conflicts.

Ronald Nowak, a now-retired Fish and Wildlife Service mammalogist, has spent a large part of his life advocating for and studying red wolves. Nowak was among the first group of biologists to study red wolves to try and figure out what they are. But he felt that science moved too slowly and that scientists published in places that only other scientists read. He recognized that the public must be made aware of the plight of red wolves and that without public support, the animals might fade into extinction. So in the 1960s and 1970s, he wrote about red wolves and his research on them in *Natural History*, *Defenders of Wildlife News*, and *National Parks and Conservation*. Few people have pushed the dialogue of red wolf conservation further into the public sphere than Nowak has.

In the late summer of 2010, I visit Nowak at his home in Falls Church, Virginia. He is soft-spoken, slightly built, and a little stooped with age. Nowak has a cerebral demeanor, and in a Louisiana accent that softens his r's, he might tell you he was born in the "fawties." We sit in his living room, which is decorated with tiny statues of forest animals. Every few minutes, he darts down the hall to his desk—above which hangs a famous photo of a black-phase red wolf from the Tensas River—to retrieve books, graphs, and papers for reference. More than a decade after his retirement, Nowak remains engrossed by discussions of red wolf origins. Deep in conversation about carnassial teeth, he dives to grab his wife's shitzsu, Tommy, to show me what they look like, then he thinks better of it. (Tommy had eyed him warily.) He hands me a copy of his most recent publication, a 2002 paper from *Southeastern Naturalist*.

"When I wrote this, I threw everything I had at the red wolf problem," he says. "This was my best shot." He thumps an extra copy onto the coffee table between us. After a very long pause, he gazes at it and adds: "I'm not sure I have anything left to offer."

This is hard to accept, considering everything he has invested in learning about the red wolf: few people have devoted more time to understanding red wolves than the man sitting across the coffee table from me, absentmindedly stroking his wife's dog.

Nowak grew up in New Orleans, and as an undergraduate at Tulane University in 1962, he became interested in endangered birds. While reading a book on the last ivory-billed woodpeckers in the swamps along the Tensas River, his eyes widened when he found references to wolves.

"Wolves in Louisiana! My goodness, I thought wolves lived up on the tundra, in the north woods, going around chasing moose and people," Nowak recalls. "I did not know a thing about them. But when I learned there were wolves in my home state, it got me excited."

His attention turned from birds to mammals. Picking up *National Geographic's Wild Animals of North America*, Nowak read the scant few paragraphs it held on red wolves, authored by U.S. Biological Survey head Stanley Young. The paragraphs occupied less than a page and overlaid an illustration of a red wolf and a black-phase red wolf bounding side by side through the woods. A two-word phrase caught his eye: "fast disappearing."

"This was the first indication that the red wolf was in real trouble," Nowak recalls. "Young wrote that phrase, even though his agency would continue to say, for four or five more years, that the red wolf was abundant. It was not declared in trouble until 1967. When I read those words, it got me wondering about what I could do to help the red wolf."

Nowak penned letters to anyone and everyone. He asked biologists and game wardens for information and surveys. He queried environmental groups and known wolf experts for help. Nowak compiled everything he learned into a report and submitted it to the FWS in 1963. It included reports from the Louisiana and Arkansas game commissions dating back to the 1950s, which stated that their large wolves were gone and that a smaller wolf was moving in from the west, though they did not know what it was. Nowak wrote that the red wolf was on the road to extinction and the FWS should address the problem. Somehow, his report found its way to a biologist named John Paradiso, who headed the endangered species section of a specimen laboratory that the FWS maintained in the National Museum (now the Smithsonian). After conducting his own surveys, Paradiso arrived at the same conclusion: the red wolf was on its way out.

After finishing at Tulane, Nowak entered the military and spent his free time holed up in the library reading everything he could get his hands on about endangered mammals. He also interviewed trappers and visited places where red wolves were said to have dwelled. When he left the air force in 1968, he entered a Ph.D. program in mammalogy at the University of Kansas, where he focused on *Canis*. Nowak graduated in 1973 and was hired almost immediately by the FWS for its new Office of Endangered Species. The FWS encouraged him to continue working on his research, and his dissertation was finally published in 1979. By then, it had become a monograph on *Canis* that covered the entire Quaternary geological time period (2.5 million years ago to today). He analyzed *Canis* specimens for fifteen skull measurements using a method known as morphometric analysis. Morphology is one of the oldest methods that naturalists and taxonomists have used to delineate species in nature; in essence, it examines an organism's physical form. Nowak measured characteristics of 5,000 fossilized, archaeological, and recent *Canis* skulls. He organized the specimens into series by both tentative or known species groups, geographic areas, and time spans when they were collected. He then analyzed their measurements to search for relationships and species boundaries.

When Nowak examined specimens from several populations of *C. lepopha-gus*, a fossil species that emerged in the United States, he noted some intriguing features in their skulls that changed over time. Populations from the Early Blancan (2.5 million to 4.5 million years ago) revealed a coyote-sized animal that had what Nowak called a "narrowly proportioned skull" that was lightly built and featured a narrow snout and a shallow jaw. But another population from Cita Canyon in Randall County, Texas, from the Late Blancan (1.8 million to 2.5 million years ago) contained skulls that were wider and broader than average. In this small population, Nowak and others saw precursors to the cranial changes that may signal the start of the evolutionary path to modern wolves. Skulls from this population showed elongated snouts, their mandibles were deeper than a coyote's, and their foreheads were broader. The bony ridge that ran along their skullcap, called the sagittal crest, was also more expressed. The sagittal crest is where chewing muscles attach, and a more pronounced crest means the animal fed upon larger prey that required a higher bite strength or masticating power. Along with other researchers, Nowak wondered if perhaps these two populations of shallow-jawed and deep-jawed canids might mark the divergence of the ancestral coyote lineage from the precursor to the lineage leading to gray wolves. This split is thought to have happened between 1 million to 2 million years ago. If true, then *C. lepophagus* may represent the last shared ancestor between coyotes and wolves. Nowak hypothesized that some *C. lepopha-gus* animals may have crossed the Bering Land Bridge into Asia, where they adapted to different environmental conditions and gave rise to a new species called *C. arnensis*. Of the *lepophagus* that remained in North America, the shallow-jawed populations may have given rise to *C. latrans* (coyotes), while he thinks the deeper-jawed populations may have given rise to a line of protowolves, now extinct, and eventually to true wolves. One of these early protowolves was *C. priscolatrans*, a coyote-like animal that Nowak recognizes as the earliest known wolf species, or protowolf, in North America. He believes the diminutive *priscolatrans* led to a more wolflike and robust creature named *armbrusteri*, which culminated in the very large and robust *dirus*, the dire wolf.

Nowak thinks that populations of *priscolatrans* also padded across the Bering Land Bridge into Eurasia, where they gave rise to *C. mosbachensis*, the species he believes generated both gray and red wolves. He thinks prototypical red wolves were perhaps spawned from *mosbachensis* by adapting to

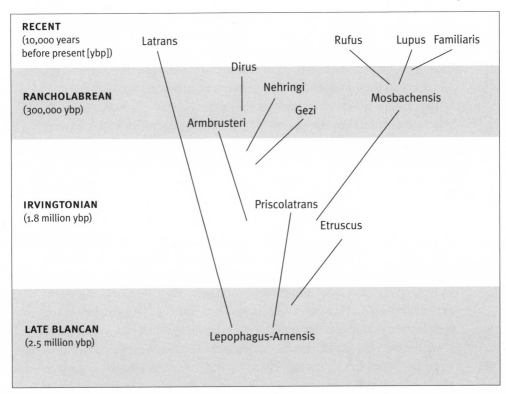

RECENT
(10,000 years before present [ybp])

RANCHOLABREAN
(300,000 ybp)

IRVINGTONIAN
(1.8 million ybp)

LATE BLANCAN
(2.5 million ybp)

Latrans
Dirus
Nehringi
Gezi
Armbrusteri
Rufus
Lupus  Familiaris
Mosbachensis
Priscolatrans
Etruscus
Lepophagus-Arnensis

Unique-Origin Theory Lineage Tree. Ronald Nowak proposed the unique-origin hypothesis, which asserts that red wolves and gray wolves stemmed from a shared common ancestor, *Canis mosbachensis*. This ancestor can be traced back to a common ancestor with coyotes, which is thought to be *Canis lepophagus*. (Adapted from Ronald M. Nowak, "Wolf Evolution and Taxonomy," in *Wolves: Behavior, Ecology, and Conservation*, edited by L. D. Mech and L. Boitani, 239–58. Chicago: University of Chicago Press [2003]. Adapted by permission of University of Chicago Press.)

new environments in Asia and that they initially reentered the New World by traveling east back across the land bridge. He speculates that this population then moved farther south in the later Pleistocene and fully speciated into *C. rufus* in what is now the central and southeastern United States. He thinks the *C. mosbachensis* remaining in Eurasia spread westward and evolved into *C. lupus* in Europe. Later, gray wolves backtracked east across Asia, entered North America, and made their way into what is now the central United States. Nowak believes that successive waves of wolf invasions occurred in North America and that this accounts for the historic range patterns of gray wolf subspecies. Other paleontologists, such as Xiaoming Wang and Richard Tedford, the authors of *Dogs: Their Fossil Relatives and Evo-*

lutionary History (2008), have suggested that *C. arnensis* (or another species called *C. etruscus*) may have given rise to gray wolves because they were the first *Canis* species to spread into Europe. While Nowak believes gray wolves did not dwell in the central parts of the United States until 10,000 years ago, Wang places their midcontinental arrival at 25,000 years ago or more.

According to Nowak, three "extremely questionable" records exist for gray wolves from the East; he considers none to be definitive. Only two were actual specimens, while one was a written record made "long before anyone had made a distinction between gray and red wolves." He found that one of the specimens was just as easily grouped with *C. dirus*, while the other, which lacked a skull, could have also been *C. rufus*.

While the majority of Nowak's study specimens were gray wolves, coyotes, and dogs, 129 specimens were red wolves. This sample included several series of red wolf skulls from different geographic regions and time periods. He assessed fossil fragments dating from 10,000 years ago as red wolves. These were from southwestern Illinois, West Virginia, and north and central Florida. Younger fossils and remains that he assessed as red wolves were found at archaeological sites dating to between 200 and 2,000 years ago in Pennsylvania, Ohio, southeastern Illinois, West Virginia, North Carolina, Tennessee, eastern Arkansas, and southern Florida. Complete skulls of red wolves from prior to 1918 were also found in Pennsylvania, southwestern Indiana, southeastern Texas, Louisiana, southeastern Oklahoma, Alabama, and Florida. (However, on the whole, far fewer fossils of red wolves have been recovered in the East than fossils of gray wolves in the West.) According to Nowak's interpretations, the fossil and archaeological material that does exist shows that red wolves lived for at least 10,000 years with a stable form that corresponds to red wolf specimens obtained between the mid-1800s to 1917. He found the red wolf skulls to be consistently intermediate between coyotes and gray wolves. But after about 1920, hybridization with coyotes became widespread in the western portion of its range—Missouri, Arkansas, eastern Oklahoma, Texas, and Louisiana— and he believes some specimens show some of this variation. By Nowak's estimation, the first hybrid population of coyotes and red wolves emerged between 1900 and 1920 in central Texas. A second hybrid population later arose in the Ozarks between 1930 and 1950 in central Arkansas to extreme southern Missouri and far eastern Oklahoma.

One of the more persuasive pieces of ecological evidence for the archaic presence of red wolves in the East is argued in Nowak's 2002 paper titled "The Original Status of Wolves in Eastern North America." After he studied carnassial teeth from fossil canids in North America, he found that their size classes corresponded to species groupings of red wolves, coyotes, and dire wolves. (Carnassial teeth are the sharp, scissor-like teeth of a carnivore that cut flesh like shears.) He concluded that fossil coyote material was found in the East up until about 10,000 years ago, when it vanishes from the fossil record. He infers that when red wolves emerged, they excluded coyotes from the eastern deciduous forests. Their ecological niches were perhaps too similar for these creatures to coexist. Coyotes are able to live in the same range with gray wolves, on the other hand, because their ecological niches are so different. In this scenario, it was only when wolves were extirpated from the East after European contact that coyotes then returned eastward.

When Nowak first investigated the red wolf issue, lumping—a term applied when biologists try to "lump" as many variable organisms into a single species designation as possible—was in fashion. (Splitting is the opposite, when numerous species designations are drawn based on slight variances between organisms.) He had originally intended to demonstrate that the red wolf was not a distinct species. "We thought we would show that it was just a small gray wolf," Nowak recalls. "Very interesting, yes. Worthy of protection, yes. An important part of the southeastern fauna, yes. But not a fully distinct species. But darn it, try as we might, we still could never bridge that gap between a red wolf and a gray wolf."

But not everyone agreed with Nowak. At about the time his monograph was published, there were no more red wolves left in the wild, and efforts were under way to captive breed them with the intention of reintroducing them within their former range. Some researchers still believed red wolves were a subspecies of gray wolf, while others had proposed that red wolves may be hybrids of coyotes and gray wolves, noting their intermediate physique. Responding to the latter idea, Nowak asserted that recent hybridization in the past century signaled the red wolf's end, not its origin. Unfortunately, hybridization between red wolves and coyotes was occurring at precisely the time that scientists had begun paying attention, and the red wolf's taxonomic identity was a tangled mess. By the early 1990s, some people hoped that newly developed genetics tools might help to untangle what a red wolf is. But far from being a saving grace, genetics studies simply increased the number of kinks in the taxonomic knot; and over time, genetics research actually produced two radically different story lines about what red wolves may be. The idea of red wolves arising through hybridization gained credence in 1991 when a surprising study came out in the journal *Nature*. Robert Wayne, a population geneticist at the University of California, Los Angeles, who harbored an interest in canids, had entered into conversations with the Fish and Wildlife Service to analyze red wolves' mitochondrial DNA and compare it to coyotes and gray wolves to uncover what the animals' ancestry may be.

The DNA inside mitochondria, which is an organelle in the cells of all animals that regulates energy metabolism, is useful for tracing evolutionary relatedness between organisms. MtDNA is passed only from mothers to their offspring, so it does not go through the genetic shuffling of sexual recombination. Genetic mutations tend to occur at a higher rate in mtDNA than in nuclear DNA. These mutations, if they occur in regions that do not code for proteins, are typically not damaging to the organism but tend to accrue, like typos in a recipe. These genetic "typos" are then replicated as the "recipe" is passed from a mother to her offspring. Their accumulation over time enables certain regions of mtDNA to serve as useful markers for tracing evolutionary changes within populations and determining relationships between populations and species.

Wayne and his study coauthor, Susan Jenks (then a postdoctoral researcher at the University of California, Santa Barbara, who was interested in carnivore evolution), analyzed the mtDNA of captive red wolves, preserved blood taken from where the captive stock of red wolves had been collected, and museum skins of red wolves collected between 1905 and 1930. They found only mtDNA haplotypes that they classified as either gray wolf or coyote in origin; they uncovered nothing genetically unique to red wolves. (A haplotype is a set of genes or a cluster of genetic sequences that are inherited together as a set from one parent.) Interestingly, they also found that red wolves and coyotes grouped together much more closely than previously thought. This conflicted with Nowak's unique-origin idea that red and gray wolves share a common ancestor: if coyotes and red wolves were distant cousins, as he posited, they should not have tested as so genetically close. Wayne and Jenks concluded that recent hybridization between coyotes and gray wolves had occurred in a zone stretching hundreds of miles wide; it would have been the largest hybridization zone known, at that time, for a vertebrate animal. The paper was a landmark study that provided the first genetic evidence supporting extensive hybridization in red wolves. (At the time, the work was state-of-the-art, but by today's standards, the study examined a small sample of genetic code.)

Jenks, who is now at the Sage Colleges in Troy, New York, said that in retrospect, she had hoped to be the first to find unique red wolf DNA but was "surprised" when she found only coyote and gray wolf material. The paper was published a mere four years after the first pairs of captive-bred red wolves had been released to Alligator River National Wildlife Refuge. It was not just red wolves' status as a taxonomic species that was at stake. If the findings were right, then the FWS "may have spent twenty years and hundreds of thousands of dollars to preserve a wild mutt," wrote author Jan DeBlieu in a *New York Times Magazine* piece. (DeBlieu's book *Meant to Be Wild* had been published the year before; in it, she chronicled the early days of the red wolf's reintroduction.) Previously, the Department of the Interior had taken a stance that Endangered Species Act protections should not extend to hybrids, but they backtracked on this the year before Wayne and Jenks's study was published. Still, the findings opened the door for uncomfortable questions about the reintroduced wolves' conservation worthiness, despite Wayne and Jenks's statement that their results did "not argue against the continued protection of the red wolf." The paper caused a huge stir in the conservation world.

Additional genetic research emerged in the ensuing years that backed the theory that red wolves had arisen as a hybrid. Among those who believed red wolves to be a historic species stretching back thousands of years, one of the main concerns was (and continues to be) whether these studies adequately characterized what red wolves may have been in the past. Critics claimed that some of the studies had sampling problems and even used specimens whose species identities were disputed. (Nowak, in particular, took issue with historic samples used in the 1991 study and a subsequent study on red wolf museum skins published in 1996.) Over time, researchers found no nuclear DNA in red wolves that was different from coyotes or gray wolves; and although they found one mtDNA haplotype that was unique to red wolves, it was only slightly different from known coyote haplotypes.

Studies from the hybrid-origin literature stream initially offered two different scenarios for how hybridization may have happened. Both scenarios assumed that gray wolves and coyotes were present historically in the Southeast, an idea that made Nowak fume. In one scenario, when European settlers arrived to the New World and began exterminating wolves and altering the environment, habitat degradation may have led to gray wolves and coyotes coming into contact and hybridizing. In the other scenario, hybridization between coyotes and gray wolves may have occurred in the Southeast much deeper in the past or at different times during both species' evolutionary history. If hybridization were a part of the red wolf's natural evolutionary path, then some researchers advocated for continued protection of red wolves. But if red wolves were a product of hybridization from recent human-induced habitat changes, then they advocated that the wolves were not a high priority for conservation. In other words, if humans had created the red wolf, it was perceived as being far less valuable than if Mother Nature had created it. Jenks strongly disagreed with this sentiment. "If the animal was adapting to environmental changes by hybridizing," she said, "then no matter what its cause, that is natural."

In 1999 a pair of researchers from the University of Oxford published a paper with Wayne in *Molecular Ecology* that used genetics to test the ideas of an ancient or recent origin for red wolves. They concluded that gray wolves and coyotes likely hybridized within the past 2,500 years to produce the red wolf, but they narrowed this down even further to infer that interbreeding had probably occurred within the past 250 years, coinciding with European settlement and habitat alterations. As the papers supporting the hybrid-origin theory piled up, Nowak dug his heels in and continued to advocate for a distinct southeastern wolf that had remained morphologically stable for thousands of years before hybridizing early in the twentieth century.

Over time, Wayne refined the scenario for how he views hybridization to have created the red wolf. He said he believes that a small subspecies of gray wolf, perhaps akin to the Mexican gray wolf, inhabited the eastern United States. As this animal was persecuted and extirpated at the time of European settlement, he believes the population of gray wolves dwindled, and they then began to interbreed with coyotes, which Wayne thinks became comparatively more abundant. The hybrids had an intermediate appearance and may have held an advantage in the transitional landscape. He thinks that this hybrid swarm became more coyote-like with the passage of time because gray wolves were eventually wiped out. "There may have been insulated pockets of populations where they were gray wolf–like, and other areas where they were more converted to coyotes," Wayne said.

The studies concluding that red wolves originated as a hybrid animal led to an erosion of support—or, at best, ambivalence—for *Canis rufus* and its reintroduction program. Confusion in the public mind as to whether interbreeding signaled the animal's beginning or its end, and a lack of understanding (at the time) about the widespread occurrence of hybridization within some *Canis* species, likely detracted from its wolfish charisma. Combined with some people's inability to visually distinguish between red wolves and coyotes, the wolf of the Southeast was mired in a vicious and heated scientific controversy. What exactly had red wolves been in the past?

If red wolves had once been genetically unique, were they now so hybridized that they were no longer distinct?

The new millennium brought a surprising turn to the north in the debate over red wolf origins. In 2000 a group of Canadian researchers announced that they believed red wolves and eastern wolves were an offshoot from a North American–evolved canid lineage that eventually led to modern coyotes. But what on earth is an "eastern wolf"?

Today, the eastern wolf of Canada is found on the northeastern side of the Great Lakes. It may have ranged more widely historically, perhaps into New England. Originally named *Canis lycaon* in 1775, this creature was later renamed *Canis lupus lycaon*. The fact that biologists have such a hard time agreeing on its relationship to gray wolves is, in part, a testament to the trickiness of its identity. Its core range is now within and around Algonquin Provincial Park, south of the French River and into southern Quebec. The park is in lower Ontario in extreme southeastern Canada. It encompasses a unique ecotone, which extends into Quebec, where deciduous forests transition north into coniferous boreal forests. White-tailed deer live in the deciduous woods, whereas moose and caribou typically live in the colder boreal woods to the north. The eastern wolf has been viewed as different because its morphology is somewhat intermediate between gray wolves and coyotes. It also is unusual because when it leaves Algonquin Provincial Park's protection, it hybridizes with coyotes to the south and Great Lakes wolves to the north and west. (Great Lakes wolves also hybridize, although there is disagreement as to whether they are hybrids of gray wolves and coyotes or hybrids of gray wolves and eastern wolves; if the latter interpretation is correct, it would mean that only red wolves and eastern wolves hybridize with coyotes.)

Canadian wildlife geneticist Paul Wilson was intrigued by these enigmatic eastern wolves. Wilson was fascinated with the potential of genetics as a tool for wildlife forensics to seek out and uncover animals' genomic secrets. Along with several other researchers, he noticed the physical similarity between eastern wolves and red wolves. As a Ph.D. student at McMaster University in the mid-1990s, he worked with his adviser, Brad White, to set up a study designed to compare the DNA profiles of red wolves, coyotes, and eastern wolves. They and several colleagues obtained specimens of wolves from Algonquin Provincial Park and its surrounding areas from between 1960 and 1965 and between 1985 and 1996; red wolf samples from the captive breeding program; Texas coyote samples; and gray wolves from the Northwest Territories. From these, they extracted DNA from the kidneys, heart, and muscle. They also took whole blood from canids trapped alive and extracted DNA from the preserved dental pulp of historic eastern wolf teeth collected in Ontario in the 1960s.

From the samples, White and Wilson's research group analyzed nuclear DNA and the mitochondrial DNA control regions (this is a region that doesn't code for proteins, but serves as the origin of mtDNA replication). In the nuclear DNA, they identified eight microsatellite markers where various alleles are present, and they found that the allele frequencies at these eight markers were similar between red wolves and Algonquin wolves, which set them apart from all the other samples. (Microsatellites are short, repeating sequences of a few nucleic acid base pairs.) White and Wilson's team interpreted these similarities to mean that Algonquin wolves and red wolves share a common origin and even a common ancestor (rather than the genetic similarity arising from both wolves having hybridized with coyotes). From the mtDNA analysis, they also found a divergent haplotype that they interpreted as being unique to eastern wolves. They reported finding little to no gray wolf mitochondrial genetic material in either eastern or red wolves. Using a molecular clock, and considering mtDNA sequence differences, they estimated that eastern and red wolves diverged from an ancestral coyote lineage between 150,000 and 300,000 years ago. This placed the coyote as a very close relative of red and eastern wolves. Their results contradicted the idea that the gray wolf had helped create the red wolf through hybridization. It also suggested that lycaon did not belong in the lupus species grouping.

White and Wilson's research team concluded that both eastern and red wolves evolved in North America independently of gray wolves. They argued that eastern and red wolves are more closely related to each other than they are to gray wolves or than either is to coyotes. They wrote that the "predisposition of the eastern North American wolves to hybridize with coyotes may represent an evolutionary characteristic unique to these wolves and suggests that the red wolf and the eastern Canadian wolf have a common origin." To explain both eastern and red wolves' tendency to hybridize with coyotes, the study authors wrote that a divergence that took place less than 300,000 years ago is relatively recent in terms of a species' longevity. It was recent enough that these wolves would be more likely to hybridize with their common relative, the coyote, than with the less closely related gray wolves. Wilson's group also believed that the smaller body size of red wolves did not drive their hybridization with coyotes (as had been suggested) because

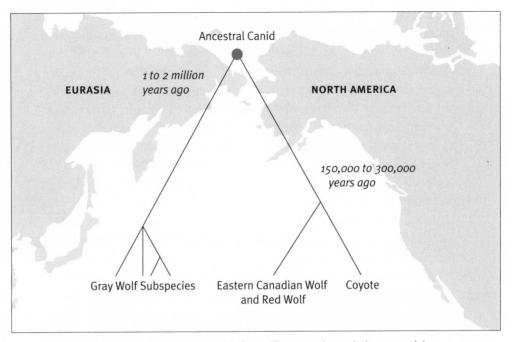

Shared-Ancestry Theory Lineage Tree. This figure illustrates the evolutionary model proposed in 2000 by Paul Wilson and others. According to this theory, red wolves and eastern wolves evolved solely in North America from a lineage leading to coyotes, whereas gray wolves evolved in Eurasia and later invaded North America. (Adapted from P. J. Wilson and others, "DNA Profiles of the Eastern Canadian Wolf and the Red Wolf Provide Evidence for a Common Evolutionary History Independent of the Gray Wolf," *Canadian Journal of Zoology* 78, no. 12 [2000]: 2156–66. © 2008 Canadian Science Publishing or its licensors. Reproduced with permission.)

in comparison, Mexican gray wolves, which also have smaller bodies, don't hybridize with coyotes. Rather, Wilson's group viewed a close evolutionary relationship as key to the interbreeding. They also suggested that *C. rufus* might be the same species as lycaon. Their results were published in the *Canadian Journal of Zoology*.

In 2003 Wilson and White and several colleagues followed up with another paper further detailing evidence for a unique North American–evolved eastern wolf. It described two historical wolf skins, one reportedly from the last wolf killed in New York State in the 1890s and one from Maine that was collected as a bounty in Penobscot County in the 1880s. They reasoned that these specimens came from a time before western coyotes were thought to have expanded into these states, so they should yield evidence of whether the wolves in this area were of gray wolf or New World origin. The team extracted mtDNA from the skins and determined it held sequences that were not of gray wolf origin. The Maine specimen held "a sequence that clustered with previously identified eastern wolf– and red wolf–specific mtDNA sequences." The New York specimen, however, contained a sequence that clustered with modern western coyotes. This forced the team to reconsider whether the expansion of western coyotes to the East had occurred earlier than previously recorded or whether it was further evidence for a common origin between coyotes and eastern wolves. But the group interpreted the Maine specimen—and its sequence similarity to those found in red wolves and wolves found in Algonquin Park in the 1960s—as support for their idea that an eastern wolf had diverged from a lineage leading to coyotes. The research team recommended moving lycaon from the gray wolf lupus lineage and reclassifying it as Canis lycaon.

In subsequent years, additional researchers at Trent University (where both White and Wilson moved to from McMaster University) published more papers arguing for the existence of an eastern wolf that evolved independently from gray wolves in the New World. In 2010 Linda Rutledge, then a doctoral student at the university's Natural Resources DNA Profiling and Forensic Centre, published a study along with several colleagues on a single wolf jawbone from the 1500s found during an archaeological dig of an Iroquois village in extreme southern Ontario. She examined the morphology of the jaw; extracted mtDNA from it; and determined that it, too, was not of gray wolf origin. She reported that it contained coyote-like mtDNA sequences, yet it lived 400 years before coyotes were known to have infiltrated that area.

In time, the Canadian researchers detailed evidence from mtDNA (maternally inherited), Y-chromosome DNA (paternally inherited), and microsatellite markers that coalesced to describe the wolves of Algonquin park as the best remaining representatives of a historic eastern wolf. The Y-chromosome sequences were interpreted as being more divergent from coyotes than coyotes are from gray wolves, which indicates a long separated lineage. People who study these animals agree that individuals within the eastern wolf population have hybridized with coyotes and Great Lakes wolves and that there may be few "pure" eastern wolves remaining. ("Pure" or unadulterated is a relative term in this context because no one really knows the exact genetic nature of the wolf that was present historically in this region.) But the wolves from Algonquin park consistently cluster separately from other wolves around the Great Lakes in many different analyses, according to Rutledge. So far, researchers have not found the same eastern wolf Y-chromosome genetic signature in red wolves, although Y-chromosome research of red wolves has revealed a signature known from domestic dogs and haplotypes known from coyotes.

In a 2012 paper published in *Northeastern Naturalist*, wolf biologist David Mech outlined three nongenetic lines of evidence bolstering the idea that Great Lakes wolves are hybrids of gray wolves and eastern wolves rather than hybrids of gray wolves and coyotes. He concluded that all three lines of evidence support the Canadian researchers' interpretation that the coyote-like mtDNA sequences found in Great Lakes wolves were derived from eastern wolves and not from coyotes. First, he argued that Great Lakes wolves' morphology more closely resembles the gray wolf than the coyote, which he interpreted to support gray wolf–eastern wolf hybridization rather than gray wolf–coyote hybridization. Second, he pointed out that while hybrids of eastern wolves and coyotes have long been reported in eastern Canada, there are no records of reproduction between gray wolves and coyotes west of there, nor has there been any genetic documentation of coyotes and gray wolves interbreeding in the West, where they live within the same range. Third, Mech stated that known behavioral interactions between gray wolves and coyotes from Michigan and to the west show that wolves always kill coyotes, whereas he found no reports of this east of Michigan. He wrote that in general, Great Lakes wolves kill coyotes, which he interprets as a behavioral barrier that prevents them from interbreeding. (The current thinking is that *lycaon* acts as a bridge for genes flowing between *latrans* and *lupus* around the Great Lakes.) In this vein, the shared-ancestry model is attractive because it meshes with how eastern wolves behave and interact with gray wolves and coyotes in the Great Lakes region today, and it explains the existence of a small southeastern wolf present in the late Pleistocene as documented in Nowak's morphometric studies.

But not everyone agrees. In 2011 Wayne published a study that offered a "genome-wide perspective on the evolutionary history of enigmatic wolf-like canids." The newest paper was a highly collaborative project with Bridgett vonHoldt (a graduate student of his at the time) and more than a dozen coauthors. It was published in *Genome Research* and surveyed 48,000 single nucleotide polymorphisms (or SNPs) from canids around the world, including wolves of the Great Lakes and red wolves. (SNPs are identifiable spots in the genome that differ by a nucleotide substitution; in other words, they have different DNA bases at that single location.) The authors also used the SNPs to investigate the recent hybrid-origin and shared-ancestry models for red and eastern wolves. They characterized the eastern wolf as having an ancestry of about 58 percent gray wolf and 42 percent coyote, while they characterized the red wolf as having an ancestry of about 76 percent coyote and 24 percent gray wolf. Using genetics, they estimated the number of generations since hybridization had occurred to create these wolves, calculating a range of 287 to 430 years ago for the red wolf and 546 to 963 years ago for the eastern wolf. "It's nice that those time estimates match up to demographic events with people, when people were hunting wolves or cultivating the land," vonHoldt said. The researchers interpreted their results to uphold the recent hybrid-origin model, and they rejected the idea of a common ancestry between eastern and red wolves.

But the Canadian researchers countered that the way the samples were structured may have skewed the results because the eastern wolf samples were lumped in with Great Lakes wolf samples, which ignored prior literature delineating the two as distinct. They also questioned whether the two samples labeled as eastern wolves were truly representative of what they considered eastern wolves to be. Linda Rutledge reanalyzed a subset of the same SNP data in a paper published in 2012 in *Biological Conservation* and found that it was completely consistent with the concept of a North American–evolved eastern wolf. "Every time someone comes out with new results, it's always nitpicked and argued over," Wayne commented. He felt his newest paper should have settled the debate on red wolf origins. "We've been working on this for more than two decades, and sometimes I just want to throw up my hands. Look at all the history here; twenty years of studying this and we're still in the same place."

Rutledge offered that one of the core issues separating the eastern wolf researchers from the hybrid-origin researchers is the interpretation of coyote-like mtDNA sequences in eastern and red wolves. These sequences aren't known to occur in western coyote populations, but they consistently cluster among western coyote sequences during genetic analyses. She said that whereas the hybrid origin researchers interpret this coyote-like mtDNA as being from coyotes, she and others interpret it as being eastern wolf in origin, tied to these wolves having arisen from a lineage leading to coyotes. "All of these North American–evolved, coyote-like mtDNA that are found in the East but not in the West are likely due to what's called incomplete lineage sorting," Rutledge said. "There hasn't been enough time for them to completely separate. Their nuclear and mitochondrial genes still work with each other. So these animals are very happy to have a coyote-like mtDNA, but that doesn't mean it came from a recent coyote hybridization event. It could have always been in the historic eastern wolf population. And there is evidence to suggest that is true."

The way Rutledge conceives of it, the eastern wolf and the red wolf were probably historically the same deer-eating wolf species that ranged throughout the East. When they were persecuted and extirpated at the time of European settlement, eastern wolves, she believes, took refuge in what is now Algonquin Park, while at the extreme southern end of their range, the last eastern wolves became known as red wolves. "It just doesn't make sense that you would have two similarly sized but different wolves in the same area," she said. "I think the eastern wolf and red wolf were one and the same." (Wayne, of course, disagrees. He is unconvinced that the eastern wolf is anything more than a geographical variety within the gray wolf species. "In a way, it's semantics," he said. "They call it a species, we call it an ecotype.")

Roland Kays, a coauthor of the *Genome Research* paper and an expert on coyotes, disagrees that genetics research supports the idea of a New World wolf lineage as an offshoot of the coyote lineage. He ascribes to the hybrid-origin school of thought. Because the unique mtDNA of eastern wolves is so coyote-like, he suspects something called mitochondrial capture occurred. This means that a coyote mtDNA got into an eastern wolf through hybridization—perhaps within the past few hundred thousand years—and then changed over time to become differentiated within the eastern wolf population. In 2000, when Wilson and White's paper came out announcing the discovery of a new haplotype unique to eastern wolves, Kays said it was explained as being a unique species. "But we now know that mitochondrial DNA capture can happen in other species," he said. "It happens all the time through hybridization, and you can end up with some very interesting DNA patterns." Kays also offered that he felt the small number of microsatellite markers used in the Canadian researchers' work was statistically weak, and he said he was "leery of their conclusions." The recent research with Wayne and vonHoldt was the "best estimate we've got," he said, for when hybridization may have formed the red wolf.

But here again, experts differ. In 2012 a taxonomy review of North American wolves published in *North American Fauna* surveyed the literature and concluded that the evidence was growing for the eastern wolf having evolved distinct from gray wolves. "I'm not saying it's a done deal," study author Steve Fain said, "but it's very convincing to me." Fain, a geneticist with the FWS Forensics Laboratory, said that if you accept the evidence for a historical, small, deer-eating wolf in the East, then "it's clear that this canid was on the landscape prior to the opportunity to hybridize." Fain commented that he remains unconvinced that historic red wolf samples have been adequately characterized with modern genetic methods, and he believes red and eastern wolves are closely related. He and his study authors chose to accept the *Canis lycaon* species designation and upheld the *Canis rufus* designation for red wolves. But they wrote that each wolf may be a subspecies of the same species—leaving the door open for a future taxonomic revision.

Lisette Waits, whose genetics lab analyzes red wolf samples for the Red Wolf Recovery Program, differs slightly from Fain and Rutledge. While she believes that red wolves share a recent evolutionary lineage with coyotes, she disagrees that red and eastern wolves are from the same species. In her view, coyotes, eastern wolves, and red wolves likely all descended from a historical canid that was distinct from the gray wolf. She thinks that red wolves hybridized with both coyotes and gray wolves multiple times in their evolutionary history within hybrid zones. But she also believes that there was a core population of red wolves in the Southeast that had an independent evolutionary trajectory. In her view, the red wolf was probably a fairly young species that shared a recent common ancestry 150,000 years ago with coyotes. "Hybridization makes it really difficult to sort out the evolutionary history now using genetics, which is why I think there has been so much debate," Waits said.

While the geneticists disagree over what red wolves may have once been, paleontologists also disagree over whether there even was a historic southeastern red wolf. Xiaoming Wang, curator of vertebrate paleontology at the Natural History Museum of Los Angeles and an expert on *Canis* natural history, said that while paleontological evidence tends to support a historic eastern red wolf, he personally finds the evidence to be weak. "The fossils are rare," he said. After a brief study of red wolf material, he said he opted to not make a formal statement about what the animal is because he was unable to "unambiguously" say that the red wolf is or is not a species unto itself. Wang said that no one has amassed as much data as Nowak has on red wolves in terms of his morphometric studies, but he believes Nowak's statistical analyses found "a red wolf morph" that is "very difficult to deal with." Wang offered that perhaps only molecular studies of ancient DNA extracted from fossils might settle the debate. However, the heat and humidity of the Southeast is not necessarily conducive to preserving DNA, which makes finding the appropriate study material problematic. Waits and Rutledge both agree with Wang that molecular studies of fossilized wolves from the East are key to settling the debate over red wolf and eastern wolf origins. According to Waits, the ideal study would use samples that represented wolves inhabiting the East before European contact, and preferably even before the time period when Wayne's research hypothesizes they began hybridizing. "But those samples may not exist," she conceded.

It is confounding that researchers have come up with such vastly different and often contradictory conclusions about what red wolves are and what they may once have been. Among the scientific community, there has been broad support of the hybrid-origin theory, but this has been challenged by the shared-ancestry theory. Despite his decades of work to untangle red wolf origins on the basis of recent molecular findings, Nowak's concept of red wolves and gray wolves sharing a common ancestor has lost support— although his idea of a unique origin for the red wolf is shared by others. Though it is controversial, members of the Red Wolf Recovery Program have embraced the theory that red wolves diverged from a New World canid lineage leading to coyotes. The disagreement over how red wolves originated has played out as an acrimonious, divisive, deeply entrenched debate spanning several decades. Supporters of each concept believe that their idea best illuminates where red wolves came from. Perhaps Wayne put it best when he said: "Maybe I'm guilty of this too, but I feel like people see what they want to see when they study these wolves."

Despite years of inquiry, the origins of *Canis rufus* remain elusive. According to Fain and his coauthors, although hybridization has influenced gray wolves around the Great Lakes, eastern wolves, and red wolves, it is the red wolf that has been the most deeply affected by it. In addition, its extreme population bottleneck, and the artificial process of selecting the founders for the captive-breeding program based on morphology, further altered its genetic makeup. The lack of consensus over what a red wolf is versus what it once may have been exacerbates its conservation "purgatory" of being officially listed as an endangered species but perpetually accused of being unworthy. Was there a diminutive southeastern wolf that evolved in North America independently from gray wolves? Do red and eastern wolves share an evolutionary lineage with coyotes? We know without a doubt that when Europeans arrived in the New World, the eastern woods held howling, chorusing wolves. But the not-so-simple question remains: what *were* they?

## CHAPTER 9
# "Dogs of the Woods" and Their Decline

When Europeans first settled the Eastern Seaboard, they encountered wild, wolflike canids almost immediately. Sometimes they spotted them from their ships. The journals, letters, and books of these early explorers and colonists offer a snapshot of the New World's rich flora and fauna. They wrote of deer, elk, hummingbirds, possums, raccoons, skunks, panthers, bears, bobcats and, yes, creatures they called wolves. In the Carolinas, most records mention wolves as an animal that existed somewhere in the background of life. They were heard "singing" from the woods more often than they were seen. Wolves, it seems, did not play a very large role in the early southern settlers' lives—except that their presence sparked fear and represented a symbolic ferociousness and unpredictability of nature that Europeans felt the need to snuff out, control, or harness for their own utility.

John Lederer, a young man from Hamburg, Germany, was the first European to produce a detailed written account of the Carolinas. *The Discoveries of John Lederer* was originally published in 1671. Lederer first set off along the Pamunkey River in modern-day Virginia, heading into the Blue Ridge Mountains in early March 1669. Next, he explored North Carolina and possibly South Carolina near the Catawba River in late May 1670. On his last trip, he pushed farther north in late August, possibly starting around Harpers Ferry (now in West Virginia).

Lederer called the piedmont the "Highlands" and recorded that the ground there was so overgrown with underwood and dense with mats of vines that travelers had to slice open their paths. He described green valleys that fed herds of elk, which outsized oxen, and numerous deer. And where there were deer, there were wolves: "These thickets harbour all sorts of beasts of prey, as Wolves, Panthers, Leopards, Lions, &c . . . and small Vermine, as wilde Cats, Foxes, Racoons." The panthers, lions, and leopards Lederer mentioned likely were eastern mountain lions, while his "wilde cats" were bobcats. On his first exploration, he spied a doe running through the forest with a bobcat clutched to its back. A Native American traveling with him shot an arrow through the cat's belly. This incident exemplifies the way that predators were viewed by early settlers as competition for protein. But once he was within the mountains, Lederer wrote that the Appalachians were "barren Rocks and are therefore deserted by all living creatures but Bears, who cave in the hollow cliffs."

In late winter or early spring, Lederer was camped in Virginia near the south branch of the Rappahannock River. "The Wolves in these parts are so ravenous," he wrote, "that I often in the night feared my horse would be devoured by them, they would gather up and howl so close about him, though Tether'd to the same tree at whose feet I myself and the Indians lay: but the Fires which we made, I suppose, scared them from worrying us all."

Nearly three decades after Lederer's adventures, John Lawson was appointed by the Lords Proprietors of the Province of Carolina to perform inland surveys because no detailed maps of the area existed then. Right after Christmas in 1700, Lawson and a small party of men set out from near Bulls Island, South Carolina, and traveled in a rough horseshoe trajectory for fifty-nine days. Near Bulls Island, he watched Native American hunters set the swamp canes afire, possibly as part of a routine to maintain habitat for species they desired, but perhaps also to flush out quarry. He described the coastal landscape there as dry land interspersed with small brooks and threaded with small runs of water that he called "percoarson," a word likely affiliated with the modern term "pocosin." His party traveled inland roughly along the Santee River. One night, when camping at the head of one of its branches, they heard a chorus of howls emanate from the surrounding woods. "When we were all asleep," Lawson wrote,

> in the Beginning of the Night, we were awaken'd with the dismall'st and most hideous Noise that ever pierc'd my Ears: This sudden Surprizal incapacitated us of guessing what this threatening Noise might proceed from; but our Indian Pilot, (who knew these parts well) acquainted us that it was customary to hear such Musick along the Swamp-Side, there being endless Numbers of Panthers, Tygers, Wolves, and other Beasts of Prey, which take this Swamp for their abode in the Day, coming in whole Droves to hunt the Deer in the Night, making their frightful Ditty 'til Day appears, then all is still in other Places.

When he visited Native Americans of the Waxsaw (Waxhaw) tribe, Lawson entered the abode of a Native man that was "dark as a dungeon and as hot as a Dutch stove in Holland." Inside, he watched as the owner expelled his dogs, which Lawson described as "Wolves made tame with starving and beating." It isn't clear whether he believed the dogs to be true tamed wolves or fully domesticated dogs that appeared wolflike.

While sailing along the Cape Fear River in 1663, a few decades before Lawson, William Hilton spied partridges, cranes, ducks, widgeon, and a flock of Carolina parakeets (now extinct) from the boat deck. He also heard wolves howling in the woods and spotted a deer that a nearby pack had recently torn in pieces. It may be one of the earlier European recordings of a wolf kill in the Southeast. Perhaps the sight of Hilton's boat made the wolves recede beyond the tree line, where their vocalizations advertised their claim to the kill.

When Lawson departed from a Sapona Indian town in this area, his men slept in the open beneath the stars. He was awakened from sleep by a wolf that came close to his fire and spooked his dog, a spaniel. One of the men fired a shot at the wolf, which howled in response, but it slipped away before the shooter could reload. The wolf approached once more, shyly this time, after the men had lain down. If the party was camped within the wolf's territory, it may have been trying to kill the spaniel interloper; or it may have simply been hungry and attracted by the smells of their supper.

Lawson was not the only explorer to have his camp visited by the East's native wolf. William Bartram was camped near Lake George in Florida in 1774 when he strung his day's fish catch upon a tree branch and made his bed below them. That night, he awoke to the "heavy tread" of a departing animal. It dove into the thickets before Bartram could see it, but then he noticed the night thief had absconded with his fish stash. While Bartram never *saw* a wolf, he clearly believed the thief to have been a wolf—and one from whose jaws he felt he'd narrowly escaped. As the incident sunk in, he reasoned that having a "rapacious wolf" steal "my fish from over my head" was much better than having a wolf leap upon his breast in the dead of night to tear out his throat, "which would have instantly deprived me of my life." He imagined that the wolf might have gutted his stomach and dragged his body off to satiate its pack mates. While Bartram embellished the danger to himself, he also marveled at the cunning that the animal had shown in plundering Bartram's meat but not awakening him until the deed was done.

Bartram was informed by others that the wolves of Florida were "frequently seen pied, black and white, and other mixed colors." But it appears that he only saw them himself on two occasions. Once, when traveling near the Alachua Savannah (which would place him in north-central Florida near Paynes Prairie), he saw a "company" of wolves, which he named lupus niger, feeding on a horse carcass. He stated that the wolves were all black, except for the females, which had white spots on their breast. (He made no mention of why he thought only the spotted ones to be females.) The wolves sat on their haunches until his men came within shooting distance and whooped and hollered at them. Though he did not count their numbers, Bartram noted that they were smaller than the wolves of Pennsylvania and Canada. The second time he saw wolves in the Southeast, his party was traveling in west Florida, an area that is now Alabama, when they rustled up a litter of young wolves. The wolves gave chase, and one man caught a lagging wolf by its hind legs. A second man used the butt of his rifle to beat out the wolf's brains. Bartram showed no sorrow over the incident; to him, wolves were not a part of the fauna that demanded dwelling upon.

Lawson revealed a similar lack of interest in writing about wolves. While he wrote a page and a half parsing the habits of bears in the Carolinas, he produced only a meager half a page describing its wolves, which he called the "Dog of the Woods." He wrote that the native wolves were smaller and less fierce than the European wolf, that they were not "manslayers," and that they hunted deer. He also wrote a baffling account describing how they were known to enter the swamps at night to eat mud, but he said they promptly disgorged this for the opportunity to consume flesh. Lawson stated that near the coast, the alligators were known to kill dogs "as they swim over the Creeks and Waters." But he did not differentiate in his tale whether the alligators killed domestic dogs or the "Dog of the Woods."

Perhaps both Lawson's and Bartram's lack of wolf descriptions speaks to the negative perception that people held regarding wolves at this time, as well as wolves' lack of utility to people. In contrast, Lawson wrote at length about animals that were good to eat. He detailed the flavors of their flesh, and how it fared during digestion. On the other hand, native wolves can't have posed a serious threat to settlers and farmers in the Southeast, or much more would have been written about them. Perhaps the scarcity of descriptive writings shows that they were merely not that significant in a settler's everyday life. This realization, of course, makes Lawson's demise slightly ironic. He was among the first killed in the Tuscarora Indian War on September 22, 1711, and several reports noted that wolves fed upon the skirmish's dead. In early November, Major Christopher Gale wrote a letter to his sister that detailed particulars of the attacks that the settlers suffered. The Indians charged so frequently and so fiercely, he told her, that the living scarcely had time to bury their dead. Gale wrote that the corpses were "left for prey to the dogs, and wolves and vultures, whilst our care was to secure the garrison for the living."

A few decades after Lawson's trip through the Carolinas, *The Natural History of North Carolina* by John Brickell was published. Brickell was an Irishman who came to North Carolina in 1729, where he visited Bath, Beaufort, and Edenton, all coastal cities. Brickell's book is viewed as an obvious plagiarization of Lawson's work. However, he sometimes offered additional information, and this is the case with his treatment of wolves. He wrote that North Carolina's wolves would follow Indians through the woods "in great droves," and when the men took only a deer's skin and left its carcass, the wolves would devour the remains. He also reported that a bounty in the area had formerly caused the Indians to bring in so many wolf heads that the counties were overwhelmed. According to Brickell, local farmers used pit traps, holes dug in the earth and baited with scent lures, to capture and destroy wolves of the woods that dared tread on their land. But the method also destroyed so many dogs, which were attracted by the bait, that many farmers abandoned it. Brickell described wolves in North Carolina as no larger than a "middling" dog, crafty yet fearful of people. They rarely gave chase to colts or horses but wreaked havoc on sheep, and they were said to kill as many of the wooly creatures as they could before they settled in to eat. Brickell made no mention of cattle, though other sources say the native wolf of the East also inflicted damage on hogs and small calves. They seemed to know when bad weather was approaching and farmers' guard dogs would be seeking shelter away from the flocks, Brickell noted, implying that the attacks on sheep showed some degree of forethought and cunning on the wolves' part. Brickell wrote that the largest groups of wolves formed in the winter, when they would "go in great Companies together in Evenings and especially at Night." His may be the earliest observation on seasonal fluctuations of pack sizes.

It's clear that Brickell did not assess the native wolves as a threat to people, but he did find human-centered uses for them. Their skins, if dried into a parchment, were said to make excellent drums. Their pelts, when flung on a bed, repelled fleas. Their dung and blood were "excellent good to expedite the Birth and after-Birth" during childbearing. Despite these numerous utilitarian practices, Brickell wrote that "it is the Opinion of the most prodigious hunters in these Parts, that if they [wolves] did not die for Hunger, or some secret unknown way, which they have for destroying one another, they would be the most numerous Beasts in America, being such prodigious breeders."

One of the more insightful records about the eastern native wolf's fear of humans comes from a Moravian bishop named August Gottlieb Spangenberg, who visited North Carolina in the 1700s. The purpose of his visit was to scout for land to create a settlement. He found wolves to be numerous. His journal from the visit is known as the "Spangenberg Diary." Wolves had been absent from England since the late 1600s, so the only knowledge English colonists in the New World had of them would have been through folklore and mythology. (It was largely the English who first settled North Carolina.) But Spangenberg would have known gray wolves directly from his central European home, where they still remained. While traveling near Upper Creek in Burke County south of Grandfather Mountain, he wrote one of the few early accounts that directly compares the Southeast's wolves to European gray wolves: "The wolves here give us music every morning, from six corners at once, such music as I have never heard. They are not like the wolves of Germany, Poland, and Livonia, but are afraid of men, and do not usually approach near them. A couple of Brethren skilled in hunting would be of benefit not only here but at our other tracts, partly to kill the wolves and panthers, partly to supply the Brethren with game. Not only can the skins of wolves and panthers be sold, but the government pays a bounty of ten shillings for each one killed."

This bounty speaks to the widely held perception—also revealed in Brickell's observations—that wolf populations must be controlled. It was a mentality that led to widespread persecution of the East's native wolves. Settlers shot them on sight; organized community predator hunts; and set pit traps, leg-hold traps, and neck snares. Anything that was carnivorous, that bore fur and sharp teeth, was clobbered on sheer principal alone.

The extermination of wolves in the West is better documented than those in the East in part due to the early nature of the eastern efforts, which were initiated by European settlers and colonists on an ad hoc basis and only later taken up by the federal government in a coordinated way. Still, records exist in counties and states along the Eastern Seaboard that clearly depict a widespread, though perhaps decentralized, pattern of wolf persecution starting as early as 1630.

The battle against North America's eastern wolves was waged slowly, but deliberately, by both legal and cultural practices devised in New World colonies. In his book *The War against the Wolf*, Rick McIntyre meticulously highlighted early records of settlers' attempts to wipe wolves from the woods of the Eastern Seaboard. McIntyre reported that a mere decade after they anchored in Massachusetts Bay in 1620, colonists passed multiple laws that created the first monetary rewards in the New World for the murder of wolves. Their bounties were raised from a livestock tax—cows and horses were taxed at twice the rate of pigs—amassed in a public treasury. An individual dead wolf could reap forty shillings, an amount McIntyre calculated as equal to nearly a month's wages for the average laborer. It also lends insight to how preciously the settlers valued the cattle, goats, sheep, and horses that were fresh off their ships from native England. (By 1643, cattle outnumbered people five to four in the Massachusetts Bay Colony, according to environmental historian William Cronon.) McIntyre wrote that by 1640, the Massachusetts Colony paid four times more for a wolf killed by dogs than a wolf caught in a pit trap (forty versus ten shillings). This reveals the depth of pathological hatred directed at wolves: those that were killed the most brutally garnered the highest reward.

Environmental historian Valerie Fogleman wrote that perhaps the early Christian colonists saw themselves figuratively as the wolves' prey based on the New Testament's anecdote of Jesus sending his followers out as sheep among wolves. Their antipathy and fear toward wolves was a physical manifestation of their spiritual protectiveness, she wrote, for "wolves were considered capable of murdering a person's soul." Wolves were also viewed through a religious and cultural lens as animals that made pacts with the devil, thereby garnering them the stigma of being full of trickery and evil. Livestock damages may have been the rational argument for clearing wolves from the woods around settlements, but wolves likely also symbolized a potent religious threat in the minds of some early colonists.

The Native Americans did not view wolves so negatively, and some even tattooed images of wolves—along with moose, deer, bears, and birds—on their cheeks and arms, according to William Wood. Wood, writing about New England in 1634, described the "ravenous howling Wolfe; Whose meagre paunch suckes like a swallowing gulfe" in a passage that imparts the belief that wolves consumed more prey than was necessary. Wood wished that all the wolves of the country could be replaced by bears, but only on the condition that the wolves were banished completely, because he believed wolves hunted and ate black bears. He also lamented that "common devourer," the wolf, preying upon moose and deer. No doubt, the colonists wanted the bears, moose, and deer for their own meat and hide supplies. Yet Wood also observed the wolves of New England to be different from wolves in other countries. He wrote that they were not known to attack people, and that they did not attack horses or cows but went after pigs, goats, and red calves. The colonists seemed to believe the wolves mistook calves that were more coppery colored for deer, so much so that a red-colored calf sold for much less than a black one.

Further south in 1642, Virginia fined colonists who failed to check their pit traps regularly, McIntyre reported. Pit traps alone did not kill wolves, though, and in his book *Vicious: Wolves and Men in America*, historian Jon Coleman recounted a powerful anecdote. In the tale, founding conservationist John James Audubon watched passively as a Kentucky farmer slashed the Achilles tendons of wolves caught in pit traps. He then drew the lame wolves out of the pit so that his hounds could "bother" the beleaguered and hamstrung predators to death. Audubon barely blinked at what, today, would be considered cruel and inhumane treatment of an animal. Folklore from New England tells of a woman and an Indian who, on separate occasions, fell into pit traps already occupied by a wolf. When the woman and the wolf were discovered, it is said they were cowering on opposite sides of the trap, neither wanting anything to do with the other, according to Coleman.

Environmental historian William Cronon observed that New Englanders also introduced a cascade of environmental changes that, in conjunction with killing wolves outright, made the land inhospitable to the animal. They leveled forests for fuel and agricultural fields and disrupted the Native American's cycles of burning the woods near their seasonal villages. Cyclical, small-scale burnings produced grassy forest floors and an edge effect that beckoned elk, deer, porcupine, beaver, and ruffed grouse. Regular burning created a mosaic of forest patches in different states of ecological succession, which kept game populations high but kept pests like ticks, fleas, and grasshoppers at bay. The colonists forever altered the native fauna and flora by introducing horses, goats, sheep, and cattle that often grazed freely.

McIntyre reported that by the mid-nineteenth century, settlers were successful in their mission of wiping wolves from most of the eastern states, including New England's woods. He notes that poet and naturalist Henry David Thoreau provided one of the first laments for the absence of the "nobler animals" such as "panthers, lynx, wolverine, wolf, bear," and moose in his home state of Massachusetts. Thoreau compared the woods near his home in Concord to observations recorded in William Wood's *New England's Prospect* more than 200 years earlier. He found that many forest creatures were few or absent. In his journal, Thoreau wrote: "I should not like to think that some demigod had come before me and picked out some of the best of the stars. I wish to know an entire heaven and entire earth. All the great trees and beasts, fishes and fowl are gone. The streams, perchance, are somewhat shrunk." By all measures, Thoreau deemed his surroundings an "emasculated country." Not all of his countrymen agreed with him, and many still pursued wolves where they existed farther south and west.

When Ronald Nowak researched the last wolves of the Southeast, he uncovered records from settlers in Louisiana who recorded wolves in the area as early as 1699, when the founder of their colony, Pierre Le Moyne d'Iberville, reported seeing them near the mouth of the Mississippi River. Nowak also found writings from a settler, M. Le Page DuPratz, who lived in New Orleans and Natchez between 1718 and 1734. DuPratz reported wolves to be quite common across the colony, writing that they would trail hunting parties for miles to scavenge the juicy entrails left behind in piles of offal. A century later, wolves were reported to be "fearful on young pigs and calves," according to an account Nowak found from Sabine Parish. As late as 1885, wolves were reported by a writer named C. T. Dunn to be found in thinly settled swamps within the state. Nowak determined that the only cases of wolves harassing people in Louisiana were when people processed alligators, deer, squirrels, and other hunted meat outdoors.

In North Carolina, colonial records show that the first wolf bounty was enacted on April 6, 1748, at a General Assembly meeting held in New Bern. It established that anyone who killed a wolf or panther was entitled to a bounty of ten shillings, while those killing "wilde cats" could earn two shillings and six pence. This early legislation reveals what the colonists considered their largest problems: the South's two apex predators and its most notorious, ambush-attacking mesopredator. To claim their reward, bounty hunters showed the head or scalp of their quarry with its ears intact, then swore that they killed the predator in the parish that offered the reward. The local magistrate then gave them a certificate for their reward and promptly burned the head or scalp, lest the bounty hunter attempt to reuse his gory prize for a second reward in a different parish. Once a year, the local church wardens paid out rewards for all outstanding certificates. (Church wardens and magistrates were fined five pounds for failure to carry out their bounty duties.) A few years later, the burden of paying the bounty reward was shifted to county courts. In 1764 new legislation was passed to restrict the range of predators taken to within ten miles of settled plantations because so many people searched far and wide for predators that it became a burden to the least populated, westernmost parishes to pay out. Because the bounty system relied on taxing people within a parish, it was rarely instated for more than two to five years. The ecological result of this, along with the ten-mile restriction, was a cycle of temporal and geographic persecution and reprieve for the area's top predators. In 1769 the parishes of Mecklenburg, Rowan, Tryon, Carteret, Bute, and Granville declared they were "much infested with wolves" and instated a bounty for wolves and panthers only, offering seven shillings apiece. In 1773 the bounty went up to ten shillings for Bute, Orange, Anson, Granville, Tyrrell, Chatham, Wake, Mecklenburg, Guilford, Onslow, Carteret, and Surry Counties. The following year, Brunswick, Rowan, Currituck, New Hanover, Tryon, Bladen, Cumberland, Pitt, Duplin, Dobbs, and Johnston Counties added their names to the five-year legislation. When the bounty was reinstated in 1777, the price for a wolf was doubled to twenty shillings, and ten shillings was paid for each pup.

On November 28, 1777, when the price on a wolf's head was at its all-time high, an anonymous Carolina planter penned an opinion letter to the *North Carolina Gazette*. He proclaimed that all previous bounties had been set too low to entice anyone to truly go after wolf eradication in a meaningful way. The correct incentive, he opined, was five pounds. "Among the many losses that attend the planter and obstruct his success," he wrote, "perhaps none are more so than the damage done by wolves, and other noxious animals among our cattle, sheep, and hogs." The planter calculated that each grown wolf enacted twenty to thirty pounds of damage in a year. But to truly exert pressure, more money must be shelled out by taxing citizens on the value of their real estate. Wolves were a burden to be borne by all. If more money were offered, the planter reasoned, then "before many years it would be a rare thing to hear of a wolf &tc doing damage among the settlements." In wolves' absence, stock animals would flourish. His vision proved prophetic, though wolves were so vulnerable to the persecution they suffered, in addition to the unprecedented changes to their landscape, that larger bounties were not necessary to banish them from the state. By the 1800s, individual counties maintained bounties on an ad hoc basis, though wolves were growing scarcer by the middle of the century and were all but gone by its end.

In far western North Carolina, near Eagle Creek, regional hunting legend Acquilla "Quill" Rose was known for telling a tale of literally falling into a "wolf nest." The story was likely passed down as oral history, but Bob Plott recorded it in his 2008 book *A History of Hunting in the Great Smoky Mountains*. According to Plott, Quill was born in 1841 and became an accomplished bear hunter who rounded out his income by brewing moonshine and collecting wolf bounties. Local lore pegged a problematic wolf that had been raiding farmers' livestock for at least three months. Farmers set out some traps; they once caught the wolf, but he freed himself by chewing his own leg off. The stump apparently did not slow down the wolf's desire for sheep.

(In truth, the injury may have made the animal more reliant upon livestock, now that he was at a disadvantage to hunt comparatively more mobile and wary wild prey by himself.) Quill decided to catch the three-legged wolf. One day, while searching for signs of the animal, he slipped from a rocky ledge and fell into a hollow behind a waterfall of Bear Creek. Something "soft and hairy" broke his fall. He felt it with his hands and realized it was his three-legged quarry. Quill grabbed the animal by its ruff and straddled it. Immobilized by the man on its back, the wolf could not resist. But Quill had no hands left to reach for his knife, so he used the weight of his body to push the wolf's head down into the water. Within minutes, the wolf drowned. Quill earned five dollars. The story is undated, but, if true, this unfortunate incident likely took place in the three decades between 1860 and the end of the wolf bounty in western North Carolina in 1891. Quill wrote of the wolf: "He had been living high off the settlements for months, til he war to fat to fight well."

. Plott told of another respected hunter in western North Carolina, "Turkey" George Palmer, who also profited from wolf bounties. Turkey lived in the northwest corner of Haywood County, surrounded by the Qualla Boundary of the Cherokee and Tennessee. He was born in 1857, lived until 1944, and killed 106 bears during his lifetime. According to Plott, he canned the meat that his family did not eat and sold it for $1.50 per jar. Turkey is said to have claimed that wolves in the area were too trap smart, so he selected strychnine-laced mutton as his weapon of choice. Though wolves were said to "plague" the valley where Turkey lived, Plott, in his book, recorded bears raiding farms in this region nearly a half dozen or more times while making reference to wolves raiding farms only once.

In addition to being an author, Bob Plott is a descendent of Johannes Plott, a German immigrant who created a special breed of bear-hunting dog known as a Plott hound. Oral history passed down among Plott hound owners in North Carolina establishes that wolves lived in the mountainous western region of the state as late as the early 1900s. When bears were scarce, it is said the hounds could always ferret out wolves, too. In a tale related in *The Story of the Plott Hound* (2007), Montraville Plott, a relative of Johannes Plott, is said to have kept a wolf on his farm in the late 1800s. He tied it to a tree, which became known as the Wolf Tree. Author Bob Plott said there was speculation that Montraville used the wolf to breed with his Plott hounds. But Bob believes this is untrue and that his ancestor likely used the tethered wolf as bait to attract other wolves, which he then killed for a bounty. One day, the captive wolf, which was described as semidomesticated but still wild, broke free and somehow got into a bind in Mrs. Plott's laundry. She whacked it with a frying pan, the story goes, until it died.

Folklore from North Carolina points to the dishonesty that bounties bred as well. According to Bob Plott, at least one hunter, trapper, and outdoorsman living in the Nantahala Forest near the Tennessee state line is said to have farmed wolf pups annually from a den whose location he kept secret. He plucked the pups for their scalps but, thinking ahead, left the parents alive so that he could collect a bounty on their litter again the following year. While bounties alone would have never rid an area entirely of wolves, they did exert serious pressure on the animals by making their deaths profitable.

It was midway through the 1800s, after several hundred years of persecution, that the red wolf finally received a scientific name. John James Audubon and John Bachman were the first to give the red wolf a true Latinized scientific name, *Canis lupus var. Rufus*, in their 1851 book, *The Viviparous Quadrupeds of North America*. They focused only on populations from Texas in their descriptions and referred to it as the Red Texan Wolf. Although Audubon and Bachman recounted several anecdotes involving red wolves stealing food from camps or feeding upon corpses after battles, their discourse lacked a detailed species or taxonomic description. However, Nowak noted that Audubon and Bachman were the first to record that the wolf of the southeastern states was "structurally different" than other wolves in the country.

The first biologist to document red wolves in the extreme southwest of their range was Vernon Bailey, a biologist with the U.S. Biological Survey. In 1905 he listed red wolves in a statewide survey of Texas mammals that was published in *North American Fauna*. Bailey was well versed in western wolves, and it's significant that he, too, assessed the wolves of eastern Texas as somehow differing from gray wolves. He noted them as *Canis rufus*, showing that he agreed with Audubon and Bachman—but he moved the animal solidly into its own species class, upholding suspicions of its otherness. (He also recognized the black phase wolf of eastern Texas tentatively as *Canis ater*, though he wondered if perhaps this was not the same animal as the black wolf reported from Florida.) Bailey also observed that Texas ranchmen differentiated between coyotes and red wolves as reflected in the higher bounty offer of ten to twenty dollars for a red wolf versus one or two dollars for a coyote.

At around the same time, in 1907, President Theodore Roosevelt traveled along the Tensas River in Louisiana and, according to a 1967 article by Ronald Nowak, "found wolves to be common" there. But in other parts of the state, wolves were in decline due to the use of pit traps, poisons, and dynamite. But Nowak reported that some red wolves likely held out in the northeastern quadrant of Louisiana, where there were dense woods and impassable canebrakes along major waterways, like the Mississippi, Tensas, and Ouachita Rivers. In these natural refuges, man was less likely to tread, and wolves could make a quiet living in the swampy wilderness.

Nowak found that by 1934, when Stanley P. Young, another biologist with the U.S. Biological Survey, visited Louisiana, he reported wolves "in considerable numbers" in Madison Parish, as well as in West, East Carroll, Franklin, and Tensas Parishes. Young also indicated that wolves were numerous in the southwestern part of the state in Cameron and Calcasieu Parishes.

Eighty-six years after the red wolf was officially named as a species, biologist Edward A. Goldman wrote the first solid taxonomic description of the animal. In a paper titled "The Wolves of North America," published in the *Journal of Mammalogy* in 1937, Goldman became the first to recognize the species as being composed of three subspecies: *C. rufus floridanus*, *C. rufus gregoryi*, and *C. rufus rufus*. (The easternmost subspecies of red wolf was first recognized by Miller in 1912 when he named it *Canis floridanus*.) Whereas previous naturalists and early biologists had noted several different types of wolves in the Southeast, Goldman was the first to fold all southeastern wolves into a single species. While *C. rufus floridanus* and *C. rufus rufus* had already been loosely, but not necessarily scientifically, described by others, Goldman focused on describing *C. rufus gregoryi* for the first time in his *Mammalogy* paper.

A few years later, in 1944, Goldman coauthored *The Wolves of North America* with Stanley Young and offered thorough taxonomic treatments of all three subspecies. He noted *C. rufus floridanus* as the largest of the three red wolf types. He recognized it as dwelling in Georgia, Florida, and Alabama. (Later, Ronald Nowak revised this range to indicate it had previously occupied land along the Atlantic Seaboard during colonial times but had since become extinct throughout its range from approximately Pennsylvania south to Florida and west through Alabama, central Tennessee, and eastern Kentucky.) Goldman noted that *floridanus* had specimens as large as the northeastern wolf, *Canis lycaon*. He was the first to describe *C. rufus gregoryi* as intermediate in size between the subspecies, and he reported that its range encompassed the lower Mississippi River basin from Mississippi and Louisiana to east Texas and north through Arkansas, southeastern Missouri, southern Illinois, southern Indiana, western Kentucky, and western

Tennessee. He also reported that a black morph was common in *gregoryi*. Based on reports from Bartram, the black phase was also common in *floridanus* within Florida as well. Goldman verified *C. rufus rufus* as the smallest of the subspecies, which he believed occupied a small range from central to east Texas.

Goldman also reported that in east Texas, "red wolf" was a common name for this animal, and, according to Nowak, he is credited with popularizing this term across the animal's entire eastern range. Goldman, too, thought that the morphology of *C. rufus* hinted at something altogether different from gray wolves. But even though Goldman saw red wolves as distinct, he was likely as stumped as the next biologist as to how *C. rufus* was related to its canid relatives. Even as he studied them, they were fading fast from the landscape. They were virtually extirpated from east of the Mississippi and were growing scarce in their range west of it.

In 1967 Nowak summarized reports of the last wolves killed in southeastern states. He wrote that wolves were extinct in Florida by the early 1900s, with the last recorded wolf killed there in 1894. The last wolf killed in North Carolina is thought to have died in the Great Smoky Mountains in 1905. In the Okefenokee Swamp in southern Georgia, the last wolf was killed in 1908. Wolves in Alabama apparently holed up in the hilliest countryside of the state, from Walker to Colbert Counties, until at least the 1920s, though the last recorded kill in the state was in 1917. On the other side of its range, the last wolf killed in extreme southeastern Kansas is thought to have been felled near Columbus in 1909. According to Nowak, the U.S. Biological Survey "helped" by killing 154 red wolves in 1927, 716 in 1928, and 1,339 in 1929. Most of these killings took place in Arkansas, Oklahoma, and Texas. In Missouri, the last known wolf was killed in 1942 in Oregon County; and in Mississippi, the last wolf was killed in 1946 in Clairborne County.

Across its range, *Canis rufus* experienced an obliteration of its kind. By the late 1800s, it had become fashionable to explode wolf dens with dynamite and to lace baited carcasses with poison, but even the wolves that avoided direct attacks by people suffered a less-coordinated assault on their habitat. By the early 1900s, wolf depredations appeared to increase in Louisiana, according to Nowak, and some thought this marked a population spike. Nowak attributed this anomaly to an influx of settlers in the 1800s and nearly a century of overhunting the local deer and felling of the virgin forests. Farmland swallowed up vast stretches of the state's native habitat, and with their natural prey gone, Nowak believes that the remaining wolves turned to livestock. The uptick in depredations may have appeared to be an increase in the wolf population, but this spike likely occurred even while the Southeast's last wolves dwindled numerically. Nevertheless, Nowak reported that the state called for more stringent measures to kill wolves in the 1930s. By the 1940s, the Louisiana Department of Wildlife Fisheries was formed, and controlling predators was high on its staff's to-do list. In 1948 they recorded taking 47 wolves, plus 38 more the following year. They killed 16 wolves in 1956 and 1957, 50 in 1958, 60 in 1959, 95 in 1960, 73 in 1961, 174 in 1962, and 162 in 1963, according to Nowak. But the following year, the agency admitted the animals they caught by the hundreds were not, in fact, red wolves but common coyotes. Their reported "wolf" population spike masked the devastating population crash that was taking place. Arkansas, Oklahoma, and eastern Texas reported similar spikes in "wolves" in the 1950s.

Also in the 1950s, a mammalogist from Sherman College in Austin, Texas, noticed that all the canids he caught appeared to be coyotes or coyote-wolf hybrids. Howard McCarley published a paper with his findings in 1959, and he kept studying the issue, searching for the state's missing large wolves. McCarley studied skulls of 117 recently deceased canids from Arkansas, Oklahoma, and Texas and compared them to known red wolf skulls. He concluded that none of the canids were true red wolves. In 1962 McCarley published a pivotal paper on his findings in *Southeastern Naturalist*. He declared that the red wolf was slipping into extinction, while coyotes — what many people called "small wolves" — migrated eastward in droves into the red wolf's now-vacant haunts. Only "isolated areas of Louisiana" still harbored pure wolves, he wrote. "Elsewhere, *C. latrans* has replaced *C. niger* as a primary predator," he declared, using an earlier name for the red wolf. Because the red wolf had been poorly studied even at that time, McCarley's study sorted through specimens of red wolves and coyotes reported in Arkansas, Louisiana, eastern Texas, and eastern Oklahoma in an attempt not only to clearly define what a red wolf and a coyote were but also to figure out the relationship between the two. He wrote that "considerable confusion exists in species identification in areas where both may occur." For the most part, people did not even notice that the wolves of their land were slowly emptied out and replaced by smaller, but similar-looking, canids. As the red wolf packs were reduced and their social networks busted, coyotes crept and then poured into the "predatory vacuum," as Nowak termed the ecological void left by the red wolf.

But the Fish and Wildlife Service was not yet alarmed. Perhaps they didn't yet notice. According to Nowak, in 1964 they submitted a report to the American Society of Mammalogists stating that between 4,000 and 8,000 individual red wolves were living in east Texas, east Oklahoma, Arkansas, Louisiana, and Mississippi. The following year, society members expressed their concern that the FWS's control efforts in Arkansas would eliminate the state's remaining wolves. In 1966 the society reported at their annual meeting that the control efforts had likely been successful.

Nowak toured parishes in northwestern Louisiana in 1965 and 1966, where he followed up on reports and rumors of wolves. He looked at carcasses that had been shot and watched taped films of animals said to be wolves. But their skull measurements came in woefully short of a red wolf's, and he assessed them all as coyotes. "The few specimens examined were too small," Nowak wrote, "and the really 'big wolves' always seemed to be reported just a little farther back in the woods or swamps. Thus [my] small effort only added to the authoritative consensus that the true wolf had become extinct in northwestern Louisiana."

In 1966 Louisiana state supervisor of predator control T. E. Harris wrote to Nowak that he had located some red wolves farther south along the Mississippi River. For reasons he did not elaborate upon, he also wrote that he believed wolves could be found in the southwest marshes of Louisiana. His trappers had caught four in Cameron Parish in 1961, and sheep farmers poisoned six in the same area, while large wolves were still reported in Calcasieu Parish. In 1966 Harris ordered his men to cease killing wolves. With an unknown number remaining, he began an "unofficial protection policy" for the highly targeted, highly misunderstood, and highly understudied red wolf, Nowak reported.

By the time the scientifically trained eyes of McCarley, Nowak, and John Paradiso began to scrutinize the red wolf, it had nearly slipped away, a victim of persecution for several hundred years and of mistaken identity for several decades. In the mid-1900s, within the span of a mere few years, the red wolf went from being called numerous to being listed (on March 11, 1967) as an endangered species under the Endangered Species Preservation Act of 1966, a piece of legislation that preceded today's Endangered Species Act. While it is significant for a species to be included under the first act, the legislation itself was toothless and represented nothing more than a list of conservationally challenged species; it offered no protections or plans for assisting them.

In 1968 Paradiso, then an FWS biologist, filed a report with his agency in which he argued there were no doubts that the red wolf had dwindled within the regions west of the Mississippi. It had been extirpated long ago from east of the Mississippi, but the regions west of the river had been reported by the FWS in the 1950s to hold stable populations of the canid. By the early 1970s, only two of Texas's 254 counties (Jefferson and Chambers) contained red wolves, and they abutted the state line with Louisiana. In 1971 Paradiso followed up with a second report, this one coauthored by Nowak, affirming the position that red wolves were distinct taxonomically from gray wolves and coyotes, but that in regions of the Edwards Plateau and east in Texas, coyotes and red wolves were found to be dwelling side by side. Paradiso wrote that "the Edwards Plateau area contains extremely varied and intermingled habitat ranging from densely forested river valleys, through sheltered canyons and prairies, to arid stony slopes. The plateau contained a mixture of life forms, the valleys being extensions of the eastern woodlands, while surrounding sectors represented the typical western semi-arid zone." Paradiso recognized that the Edwards Plateau contained a unique environment where eastern habitat intermingled with western habitat in a mosaic that could lead eastern red wolves and western coyotes to come into contact. While distinct specimens of each could be found in the plateau, so, too, could puzzling hybrid forms. "This hybrid swarm," Paradiso wrote,

> apparently formed first in central Texas and then spread to the east and filled the niches created by man's disruption of the habitat and extermination of the red wolf. A massive breakdown of ecological isolation and greatly increased gene exchange along the former border between *C. rufus* and *C. latrans* did not necessarily develop. Rather, our evidence indicates a geographic expansion of the hybrid animals themselves, reinforced by a constant movement of *C. latrans* to the East, into a niche left vacant by the decimation of *C. rufus*. There is no indication that hybridization occurred to a large extent anywhere except in the central Texas area, where the peculiar natural conditions of "eastern" and "western" habitat types supported the phenomenon.

Paradiso's take on why hybridization became widespread was a very different interpretation than the idea that simple habitat destruction and alteration had frayed existing social structures and allowed hybridization, which implied that a behavioral-ecological barrier had previously prevented interbreeding. What he argued was that the unique mosaic of eastern and western habitats in the Edwards Plateau allowed coyotes an unusual gateway through which to spread eastward. Within the plateau, they intermingled with a shrinking population of red wolves under pressure from habitat destruction and persecution. The red wolves' dwindling numbers may have been what drove it to breed with coyotes within this mosaic habitat where they came into contact. The resulting hybrid swarm then placed an extreme biological pressure on the remaining true red wolves that dwelled in the swamps and no-man's-land along the Texas-Louisiana border.

But the red wolf's luck was about to change dramatically. One man in particular built upon the detective work of Nowak, Paradiso, and McCarley to lead the red wolf out from the gaping jaws of extinction. When FWS agents began looking for someone to head up a field station in southeastern Texas to manage the last wild red wolves, Curtis J. Carley's skill set was deemed the most qualified. Carley, a coyote ecologist with a highly analytical mind, could track and catch song dogs with ease. His superiors gambled that he could use his coyote knowledge base, as well as his muddy-boots field biology know-how, to morph into a red wolf expert. *Canis rufus* sure needed one.

## CHAPTER 10
# A Biologist's Zeal for Recovery

Curtis J. Carley was a stickler for doing things right; "shortcut" was not in his lexicon. However much time and elbow grease a project took, that's what he gave. Carley became involved with endangered species eight years into his Fish and Wildlife Service career. History rarely credits Carley for the groundwork he laid to save the red wolf, perhaps in part because he never sought praise. But *Canis rufus* benefited in a timely and dramatic way from Carley's personality traits and knowledge. His meticulous attention to detail, systematic problem solving, and analytical critical thinking coalesced with his deep knowledge of coyote behavior and ecology to create unique triage-based field methods. Depending upon the lens though which you look at history, Carley either saved what was left of the red wolf or inadvertently shifted the red wolf to a more wolflike morphology.

This modest man from Kansas didn't grow up dreaming of becoming a red wolf biologist. He yearned to be a pilot, but his older brother talked him into trying college first. Carley found biology to be the easiest subject of his load due to his severe dyslexia. He learned to circumvent his disability by drafting copious notes. He wrote and rewrote them until the content lodged in his brain. Once there, it rarely left. Frequent note taking became one of his lifelong habits. Even long after his retirement, he often stayed up for hours to write detailed reports on phone conversations and his day's activities.

Upon graduation from Fort Hays State University in 1963, Carley continued on to graduate school, where he refined his zoological knowledge base. He fell in love with small mammals, especially mice and rodents. He also fell in love with a music student named Sara Hanson. When he finished school in 1965, Carley took a job with the FWS and moved Sara, now his wife, to Cornelius, Oregon, and then to San Antonio. It was in Texas that he began his career as a wild canid ecologist in 1967. For six years, he studied coyote ecology and control methods at the Predator Ecology Research Station. This job taught him about trapping, animal damage-control politics, and how to use radio telemetry and an electronic siren to census wild canid populations. He also learned to keep his side of an unspoken bargain and shoot every snake he encountered on a cattleman's land (especially rattlers). It was the Texan way of saying "thank you."

In mid-1973, Carley was tapped to start up a new field station in Beaumont, Texas, where his assignment was to survey and protect the last remaining wild red wolves from an advancing hybrid swarm. "Knew I'd be assigned as soon as the Endangered Species Act was passed," he wrote in one of his first monthly reports. Though he officially started his new position as the Red Wolf Recovery Program project leader in late October, two months before the act's passage, he worked informally from afar as early as September. There was still time, his superiors assured him, to establish a buffer zone and halt the oncoming tide of wolf-coyote hybrids and pure coyotes.

The proposed buffer zone extended fifteen miles north of a theoretical line drawn five miles north of, and roughly parallel to, U.S. Highway 90. The line extended from Lake Houston in Harris County to the Sabine River in Orange County, which formed the border with Louisiana. His superiors considered land below the line to be a management area for red wolves. They wanted his field team to clear the buffer zone of any coyotes and hybrids to prevent hybridization of the last wolves farther south. Another plan was to build a canid-proof fence. This idea, as impractical as it may now sound, was inspired in part by the 2,000-mile-long rabbit-proof fence Australia erected to keep invasive lagomorphs out of their country's western reaches.

Carley's first tasks were to figure out how many red wolves were left in the wild and to scout out what kinds of canids lived within the proposed buffer area. But censusing techniques at the time were weak and unreliable. Then there was the problem of impassable wetlands and gaining access to privately owned properties. To help the new red wolf field team learn the lay of the land around them, NASA donated $800 worth of nine-and-a-half-inch-square aerial infrared photographs of the region, with the intention of helping the crew pinpoint likely red wolf habitat and identify ways to access it. But the photographs were transparencies, and it was months before Carley could secure a light table so he could utilize them. Once illuminated, the aerials afforded Carley's team critical knowledge of the swampier regions of southwest Louisiana. Carley secured a boat to reach some of the locales.

In 1970 Ronald Nowak estimated that perhaps only 200 red wolves remained in southeast Texas, with no more than 100 in other areas. In 1972 a doctoral student from Yale estimated from a howling survey that perhaps only 100 red wolves remained in Texas. Famed wolf trapper Roy McBride estimated that no more than 300 red wolves lived in Texas, based on field observations. No matter the method, anyone who looked into the situation concluded that the red wolf population was small and ever shrinking due to hybridization.

The dense vegetative cover of the region ruled out aerial surveys, so trapping and howling surveys were Carley's two most useful censusing techniques. He was well aware of their limitations. First, he had to figure out how to catch a wolf without hurting it. Up until then, the FWS had mostly focused on how to kill wolves. Trap injuries did not matter when death was the goal. But with conservation as the new goal, injuries mattered. Carley experimented with modified leg-hold traps but was disheartened when they injured animals at the same rate as unmodified traps. While employed at the Predator Ecology Research Station, Carley had learned to attach to the traps a fabric-wrapped tab that contained a tranquilizer. When coyotes were trapped, they often chewed at their trapped leg. But by tying tranquilizer tabs to the trap, the chances were increased that the animal might lick or bite into the tab and then slip into grogginess. A drugged animal was less likely to struggle and inadvertently slice their tissue to the bone or chew off a foot. Carley taught his field team how to use the tranquilizer tabs when they trapped red wolves.

Carley's team originally consisted of an FWS biologist named John Dorsett and a predator-control agent who had been stationed in the area for several years prior to the creation of the Beaumont field station. The landscape where the team laid their traps was a mosaic of densely vegetated coastal prairie interspersed with wide-open rice farms laced with canals. In the summer it was hot and rainy, and the air vibrated with mosquitoes. The land itself was difficult to travel across, except for where roads had been built from piles of oyster shells. According to Dorsett, the team most often trapped along these shell roads and at canal crossings where they often found canid sign. "There were definitely some animals that just looked different. They were definitely a different animal than a coyote," Dorsett later recalled. "They tended to have bigger snouts and longer legs. They were just more massive overall, especially in the head. They sure *looked* like wolves." Dorsett also noticed that whereas most of the time they'd only catch individual coyotes once, they'd often catch individual red wolves multiple times each.

After just a few months on the ground in southeast Texas, Carley developed a bad feeling in his gut. It became obvious to him that his superiors were badly misinformed. Through the team's trap lines and howling surveys (both within the buffer zone and the red wolf management zone), they found evidence of coyotes, coyote-wolf hybrids, and what Carley felt were scant pure red wolves. But while Carley could tell the larger wolves from the coyotes, he was as uncertain as anyone as to the quantitative criteria constituting a true red wolf in the scientific sense. (Nowak's monograph on *Canis* was still several years away from publication.) "We had all been led to believe that there was a viable population of wolves remaining on the coastal prairie of southeast Texas and adjacent areas of Louisiana," Carley later reminisced. "We were led to believe, too, that a technician on my staff had the ability to identify wolves. Within just a few months, it became obvious that neither case was true." Carley was frustrated by what he perceived as inconsistencies in his staff's ability to classify the different kinds of canids. He knew the group needed a concrete, measurable way of telling the wolf hybrids and wolves apart.

Carley was also quickly overwhelmed by the volume of animal damage complaints, which he and his team were obliged to respond to on a weekly basis. The new red wolf project was a cooperative venture between the FWS and the Texas Division of Wildlife Services. As such, they had to deal with livestock damage complaints and pacify the local ranching community. But Carley recognized the opportunity for rapport building by being in contact with landowners, and he made a point to talk to them about wolves and the meaning of the new Endangered Species Act. Trapping wild canids off private land also gave him a chance to survey areas he couldn't otherwise access, as well as a chance to win landowners' trust. Some even asked him for signs to post declaring that their land was being trapped so that hunters wouldn't trespass and run their hounds illegally.

Carley believed in listening to locally affected people, and it showed. He had a strong understanding of agriculture that was rooted in his teenage experience as a summer farmhand. Both of his parents were also raised on farms. When he talked about his time spent growing wheat and working cattle, he connected with the locals. "The importance of the landowner and his attitude cannot be over emphasized," he said. "The landowner controls the land and maintains the habitat. Without the land, and the habitat, the wolf cannot exist."

Carley learned quickly that the office activities operated by the light of day, but the wolves operated under cover of darkness. He left home around

7:00 A.M. most mornings and returned by 7:00 P.M. for dinner with Sara and their children. After dinner, he headed back out into the night. He drove country roads, hiked through prairies, and slogged across marshes, where he broadcast the sounds of a Smith & Wesson Magnum IV electronic police siren into the inky darkness. As the minutes bled into nocturnal hours, he listened for wolves howling back. Carley collaborated with Howard Mc-Carley from Austin College to record the response howls with a twenty-four-inch parabolic reflector. They wrote a tentative species identification in their field notes after each howling session, along with the time, place, and weather conditions.

Later, McCarley analyzed the recordings sonographically, and the data gave the men important clues about the number and kinds of wild canids living on the landscape. When experienced personnel were involved, Carley noted, the species identification seldom differed between the field ID and sonographic analysis ID. Although they performed howling surveys over the entire 2,000-square-mile area in the winter of 1974–75, they focused their attention on central Chambers County later in 1975 and censused it heavily. They found thirteen canid groups there, with one to four individuals per group. With time, they identified eight (29 percent) as red wolves, sixteen (59 percent) as hybrids, and five (12 percent) as coyotes. While this amounted to a bleak assessment for the red wolf, Carley liked that their howling census data matched the approximate percentage of red wolves calculated to be present by a second census method: spot trapping and physically examining wild canids. He felt that because both methods arrived at a similar proportion of the canid population identified as red wolves, they validated each other. By scrutinizing recordings of both spontaneous and elicited howls, McCarley wanted to delineate differences in decibels, duration, and howl type that could be used to separate coyotes, red wolves, and their hybrids. He began in 1972 by recording howls of known red wolves and red wolf–coyote hybrids in the Oklahoma City and Point Defiance Zoos. But he found their cries to be different from those of wild canids.

As soon as Carley began capturing wolves, hybrids, and coyotes around the Beaumont station, he had introduced a system of identification cards with which to track them. His team recorded the animal's capture location, sex, weight, and eye color and the types of parasites it carried. They listed its body measurements, such as the length and width of its front and rear foot pads, its overall length, the length of its tail and ears, and its shoulder height. Diagnostic DNA tools were yet to be invented, so the men used rulers to carefully measure physical features and develop characteristic ranges that classified red wolves from coyotes and their hybrids. For good measure, they took a photograph of each animal and attached it to the ID card. McCarley used these cards to match the locations of his wild canid recordings to capture locations, and presumably the home ranges, of actual animals. This gave him a second line of evidence to confirm, in most cases, each vocalization's species identity as a red wolf, a coyote, or a hybrid. Carley liked the idea of creating systematic, quantifiable methods by which to tell the animals apart.

While Carley felt confident that he could tell most hybrids from true wolves by sight alone, some hybrids approached the size and look of red wolves. This was especially true when his staff squabbled over classifying an animal as a hybrid or *Canis rufus rufus*, the smallest of the red wolf subspecies. And it was these enigmatic wolflike hybrids for which Carley most desired measurable criteria to suss out their lineage. He and his staff found *Canis rufus gregoryi* easier to classify, and it was less likely that hybrids approached it in size. The area of their red wolf management zone spanned the ranges of both subspecies.

After a couple of months spent trapping, Carley realized with a sinking feeling that the buffer-zone plan was worthless. He'd gotten a slow, frustrating start on the field work due to excessive rain washing out every trap that his team buried. In January 1974 alone, storms dumped 8.81 inches of rain on Beaumont, about 4.75 inches more than normal. The ground was already saturated from December rains. At a minimum, the traps' pans were exposed. Those not sabotaged by rain were sprung by wandering cattle. Carley's team used horses when trucks couldn't maneuver over the sodden ground. But in February, the deluge slacked off, and he and his men trapped seventeen canids within the buffer zone. All were hybrids or coyotes. They also worked by horseback to locate wolf dens in hard-to-reach coastal prairies and marsh with difficult terrain. But the prairies and the marsh were only a small part of the habitat within what was recognized as red wolf range. Soy and rice farming had led people to plow most of the coastal prairies under, and rich oil deposits had led to heavy settlements in some areas. Carley noted that while red wolves would use cattle walkways and oil-field roads to move deep into the marshes, it didn't appear to be ideal habitat for them. Red wolves were more likely to use the marshes regularly only in winter when the cold abated the mosquito population and migrating geese might provide a quick meal. However, swamp rabbits and nutria were found in abundance in the marshes year round, and Carley suspected that the wolves hunted within them at night, even if they weren't actively living there.

They also pulled seven male and three female canids from land near Pasadena and southwest Houston, which was within the red wolf management area. Again, all ten were either a hybrid or a coyote. Technically, the area was mapped as the range of *Canis rufus rufus*, but Carley began to fret that *C. r. rufus* may not exist anymore. He and his men trapped four red wolves—three from southeast Jefferson and southern Chambers Counties—while answering animal damage complaints there. "These animals were very impressive and came from an area of deep southeast Texas in which we've not trapped before," Carley wrote in his February 1974 report. Having trapped coyotes for six years, Carley also found red wolves to be easier to catch. They struck him as a bit less crafty. In March the Beaumont team removed twelve canids from the buffer zone. None of these were wolves. But they found six red wolves within their month's haul of seventeen canids from the management area where Carley had devised a system of "intensive spot trapping" based on the howling surveys. By April, the team's trapping and howling surveys revealed red wolves, hybrids, and coyotes living side by side as far south as Anahuac National Wildlife Refuge. Worse, they discovered that this situation had been going on since at least 1969. The red wolf was in more trouble than anyone had imagined. Carley warned his supervisors that they must restructure their management plans to adapt to the reality on the ground.

By May 1974, Carley had convinced his superiors that implementing the buffer zone was not just wasted effort but also harmful. "To seal off the area with a buffer zone would be locking the burglars in the house," he told them. They listened and eliminated it as an option. He began to realize that preserving the red wolf in the wild was no longer tenable, but preserving it in captivity was within reach. His biggest hope was that his team had found red wolves in Chambers County (on the eastern side of Galveston Bay) and southern Jefferson County (along the state line) in Texas. He had also received good reports of likely red wolves between lakes Sabine and Calcasieu in Louisiana. But his FWS Southwest region ended at the eastern Texas state line. Louisiana was under the purview of the Southeast region, so he asked his supervisors to work out an agreement for his team to access a few counties.

"We do not know if the red wolf can be preserved as a viable species in its present range, but we would be negligent in our responsibilities if we did not try," Carley told a crowd of colleagues at the Southeastern Endangered Species workshop in September 1974. And try he did. Carley instructed his team to use radio telemetry collars to track newly collared "Judas" wolves to learn the locations of their dens and packs, as well as to study their behavior and habitat requirements. The studies showed that one seventy-six-pound male wolf spent most of his time in the pimple mounds of Oyster Bayou (three- to five-foot-tall sand mounds about two feet in diameter), where the animal ranged three to four miles per night. When he left the mounds, he struck out northeast and moved though agricultural lands under the cover of weeds that grew along canal banks. A fifty-eight-pound collared female red wolf also used farmlands. She preferred a rice field near Bayou Bay. When crop dusters inadvertently flushed her, she fled into Oyster Bayou. By March 1975, the team had collared and released eight male and five female red wolves. The male red wolves appeared to use ranges that averaged forty-five square miles, while females averaged slightly less. The wolves were most active from 8:00 P.M. to midnight, and again from 3:00 A.M. to dawn. Carley had observed similar bimodal activity patterns in south Texas coyotes. The team learned that the wolves preyed primarily upon nutria, swamp rabbits, cotton rats, raccoons, and carrion. Sometimes, they killed young calves and hogs and other small domestic animals. Carley enjoyed the telemetry studies because they added to the small trove of field data that he was accruing. But the telemetry work took a backseat to his mandate to respond to livestock damage complaints, and Carley could only commit to it as time permitted.

The wolves that his men found were in terrible shape. The coastal sawgrass razed the fur off of their tails and sides until many looked like Pleistocene-sized rats. Forced into swampy habitat that they may not normally have occupied, the wolves became an all-out feast for parasites. The animals were riddled with sarcoptic mange, hookworm, tapeworms, and ticks. Heartworm was found in almost every wolf older than three. One study documented 500 heartworms in a single wolf. Sometimes, when a group of wolves were held temporarily in captive pens, individuals that became startled fell over and collapsed. Their heart and pulmonary vessels were so choked with the parasitic roundworms that their brains and muscles were temporarily starved of oxygen. Some of the wolves' hearts became physically deformed by the masses of heartworms. Treating heartworm could endanger the life of the patient, and red wolves were so rare that Carley and his crew didn't dare try. Luckily, by breeding heartworm-infected hybrids, the team verified that offspring were born uninfected.

Since nearly all the red wolves the team found were infected with heartworm, they were shipped without prior treatment to Washington State, where a captive breeding effort was being spearheaded by the Point Defiance Zoo. But the zoo couldn't admit wolves that had mange to captive breeding in fear that it might spread to the other animals. In Texas, a local country vet, "Buddy" Aaron Long, teamed with the program and worked painstakingly to develop a system for curing wolves with mange. The only medicine available for dogs was too weak for the scale of infection in the wolves. Long washed the mange-infected red wolves with a gentle insecticidal shampoo that cleared their skin of scabs and encrustations, which in turn exposed the mites. Then he rubbed a heavier benzyl benzoate concoction across their skin and into their many creases. This medicine was so strong, and the wolves generally so weak, that he only dared to wash their bodies one-quarter section at a time. The process was repeated every five to seven days until the animal was healed. After ridding captured wolves of parasites, the team also inoculated them against rabies, distemper, hepatitis, and canine leptospirosis before either releasing them back to the wild for telemetry studies or holding on to them for captive breeding. Because they often held wolves in pens either at the Beaumont station or at Long's clinic, Carley and his team were often pressed to hunt nutria and raccoons for food. Some of the wolves refused to eat anything except wild meat.

Carley received countless unsolicited proposals from scientists wishing to study the red wolf. He joked to his wife that if he fulfilled all of the requests for teeth, bones, and tissue samples, they'd have nothing left of the red wolf but a tuft of fur. He cast a critical eye on the proposals and carefully weighed whether they were needed, would help the species' conservation, and were feasible. He was unafraid to comment negatively if he thought that a study proposal was baseless or needed improvement.

As time passed and his team pulled more and more hybrids from Jefferson and Chambers Counties, Carley became ever more convinced that breeding the red wolf in captivity was its last chance. He sought a change of supervision from the Texas Wildlife Services state supervisor to someone in the FWS's Southwest regional headquarters in Albuquerque who could give him the support he needed to do the unthinkable: make the red wolf go functionally extinct in the wild by removing every single one they could find for breeding in captivity. Doing so would require a complete change of the project's goals. Though Carley had recognized the extent of the hybridization problem right off the bat, his institution needed weightier evidence than his gut reaction in order to change their goals from protecting the last remaining wolves in the wild to rounding them up for a desperate act of species salvation. It took him a year and a half to document the geographic extent of hybridization but far less time than that to develop a set of morphometric criteria combined with howling profiles to define what he thought a red wolf was. If the live-trapped animals failed to meet a single established characteristic, they were excluded from the breeding program. Carley recognized that they may be excluding genetically "good" wolves by using such a stringent filter, but he was afraid that if they loosened the criteria, it may allow wolflike hybrids to slip by. Whether or not Carley inadvertently shifted the remaining red wolf population to a more wolflike phenotype is still questioned today.

Fortunately, Carley had learned an important lesson: when in doubt, act first and ask questions later. Although official word of the project's goal change from wild preservation to captive breeding came on July 1, 1975, Carley had operated the project as if captive breeding were the main goal since spring of the year before. The FWS had started down this path as a last resort. The same month that Carley was hired, the FWS had partnered with the Point Defiance Zoo to maintain a captive population of wild-caught red wolves as a backup plan. But even then, no one conceived of the captive population as the only thing keeping the species from the oblivion of extinction. Carley's superiors were not even sure that what he wanted to do would be legally supported under the Endangered Species Act. He was supposed to *save* the species, not make it go extinct in the wild, they told him. No one had ever done this before, and he tussled with his superiors for months. He saw the shape of things to come in the unfolding calamity in eastern Texas and did everything within his power to communicate why it was necessary to round up the last red wolves and breed them in captivity. It took eighteen months of continual pressure from Carley—and a bombardment of his monthly field reports—for his superiors to come around. When they did, it may have marked the first time that an FWS program was designed to control a listed species' functional wild extinction with the express purpose of later reintroducing it to its former range from captive stock.

At the time, Point Defiance Zoo and Aquarium was the only facility in the nation that was equipped with the necessary facilities and had expressed a sincere interest in helping the red wolf program. It was also one of the few places in the nation, at the time, that was free from heartworm. The staff constructed three breeding pens that were thirty-five feet by 200 feet. Two additional 100-foot-square pens were offered by a nearby mink farmer, Dale Pederson, who was a member of the Tacoma Zoological Society and participated on their mammal committee. He leased his land to the red wolf program for a dollar a year. By October 1974, all of the original pens were full, and the zoo worked out an agreement with Pederson to build more pens on his land. Carley pressed the FWS to figure out a way to pay Pederson a market-based lease rate.

Hand selecting red wolves to place in captive breeding was Carley's sole responsibility, which is one reason he scrambled so hard from the beginning of his appointment to come up with metrics to classify the animals. A full year into it, Carley developed a set of morphometrics to classify red wolves, along with comparative howling profiles. A wild canid was considered a red wolf if Carley's team measured its skull length to be approximately 215 millimeters for males or 210 millimeters for females. The zygomatic breadth had to be 110 millimeters for both sexes, and the weight at least fifty pounds for a male and forty-two pounds for a female. Males were at least fifty-three inches long and females fifty-one inches. Males measured at least twenty-seven inches tall at the shoulder, and females were half an inch shorter. The hind foot of a male red wolf measured at least nine inches, the female's eight and three-quarter inches; and the ear of a male was at least four and three-quarter inches and a female's four and a half inches. The only area in which red wolf females measured higher than males was their brain volume–to-skull ratio, which was twenty-three and a half versus twenty-three.

These numbers were hard won. Carley couldn't get at the most useful information — cranial measurements — using live animals. For that, he needed skinned and defleshed skulls emptied of all brain tissue — easily obtained in a museum, perhaps, but harder to come by when you needed the wild specimens kept alive for breeding. In a random stroke of blind luck, Carley gave a presentation to the Houston chapter of the Sierra Club one night in February 1974. A man named Donald Schaefer was in the audience as Carley described the conundrum of cranial studies on a live animal, and how they needed these metrics to discern hybrids from true wolves. Schaefer was a radiologist, and sometime later he approached Carley and proposed using X-rays to measure the skulls. Carley seized on the idea. Schaefer's wife also got involved, and in May 1974 Carley had some defleshed skulls and frozen canid heads sent to the Schaefers for practice. Meanwhile, back at the Beaumont station, Carley's assistants used a pressure cooker to coax the flesh from skulls of known coyotes and hybrids, which they used to study brain volume–to-skull ratios. This was a metric that Carley felt sure was a key diagnostic for telling wolves and hybrids apart. On days when the pressure cooker was being used, neighbors called with complaints about strange odors emanating from the office.

By July 1974, the Schaefers had X-rayed sixty-two canid skulls at Hermann Hospital. By the end of the year, Carley had an X-ray station installed in the Beaumont field office, and another hospital agreed to process their film pro bono publico. The Schaefers worked out a system whereby the biologists could take scaled measurements accurately from the radiograph films. They created a database of cranial measurements taken from their captures. The Schaefers received permission to X-ray all of the red wolf skulls in the National Museum's collection, which were shipped to Hermann Hospital in batches. The collections of known red wolf skulls gave them a reference data set to compare with the wild captures.

In 1975 Carley sent a fake X-ray of a red wolf skull to the FWS's Southeast regional director, who was toying with the idea of using his region for red wolf reintroduction if captive breeding succeeded. Where the animal's brain should have been, Carley placed gears and keys. In typical veiled humor, he wrote: "On the basis of the attached X-ray, we feel we are rapidly approaching the time when we can say, without fear of contradiction, that we truly understand what makes these wolves tick!" But, while useful, the brain volume–to–skull size ratio did not prove to be the diagnostic windfall that Carley had hoped for. There were still problems trying to separate out *Canis rufus rufus* specimens from hybrids that approached them in size. Carley consulted with McCarley and Nowak, who both felt that this subspecies was now lost and that the smaller-sized, wolflike animals Carley's team were finding were likely all hybrids. Because they also captured coyote-dog hybrids, the team worked out cranial differences to tell even these hybrids apart.

Despite working collaboratively to develop a range of *C. rufus rufus* and *C. rufus gregoryi* physical measurements, brain volume–to–skull ratios, and sonographic profiles of howls, Carley was dogged by the knowledge that wolflike hybrids might still make their way into the captive breeding program. "Some of these animals may be 'good' red wolves; however, it is conceivable that even the most wolflike of these canines are simply hybrid forms exhibiting the wolf characteristics of their ancestors," Carley wrote in a report. "The existence of the red wolf can be proven only through strictly controlled propagation and genetic study." So in December 1974, he and Long traveled to Point Defiance Zoo to assess the captive red wolves held there. They applied the metrics they'd developed in the field to the captive population as part of a standard procedure to certify all animals that were thought to be red wolves but had uncertain backgrounds. At this point in time, the precertification breeding program consisted of a total of eighteen red wolves, some of which had been acquired from federal trappers and other facilities. Only three of these originated from the Texas field station; all three later became founders in the certified breeding program. At least one red wolf had been acquired from the Oklahoma City Zoo (although certified for the captive breeding program, she died before reproducing), five puppies had been born the previous spring, and three pups had been born over the previous two years. Carley and Long weighed, measured, and X-rayed sixteen of the eighteen wolves and recorded their vocalizations. (Two wolves were off-site and could not be accessed.) To Carley's dismay, of the six original animals provided to the zoo, three did not meet his qualifications for being a red wolf. Carley even described one of the six as "coyote-like." Even worse, three of the suspect animals had bred successfully, resulting in Carley deeming that eleven of the eighteen total animals merited removal. Not only were coyotes and hybrids subsuming red wolves in the wild, but hybridism had also penetrated the captive genetic pool they were trying to create. Carley was devastated. He ordered the eleven hybrids destroyed. It was a hard pill to swallow, especially for the animal caretakers that tended to them. The zoo staff was so upset over his decree that, according to his notes, some refused to carry out the order. Carley had to destroy many of the animals himself. It wasn't a job he enjoyed, but in carrying it out, he recognized that it brought the program closer to the goal of breeding true red wolves.

At the same time, Carley also became aware that zoos across the nation were displaying animals that were labeled as red wolves but were likely hybrids or coyotes. The animals were obtained through dealers, private trappers, predator-control programs, organizations, and zoological gardens, but often the people receiving them did not know how to tell red wolves and coyotes apart and were often even unaware that the two species hybridized. Carley set to work notifying the nation's zoos through an announcement placed in two newsletters of the American Association of Zoos, Parks, and Aquariums. Institutions holding red wolves, or that had in the past, were asked to contact Carley so he could personally examine their animals. In cases where the animals were no longer present at the zoo, Carley asked for records indicating when the animals had been there and what had happened to them. Twenty-one organizations or individuals, which collectively owned more than fifty captive "red wolves," eventually contacted him.

According to one of his reports, Carley in short time sorted out that the Kansas City Zoological Gardens in Missouri had one male hybrid and one deceased female hybrid. The Ellen Trout Park Zoo in Lufkin, Texas, had one male and one female hybrid, along with their four hybrid pups. The University of Oregon had six male and four female hybrids, on which they conducted behavioral research. The Oklahoma City Zoo had one true red wolf, which they willingly donated to the captive breeding program—but not before she'd bred with a hybrid and produced a second-generation female hybrid that was given to the City of Detroit Zoo, which had unknowingly purchased a second hybrid animal, also from the Oklahoma City Zoo. The Gladys Porter Zoo in Brownsville, Texas, unwittingly acquired two male and two female hybrids, which produced seven hybrid pups. The Dickenson Park Zoo in Springfield, Missouri, had one male hybrid and a deceased female hybrid. The Shank Painter Children's Museum in Provincetown, Massachusetts, had one male of an uncertain status. The Hogle Zoological Garden in Salt Lake City, Utah, had a male that they had bred to a female who had produced two pups; Carley determined all four animals were hybrids. But the zoo had another female, identified as a hybrid at the time of her capture, which had recently escaped and was living wild somewhere in Utah.

The National Zoo in Washington, D.C., had owned two animals, long deceased, and one turned out to be a coyote. The World Wildlife Safari in Winston, Oregon, thought they had a mated red wolf pair, which had produced two offspring, but all were hybrids. The San Antonio Zoological Gardens also thought they had two red wolves, but they turned out to be a female hybrid and a very wolflike male hybrid. In Pasadena, Texas, the E. A. Dickerson Zoo had a mated pair with two offspring, all of which were hybrids. In Little Rock, Arkansas, the zoological gardens displayed what they said were two adult black phase red wolves, but Carley assessed them both, and their nine puppies, as melanistic coyotes. Two of these pups had been given to Overton Park Zoo and Aquarium in Memphis, Tennessee, as red wolves for display—a testament to how the unknowing keeping of hybrid animals or coyotes under the label of a red wolf threatened to undermine the rigorous captive breeding effort under way in Tacoma.

Animal by animal, zoo by zoo, Carley analyzed dozens of reported specimens labeled as red wolves, but he determined every one—except for the single red wolf from the Oklahoma City Zoo—to be either a hybrid or a coyote. If the zoos could not bear to destroy the hybrids, and if they did not want to change the display animal's description to "hybrid," then Carley offered to ship the animals to his field station or the captive breeding program, where they were euthanized. The experience also made it clear to Carley that, while zoos may want to cooperate in a well-meaning way, any donated "red wolves" had to be carefully assessed and their origin vetted. "It is imperative that acquisition, breeding, and dispersal of captive red wolves be conducted under the auspices of a single institution," Carley wrote. "This institution must have the ability and the unquestioned authority to judiciously select competent organizations for inclusion in the Red Wolf Captive Breeding Program." He expressed full confidence that the Point Defiance Zoo could fill this role. The relationship between the FWS and Point Defiance was among the first programs to establish a network of captive breeding facilities administered by the American Association of Zoos and Aquariums. (In time, the network of facilities cooperating to breed red wolves grew to forty-one members.)

The Beaumont field station closed in the summer of 1980 when it was apparent there were no more red wolves that could feasibly be caught in the coastal prairies and marshes. At that time, Carley pronounced that if there were red wolves left on the landscape (and he suspected there *were* some in the truly remote and inaccessible places), they would likely be absorbed into the hybrid and coyote populations over time. The FWS declared the red wolf functionally extinct in the wild; the evolutionary trajectory of the species had nowhere left to go. The field team had removed some 400 animals from Texas and Louisiana over the course of six years. Of these, forty-three were considered to be morphologically true red wolves. After assessing the offspring of these animals, only seventeen were admitted to the captive breeding program as true red wolves. When the team was uncertain about the identity of some animals, they bred them and assessed the offspring. They believed that hybrid litters showed more variation than pure litters. Of these seventeen animals, only fourteen were able to breed. There were nine males and five females in the group, but they had the functional genetic equivalent of eight and a half individuals. (They all came from areas that were so close geographically that it's likely some of the animals were related.) All of the other animals were destroyed.

After several generations of red wolves whelped in captivity and their pups survived, the red wolf project team breathed a collective sigh of relief at the budding knowledge that, yes, red wolves could be preserved in captivity. The question burning in everyone's mind was now whether the captive-born animals could readjust to life outside the confines of their fences and human care. Worried that the wolves may lose their wildness and vitality in captivity, Carley had come up with an innovative scheme to breed ideal candidates for reintroduction. Red wolves would become wild island wolves.

## CHAPTER 11

# Wild Island Adventures

With the captive breeding program on firmer footing, Curtis J. Carley and the red wolf project team set their sights on broader horizons. He wanted to test reintroduction outcomes and come up with a safety net for ensuring that some of the wolves kept their wildness. After all, what was the point of investing time, money, and resources on breeding red wolves in captivity unless the Fish and Wildlife Service was sure the animals could be successfully reintroduced to the wild? Carley envisioned setting up a series of experiments to test release and tracking methods and to gauge the spectrum of public sentiment.

Nothing captured Carley's attention more than the possibilities he saw in southeastern coastal islands under the control of state or federal wildlife agencies. When he made a list, the advantages of these sites dripped off the page. They were geographically confined, which meant that mated pairs of wolves could be placed on small islands and left to breed. Protected islands had low densities of humans, which minimized the potential for wolf conflicts with pets and livestock. Protected islands generally had healthy ecosystems and, as long as there was enough prey, wolves should be able to make a living there. Islands also simplified the problem of isolating reintroduced red wolves from coyotes. It was only a matter of finding an island that was the right size and had the right habitat requirements of dense vegetative cover.

As early as mid-1975, Carley put out feelers within federal and state public-lands programs to seek wildlife refuges, parks, and forests that were interested in participating by allowing experimental red wolf releases of a nonpermanent nature. In May 1975 Carley toured Bulls Island, a 5,000-acre strip of ancient barrier reef that is part of the Cape Romain National Wildlife Refuge in South Carolina. Just three miles from the mainland, it adjoined the coast tentatively through a mosaic of salt marsh and creeks. But it was isolated enough. Carley thought the island was capable of holding a mated red wolf pair. All that the wolves really needed, he reasoned, was a fresh water source, reliable prey, dense vegetative cover, and a lack of coyotes. Marsh rabbits, and a sizable herd of white-tailed deer in want of a predator, were also present on the three-mile-long, one-and-a-half-mile-wide island. It was from the same area—covered in a forest of live oaks, magnolias, pines, and a palmetto understory—that explorer John Lawson had launched his fifty-nine-day trek through the Carolinas. Carley liked Bulls Island for its small size and for the functional fact that it was operated by his regulatory agency, which he thought would help a translocation project go smoothly. Also sweetening the deal was the fact that the South Carolina Wildlife and Marine Resources Department had consented to cooperate, offered to provide personnel and, most important, expressed deep excitement for the project.

Carley knew that he was taking the red wolf project in the direction of many unknowns, and he freely admitted this in public talks. The translocation to Bulls Island was "designed to determine means of overcoming several problems associated with wolf translocations," Carley assured the public, and not an attempt to establish a permanent population on the island. Specifically, he wanted a dry-run attempt to test the best methods for releasing a wolf to a specific area and making sure it would not disperse elsewhere. He also wanted to test methods for tracking released wolves in difficult forest- and marsh-covered terrain, as well as test the wolves' abilities to find water and shelter, hunt their own food, and reproduce successfully.

In June 1976 Carley received approval to place a mated red wolf pair on Bulls Island. He assuaged worried citizens with the knowledge that the FWS would recapture or even kill the translocated wolves if they reached the mainland. But this announcement caused emotional shock among his collaborators and left them feeling alienated. The only reason he made the lethal promise, he explained, was because he felt the necessity of carrying it out was extremely remote. "In working with endangered species, I cannot overstate the importance of not being afraid to try," Carley said.

If the translocation to Bulls Island worked, Carley foresaw treating the island as one large breeding pen. The mated pair's offspring could be caught and moved to a permanent reintroduction site (when they had one) and augment the wild gene pool. Carley understood the potential problems of reintroducing captive-bred wolves into a permanent reintroduction site— who knew if they would lose their wild instincts?—and farming wild-born pups from island propagation sites could improve their odds by reintroducing woods-wary wolves. At one point, Carley calculated that if all feasible southeastern coastal islands were employed in the red wolf project, then 100 to 150 red wolves could occupy them, all pumping out pups that could be rounded up for release elsewhere. But he readily admitted that this scenario opened up new challenges to managing the family units to prevent inbreeding within each island family group.

When the island project was approved, Carley sought a pair of red wolves that were mated in the wild, preferably from Jefferson County, where most of the morphologically true red wolves had been found. His team was finding few red wolves in the canids they trapped that summer, though, and they were again hampered by bad weather and too much rain. They came up empty on his request. Carley finally settled on using a mated pair trapped together about three miles west of Sabine Pass, Texas, on January 21, 1976. They had been in captivity at the Point Defiance Zoo since then. The pair were nicknamed Buddy and Margie, after the project's longtime friend and country vet, Buddy Long, and his wife. To the captive breeding program, they were known as wolves #76040 and #76045.

On the island, a fifty-square-foot acclimation pen was carefully prepared, with chain-link skirting dug well below the ground. Starting on November 5, 1976, the pen was Buddy and Margie's home. They were carried to the island by plane, truck, and boat. Staff provided them with nutria, raccoon, rabbits, and road-killed deer. They also placed radio telemetry collars around their necks. When the appointed day of their release came, Carley and his staff found themselves managing not only the two wolves but also more than two dozen reporters and television cameramen. Carley's planning was so detailed that he even had a chain-link raceway built to guide Buddy and Margie out of their pen and away from the gawking media.

At 11:35 A.M. on December 13, Cape Romain National Wildlife Refuge manager George Garris opened the gate to the wolves' pen. The pair took off at a quiet lope. Carley and his crew grabbed their telemetry gear. They'd rigged an open-air, off-road Jeep with telemetry receiver antennas on its frame rails to tail the wolves. No one had any idea what Buddy and Margie would do. Carley and John Dorsett took twelve- and eighteen-hour shifts to monitor their whereabouts.

Buddy and Margie traveled north and then split up for a few hours. The next morning, Margie visited a dump where archery hunters had left deer carcasses and entrails. Later, she moved close to a water-control structure, and an American coot was heard screaming near her in Bull Harbor. She and her mate bedded down less than a mile apart in the evening, and during the night, Buddy also visited the carcass dump. On December 16, the team found coot feathers in Margie's scat, deposited at a scent post on the north end of the island. Despite Margie's short stint in captivity, there was nothing wrong with her hunting instincts. That night, Buddy and Margie slept in the sand dunes together at the southern end of the island from about 10:00 P.M. to 3:30 A.M. Then they jogged back to the north end of the island, hunted, and bedded down again by 10:30 A.M. The next day, they continued their exploratory forays and tested their new environment. They checked out the northeast section of the island before heading south again. From what Carley and Dorsett could tell, the wolves spent their time foraging for food in the evenings, hunting small birds and rodents, and generally doing what red wolves do before resting and hiding during most of the day. Their activities were not all that different from those of the wolves observed in eastern Texas.

On December 19, Margie got bold. She left Bulls Island to the south, and swam across Price Inlet at high tide. She trotted up onto the beach of Capers Island, which she explored south to its tail end. Carley's team got nervous and turned her back with cracker shells fired over her head. Though she retreated, they weren't sure she would return to Bulls Island. The following day, no one could find Buddy on Bulls Island. An aerial survey finally discovered him in a clump of trees on Dewees Island, a privately owned islet south of Capers. The owner did not mind Buddy there, so the team let him be. Still, it didn't sit well with Carley, because the next island south contained the populated resort town of Isle of Palms.

But Margie was not to be found on Bulls, Capers, or Dewees Islands. She'd flown the coop. They finally located her on a small palmetto-covered patch of land 200 yards north of the intracoastal waterway between Capers and the mainland. Using a helicopter, the biologists tried to push her back to Bulls Island. When that didn't work, some of them slogged through the marsh on foot to haze her. But their effort backfired. She made a break for the mainland. By dark, she was last spotted bogged down up to her shoulders in sucking-marsh mud a half mile from shore. That night, the temperatures dropped, and the wind and rain picked up.

The next morning, Carley was nervous about both wolves encountering people. He made the decision to recapture them and place them back in their pens. The men shot cracker shells at Margie, hoping to push her back across the marsh to Bulls Island, but she hunkered down in the woods under deep leafy cover. The team set traps, hoping to catch her quickly, but their activity pushed her closer to U.S. Highway 17, which she crossed and moved to the northwest. It appeared she was on a beeline for the Francis Marion National Forest. On December 22, Carley decided to shoot her with a tranquilizer dart. If that didn't work out, he'd just plain shoot her the next day.

Luckily, a gunner in a Bell JetRanger helicopter lodged a dart in Margie's back end by 1:00 P.M., saving Carley from having to make a fatal decision. By 3:00 P.M., she was back in her pen on Bulls Island, groggy but alive. The incident marked the first time in the lower forty-eight states that a live wolf was shot with a tranquilizer dart from a helicopter. (It worked so well that Carley began renting helicopters to flush and dart wild canids in the inaccessible marshes and swamps that neither horses nor boats could help his team penetrate in Louisiana and Texas.)

The next afternoon, they caught Buddy, too. He had returned to Bulls Island, likely in search of Margie. With both wolves safely in their pen, Carley quipped to his team that the wolves were in better shape than their keepers. He and Dorsett were flat tuckered out. Though everyone laughed at his joke, Carley felt they all looked at him askance. They knew he had been prepared to shoot Margie. "Although it was 'we' who decided the statements [to shoot escaped wolves] should be made and adhered to," Carley wrote in a field report on the incident, "in looking around after the recapture of the wolves, I had the distinct uncomfortable feeling of abandonment, and that 'we' had suddenly narrowed to 'I.'"

They never knew exactly what had spurred Margie to take off. Perhaps after exploring the island, she decided to set out and find her original home back in Texas. Perhaps she encountered an alligator, not uncommon in the marshy intracoastal there, and fled from fear. Maybe she didn't like the hunting grounds. Carley pondered whether she'd encountered the German shepherd that was later found to have been living on Little Bulls Island; perhaps the two had fought. He believed her rapid departure was a fright-flight response.

But the team also wondered if perhaps holding the wolves for longer in the acclimation pens would increase the odds that they would come to see the area they were released into as their home range. Everyone chalked the episode up to experience. They hoped to rerelease Buddy and Margie after holding them a little longer. Carley toyed with the idea of confining them throughout the following spring with the hope that they'd breed in their pen. Then he could release a whole family. But Margie developed a uterine infection and died suddenly on April 1, 1977. Buddy was shipped back, alone, to Point Defiance Zoo. Margie's unfortunate death meant that the team had to again search for a candidate pair to release. Carley settled on using a mated pair trapped on the Grey Estate Ranch in Calcasieu Parish, Louisiana, in March 1977. The area they were captured from was coastal prairie with woods and marsh nearby.

The female of the pair was given the identification number #77044, and she was estimated to be three to four years years old. She had a tall stature, a large angular head, tawny pelage, and large ears that hung at the characteristic forty-five-degree angle, and her eye color was noted as yellow. When caught, she had a small one-inch-square patch of hair missing above her right eye and mites were observed on her skin. But she was otherwise in excellent health. Her belly was so large that the biologists suspected she was carrying pups. Her mate, given identification #77045, was tall and had a large blockish head, large ears, and a tawny pelage with characteristic black guard hairs. His eye color was recorded as "straw." Other than a growth at the base of his penis, he, too, appeared to be in excellent health. As was standard procedure, the pair were photographed, measured, weighed, and X-rayed, and their blood was drawn. The female was a healthy fifty-two pounds, and her mate weighed four pounds more. A vet from Texas A&M University examined the male's unusual growth, but no records indicate it was problematic.

The pair were nicknamed John and Judy after John Dorsett and his wife. Carley saw that the media liked human names for the animals rather than the numeric identification numbers tattooed inside the wolves' ears. (They were actually the second pair to receive this nickname, as the female mate of the originally named pair selected from Point Defiance Zoo died suddenly before she could be transferred to South Carolina. A necropsy revealed an infestation of heartworms.) The team repeated the prerelease protocol with John and Judy, but this time, they held the pair in an acclimation pen for six months. They also built a fixed-position telemetry antenna receiver on a 110-foot-high fire tower on the island. This freed them from needing to use the jeep to tail the wolves, which Carley feared may have proved too intrusive. The fixed-position antenna held a ten-mile range. Carley attached a portable telemetry antenna to an eighteen-foot speed boat in case they needed to pursue the animals across the inlets or open water—a possibility that Margie had proven likely. As a joke, Carley also posed by John and Judy's kennel box with a long sheet of paper, from which he read aloud while a colleague snapped photos. "Since the animals seem to understand more than they let on, we did another thing differently" the second time around, Carley quipped while showing the photo in a public presentation. "We read them The Plan."

On January 5, 1978, John and Judy were set free at 11:25 A.M. They headed north toward the marshes, where the red wolf team had set out two fresh deer carcasses to help them get settled. They found one and consumed it almost immediately. John and Judy made exploratory forays similar to those of Buddy and Margie. Within a few days, they swam across Price Inlet and stayed on Capers Island two weeks. Over the next few months, the pair proved to be masters of camouflage. They were rarely seen. Even finding their scats proved difficult. Of the few the team found, they discovered deer hair and remains of marsh rabbits, squirrels, fish, insects, birds, and small mammals. They even found wool that was presumably from feral sheep that wandered Capers Island. The pair created a pattern of rotating between Bulls and Capers Islands every ten or fourteen days. In April they stayed put on Capers, and for good reason—Judy whelped. However, the pups were lost at an early age, possibly to hookworm or parasites.

After eight months, Carley decided to halt the experiment on Bulls Island due to funding and personnel constraints. They had proven that island translocations and releases could be successful. When they caught Judy, she was three pounds heavier than when they'd released her. John proved more trapwise, though, and it took two months longer to catch him. He was smart enough to drag trap-baited carcasses away, thereby avoiding the stinging metal dug around them. Carley finally rented another Bell JetRanger helicopter and, after a fifteen-minute pursuit, the chopper flushed John into a tidal marsh. As the helicopter chased, John took off running over the beach at low tide. Carley snapped a picture from the chopper as the wolf sprinted at full hilt, his back legs stretching forward of his forelegs, then pushing off. The sun's glare on the half inch or so of water gave the appearance that John raced over the ocean's surface. "The wolf that ran on water," Carley later chuckled over the photo. John was also in excellent health and had gained a dozen pounds since his release.

The second island experiment marked the first successful translocation of a wolf in the United States. Other attempts had been made, but the animals never stayed put. Carley attributed John and Judy's behavior to two things: the use of a mated pair and their long acclimation period. He felt that the acclimation period reduced the likelihood that the wolves' homing instinct would drive them back to where they had come from. The experiments also impressed upon him how reliant the field team was upon the radio telemetry gear for locating the animals.

With the fundamentals of red wolf releases and island propagation sites ironed out, the red wolf team's attention turned to finding a mainland reintroduction site for a permanent population of wolves. By August 1978, Carley moved from Beaumont to Albuquerque, and John Dorsett took over closing the Beaumont field office by 1980. The program continued to search for coastal islands to realize Carley's vision of multiple island propagation sites that could supply wild-born pups and yearlings as reintroduction candidates to the permanent population. From Albuquerque, Carley continued to oversee red wolf captive breeding for a few more years, and he went on to contribute to recovery programs for the Mexican gray wolf, the Sonoran pronghorn, and the Ozark big-eared bat.

In an informal memoir of his red wolf days, Carley wrote: "This is the most gut-wrenching, frustrating, humiliating, and rewarding job I had in my career. It is the job I am proudest of." In many ways, he is one of the red wolf's unsung heroes in terms of his contributions to its conservation. But Carley was modest and did not like to toot his own horn. He was uncomfortable with media attention and praise. The bulk of his achievements—identifying and capturing the last red wolves—are generally attributed to the Fish and Wildlife Service as a whole rather than to the small field team that Carley supervised and managed intimately for six years.

It didn't help Carley's legacy that he tangled with his own supervisors over the red wolf's reintroduction plans. He voiced opposition to their decision to not actively manage for invading coyotes in North Carolina. Later, when he worked on the Mexican gray wolf reintroduction project, he argued vociferously against corners cut by his own agency, according to his widow. The FWS reassigned him to the National Wetlands Inventory Program in 1986. But red wolf team members continued to solicit Carley's opinion and advice on an individual basis even after his retirement in 1996. Carley's knowledge of red wolf and coyote behavior, and the nature of their interactions, was deeply valued among his peers. He never ceased warning his successors of the animal's propensity for hybridization. But his warnings went unheeded, lost in the dramatic heat and hope of returning captive-bred red wolves to their historic southeastern range.

## CHAPTER 12
# North Carolina's Reborn Native Wolf

The first time that Warren T. Parker laid eyes on a red wolf, it hung lifelessly from a federal trapper's hands. It was the 1960s, and Parker was a new employee with the Fish and Wildlife Service. His first task was to survey wildlife of the Red River, so he spent three weeks at a stretch living the rough life deep in the bottomland forests of southwestern Arkansas near Texarkana. He worked from a canoe and curated his notes in a tent. The forest animals were his only companions. One day, as Parker counted birds along the Sulphur River, he ran into a trapper. Lonely for human contact, he struck up a conversation. It turned out that the man was a fellow FWS employee who was on a work detail that served ranchers and farmers by killing local predators. The trapper recounted to Parker how he'd caught a live wolf that morning in a steel leg-hold trap and then shot it. Parker admired the animal's broad, melon-like head and copper-infused coat. But when he ran his hands through the dead wolf's ruff, he could not have foreseen that two decades later, he would supervise the first reintroduction of red wolves back into their native range.

Parker grew up in Virginia. Most mornings, he carried his hunting rifle to school and stashed it in the coat closet. Come afternoon, he'd fetch it and while away the remaining sunlight hunting squirrels. When he was in high school, his family relocated to Raleigh, North Carolina. In time, he earned degrees in wildlife and forestry from N.C. State University. After a short stint as an air force pilot, Parker did graduate work studying deer biology at Virginia Polytechnic Institute and then joined the FWS. After he surveyed the Red River, Parker joined the FWS's southeast regional office in Atlanta. At the time, the regional director was Jim Pulliam, one of Parker's N.C. State classmates and also a friend. Pulliam singled Parker out in 1973 to be on a committee tasked with figuring out what the Endangered Species Act (ESA) would mean for the FWS. "No one fathomed the complexity the ESA would bring to a deer and duck biology club," Parker later joked about the act's implications to the focus of the FWS. Nevertheless, the committee set up field offices throughout the Southeast to deal with the legislation and wildlife management it entailed. The main office was set up in Asheville, North Carolina, and Pulliam assigned Parker to oversee it. One of his first tasks involved mediating with the Tennessee Valley Authority (TVA), which had encountered delays on several projects due to endangered species and environmental concerns.

When Curtis Carley contacted Pulliam about releasing red wolves on coastal islands in the Southeast, Pulliam sent Parker to oversee Carley's fieldwork at Bulls Island. It was more of a technicality than anything, according to Parker, who said that his boss just wanted to be kept in the loop as to what someone from the Southwest region did while working within the Southeast. It was atypical at the time for workers from one region to work in another. Parker stuck to the background of the island experiments, but he greatly admired Carley's work ethic and became friends with him. After the translocations were declared successful, the FWS became more serious about reintroducing red wolves. Riding a wave of positive news, the FWS began openly talking up the prospect of reintroducing red wolves somewhere in the Southeast.

When Parker's contacts at the TVA got wind of the brewing reintroduction, they approached him with an offer. They just happened to hold title to a 170,000-acre parcel of forested land that straddled Tennessee and Kentucky. The Land Between the Lakes was a seminatural peninsula, bounded on two sides by the Tennessee and Cumberland Rivers. A major highway formed the peninsula's southern boundary. The TVA ached for good press related to endangered species. They courted Parker aggressively to put wolves on their land. The space was large enough and, to Parker, it looked like a godsend just when he needed one.

Parker negotiated with the TVA for many months. When their plan took a solid form, he set up a series of public meetings in Louisville and nearby small towns. But the closer they got to the Land Between the Lakes, the more hostile the crowds were. Families who lived near the proposed site still remembered when the federal government had enticed (and sometimes forced) their parents, grandparents, and great-grandparents to sell their homesteads. The idea that the FWS wanted to release wolves mattered less, it seemed to Parker, than the fact that the FWS proposed to do anything at all with the TVA. But for Parker, the nail in the coffin came when a young environmentalist stood up during a meeting and asked what would happen to the coyotes that lived in the Land Between the Lakes. Parker replied matter-of-factly that they would possibly have to be removed. The man replied sharply that if the coyotes were removed, his organization would sue, and he sat down. Even worse, according to Parker, the Tennessee legislature told their state wildlife agency director that if he supported the wolf project, they'd fire him.

Around the same time, Parker figured that Carley would be named the red wolf reintroduction project's coordinator, and that he'd move out East. But two things happened: Carley's wife put her foot down and didn't want to move again, and Pulliam wanted to appoint someone familiar with the Southeast and the ESA. He once again pointed to his old classmate. In early 1984, Warren Parker was named the red wolf reintroduction project coordinator. Pulliam told Parker that he wanted him to become a wolf specialist. The deer biologist from Virginia who had recently turned into an endangered species specialist took the job reluctantly because he felt the probability of "getting a mixed bag" out of the captive breeding program was pretty high. But Parker came to embrace the new calling. In taking the job, Parker also became the first wolf reintroduction project leader in the nation.

The FWS arranged for Parker to be trained in the field under David Mech, a North American wolf biologist based in Minnesota. Under Mech's guidance for a few months, Parker learned how wolves hunt and raise their young, how they communicate through howls and scent mark their territories. He learned how to track them by ground and by plane and how to fit telemetry collars, as well as the basics of their captive management. After his time in Minnesota, Parker returned home bursting with knowledge about red wolves. All he needed was a place to put some. Parker knew he couldn't kick-start the very first wolf reintroduction in the United States with a lawsuit, a fired state wildlife agency director, and hostile neighbors who resented the federal government to the core. He conferred with his superiors, and they agreed: the Land Between the Lakes proposal was dead on arrival. When it was all said and done, Parker had blown a year negotiating with the TVA and gotten nowhere. He returned to his downtown Asheville office and collapsed at his desk. "Where can I go next?" he asked himself over and over again. For days, he pored over maps and made phone calls.

And then Parker got lucky. Just as the Point Defiance Zoo had stepped in to help when the FWS needed a captive facility, The Nature Conservancy stepped in when the FWS needed land. The conservancy had worked with the Prudential Insurance Company for several years to broker a land donation of 118,000 acres that the company had bought on the Albemarle Peninsula in northeastern North Carolina. Seeking to offload it, the company worked with the conservancy to donate it as a tax break. The Nature Conservancy approached the FWS with the option to turn the land into a wildlife refuge. It was a month after the Land Between the Lakes deal disintegrated. Parker pounced. If he thought the Land Between the Lakes had looked like a godsend, then the land proffered at Alligator River smacked of divine intervention. Alligator River National Wildlife Refuge moved from an idea on paper to a reality on March 14, 1984. By the end of that year, the FWS drafted solid plans to release red wolves there; and by 1986, the plan was codified in the *Federal Register* as a "Final Rule," which contained legal language that detailed how a reintroduction would be performed. The red wolf finally had a home where it could be biologically and legally reborn in the wild.

The "Final Rule" described the red wolves that would be let go as a "nonessential experimental" population. This was a new category of the Endangered Species Act that was created in a 1982 amendment and spelled out under section 10(j). It allowed some populations of imperiled species to be treated as expendable. The nonessential experimental designation allows for "take" under certain circumstances. ("Take" is loosely defined as harassing or killing a federally listed species.) It was meant to be a concession to landowners and land managers so that they wouldn't be restricted from engaging in lawful activities on their property, like logging or hunting, despite the presence of a listed species. This was intended to make the wolves' reintroduction socially palatable. The wolves could even be shot if they threatened life or property. The captive population remained fully endangered, however. The nonessential experimental designation was originally created by the FWS in a good faith effort to allow the agency's biologists to better recover populations with tricky management issues. No one foresaw how badly the listing status might be misused and abused in the future.

The Alligator River refuge lies entirely within mainland Dare County, which held about 1,000 people in the mid-1980s. The largest community, Manns Harbor, lies between Highway 64 to the south and Mashoes Marsh to the north. East Lake lies to the west of Manns Harbor, and Stumpy Point lies to the south. All of these communities bordered the new refuge. At most, the land was twelve feet above sea level. Bald cypress, Atlantic white cedar, black gum, and loblolly dominated the western side of the refuge, while the eastern side held pocosins dotted with pond pines and low evergreen shrubs. There were too many ticks, chiggers, and deer flies in the thickets and briers for most folks to understand why the FWS wanted to mess around with putting wolves there.

But the more Parker examined it, the more fitting the land appeared to be for red wolves. Small mammal and prey surveys performed by mammalogists from the state natural sciences museum in Raleigh returned favorable densities of rabbits, rodents, raccoon, possum, and deer. Their survey for canids turned up no feral dogs or coyotes.

But beyond the biological parameters, Parker and the FWS had absorbed key lessons from their defeat at Land Between the Lakes. First, they realized they must be more proactive and talk with the locally affected people earlier in their planning process. Second, they learned they must educate people about the shy, elusive nature of the red wolf. Years earlier, Carley had foreseen investing in such public outreach: "It will have to be a continual bombardment of information striking at the root of the myths. In other words, we must tear down most of what the public 'knows' about red wolves and replace it with current information. Although pig tails have been found in wolf scats, remnants of stick houses have been conspicuously absent. To date, we have not identified any scrap reminiscent of a little red cape."

In early 1986 Parker set out to hold a series of public hearings in the affected towns near the new refuge. He found that people were primarily concerned with whether or not their traditional uses of the land—hunting and trapping—would continue. While some were concerned about their safety if wolves were released, this fear took a backseat to the perceived threat of being deprived of their hunting grounds. The refuge personnel worked out agreements allowing locals to continue hunting and trapping in defined places at certain times of the year. But there was still some grumbling—especially when it was announced that the refuge would be closed to running dogs in the summer, when most deer hunters trained their hounds. But Parker felt emboldened by the communities' wait-and-see response to the wolves. He believed that he could work with the locals to earn tolerance for the red wolves.

Even before the first wolves were released, the recovery team eagerly eyed the 46,621-acre Dare County Bombing Range, which was encircled by the southern portion of the Alligator River refuge. It was a training site for the U.S. Navy and Air Force, and the state natural resources department had recently helped create buffer zones around it that were registered as Natural Heritage Areas. If the wolves could learn to tolerate the fighter jet and plane engines growling overhead, Parker wondered if they might take advantage of that land, too. But first he had to get wolves on the ground in Alligator River.

The most exciting step toward that goal happened in November 1986, when eight red wolves were flown to Dare County. Three years after starting his search for red wolf habitat in the Southeast, Parker waited at the local airport with a flock of national media anticipating the arrival of the first red wolves to be shipped to the Southeast with the intention of reintroducing them within a portion of their former historic range. The wolves were packed into kennels and flown in the cargo hold of a commercial airliner from Point Defiance Zoo and Aquarium in Washington State to the Raleigh-Durham Airport. At the time, only seventy-four red wolves existed in the captive breeding program. In Raleigh, a storm delayed their connecting flight, which meant the reporters and journalists were kept waiting. Parker was so nervous that he later joked he was sweating blood. If the wolves couldn't make it that day, what was he to tell the dozens of network newspeople who were awaiting a show? But the coast guard got wind of the dilemma and dispatched a helicopter that was able to fly below the storm. It picked up the wolves and ferried them to their destination.

FWS employees carried the gray kennels stenciled with ENDANGERED RED WOLF labels from the helicopter into waiting trucks. The plan was to put the wolves—all mated pairs—into large acclimation pens at remote spots sprinkled throughout the refuge. Over a six-month period, they would hopefully learn to see the landscape as their home—a hard-won lesson learned from Carley's island translocation experiments. Come May, the red wolf team planned to release the bonded pairs. As film crews and reporters looked on, the wolves were fitted with telemetry collars and let go into their new pens.

Over the next half a year, newly hired red wolf biologists were stationed in shifts at each pen in the remote backcountry. Their primary function was to feed and care for the red wolves, but Parker also wanted their physical presence there to deter people from gawking or harming the rare animals.

Jan DeBlieu, an Outer Banks resident, writer, and red wolf project volunteer, recorded the intimate lives of the first red wolves as well as the learning curve of the recovery team in her book *Meant to Be Wild* (1991). With a poet's eye for detail, she traced the reintroduction up to the fall of 1989, while exploring the theme of whether or not captive-reared animals could regain their wild edge. DeBlieu described how Chris Lucash lived on a houseboat on South Lake near his two charges as they became acclimated to the land. He fed them dry dog food and plucked scats from their pens. But for the most part, the biologists were supposed to avoid the pens and discourage the wolves from learning to approach people. According to DeBlieu, one day, as Lucash drew near with food, the female wolf he tended walked up to him. She wagged her tail excitedly and lowered her head. In the world of canid body language, she was advertising her desire to get acquainted. Lucash "snarled at her and threw the food buckets in her direction." She fled. The team responded by erecting wooden screens over parts of the acclimation pens to thwart the wolves from befriending the biologists or associating their presence with food. From then on, the biologists dumped the wolves' food over the fence from behind the screen.

Parker hired a biologist named Michael Phillips to serve as the red wolf reintroduction director. Phillips oversaw all aspects of the fieldwork and supervised the program's biologists. (Phillips would later go on to head the Yellowstone gray wolf reintroduction.) Perhaps it was because they were gun-shy after the failure of Land Between the Lakes, but the red wolf team wanted to approach the local people with a peace offering, something that might increase their tolerance for the wolves on the landscape. Parker found out that his mentor, David Mech, had previously cooked up an idea for a "recapture collar." The device contained typical telemetry gear but also two darts filled with a tranquilizer dose, positioned to fire into the neck muscles to the left and right of the spine. The darts discharged their drug load by remote detonation. Parker understood that people were afraid that wolves might harass kids at bus stops or threaten their pets, so he wanted to show them that these perceived threats could be eliminated if the program could control the wolves from afar.

Mech had entered into conversations with 3M Corporation about manufacturing the recapture collar by way of one of his graduate students. The company foresaw potential for spinning off the technology to other applications. When Parker first talked to Mech about using the specialized collar on the red wolves of Alligator River, it had been field-tested on creatures in captivity, but it had not been well vetted on wild animals. "I was skeptical if it could or should be tried down there," Mech later recalled, "because the project was so critical." Nevertheless, Parker sold the locals on the idea, and he felt that it assuaged many people's fears and made the reintroduction more socially acceptable.

However, early tests of the collars at Alligator River showed they had a very short signal range for the device that triggered the drug-filled darts. On more than one occasion, the red wolf team borrowed mutts from the Dare County pound and fitted them with the test collars. When the system worked, the dogs yelped, teetered drunkenly, and then collapsed after a few minutes. Unfortunately, the darts' signal range was too short to be practical for fieldwork from the ground, where the terrain, thick scrub, and even the wolves' own bodies weakened the signal. It was a far cry from the four- or five-mile range that the red wolf team desired.

The first date for the releases came and went in May 1987 as the 3M engineers tweaked their designs to make the recapture collars work in Alligator River. But when the delays dragged across the summer and into late August, Parker knew he had to release the wolves soon. If he waited any longer, they'd bump up against the opening of deer season. The last thing the team wanted was naive wolves in close range of gun-toting hunters. Even though Parker knew the recapture collars weren't perfected, he crossed his fingers and signed off on sending the wolves out in early September. According to DeBlieu's account, Parker decided the wolves would wear the recapture collar and a standard telemetry collar when they were let go. One way or another, he was determined to have a bead on every single red wolf that roamed free.

To prepare for the release of the first pairs of red wolves, the biologists several months earlier had begun giving the wolves wild fare instead of dog food. Every few days, they pitched dead raccoons, possums, muskrats, rabbits, and road-killed deer over the pen fences. But it was uncertain if the captive-born wolves still had their wild chase instincts intact. To test this, the biologists experimented by heaving live prey into the pens, starting with raccoons and nutria and culminating in a deer. When the wolves successfully chased and killed their confined prey, the team had good reason to be hopeful. (Today, the biologists say they would never repeat an experiment like this for fear of lawsuits from animal-rights groups, but it reflects the deep unknowns in the early days of the program.)

Once the wolves were released, the biologists wanted to be able to study the scats of individual red wolves to learn what each one ate. (DNA tools were still in their infancy.) But how to identify the scat of one wolf from another? The team settled on using weak radioactive markers. Two small pellets were implanted beneath the skin of at least one red wolf from each pair. The pellets leaked a unique radioactive signature into the wolves' tissues, a signature that could be read from their droppings. Collected scats could then be linked to the wolf that deposited it, and collecting multiple scats from the same individuals would help the biologists piece together the spatial limits of the wolves' home ranges.

The moment everyone had been anticipating finally came when, at a quarter past nine in the morning on Monday, September 14, 1987, Parker walked up the trail to the pen at the South Lake location where Lucash had been stationed. In contrast to the media frenzy surrounding the wolves' arrival in North Carolina, only Parker and four others—Roland Smith, from the Point Defiance Zoo; John Taylor, the Alligator River refuge director; Michael

Phillips; and Chris Lucash—were there to witness the release. According to DeBlieu's writings and Phillips's field notes, Taylor and Parker walked up the sodden trail to the pen where the wolves sloshed through mud puddles against the far fence. Parker tossed some deer meat into the enclosure, as if it were any other regular feeding. Then he did something entirely different: he secured the gate wide open with a heavy chain. He and Taylor turned and walked back down the trail to rejoin the others at the Boston whaler that had ferried them to the remote spot. Phillips noted that "Parker uttered, 'We did it. We let them go.'" Parker would reminisce of the moment later in his life that he couldn't believe he had "scratched something out of the dirt, and it worked."

But after securing the pen door open, and once Parker's tension dissipated, it was an anticlimactic moment. The wolves did not sense freedom and rush out. Rather, they stayed in their pen for several days, perhaps wary of the open gate. On the fourth morning, the female wandered out and traveled two miles. It took the male a week to move beyond the safe vicinity of the enclosure that had been his small but secure territory. The first two red wolves to be released back to the wild were free. But what would they choose to do with their freedom?

On October 1 the team released three additional mated pairs. Eight red wolves now wandered within Alligator River National Wildlife Refuge. The biologists busied themselves trailing the animals and making detailed reports of where they traveled and what they did. They took to naming the packs after geographical locations. There was the South Lake pack, the Phantom Road pack, the Pole Road pack, and the Point Peter pack.

The one time the team tried to fire a dart on a recapture collar (in mid-October 1987), the system failed. The male South Lake wolf had taken to wandering until one night he padded into Manns Harbor. DeBlieu wrote that the wolf trotted "between houses, sniffing at flower gardens." When he loitered near the post office, a recapture team quickly gathered and fretted over his proximity to people. DeBlieu recorded that the team chased him through the evening as he ran in and out of people's yards. They tried several times to trigger the drug-filled darts on his collar but nothing happened. Luckily, they had air rifles and tranquilizer darts on hand. After several attempts, Parker finally got a clear shot and successfully darted the South Lake male at around 5:00 A.M. Later, it became evident that the 3M engineers may have failed to take into account the salty coastal air, which corroded some of the recapture collars' connections. Rather than notify the public that the specialized collars were a bust, the red wolf program measured the relative risk that the wolves posed and then decided to quietly let people forget the collars existed, according to Lucash.

The first few months after releasing the wolves, the red wolf team fielded hundreds of phone calls about red wolf sightings. Lucash regretted that some of the wolves "acted like abandoned dogs." They loped up and down the main highways; some even chased cars and trucks. This was the naive behavior of animals reared by human hands. Red wolf sightings were reported by motorists a total of seventy-four times in the first eleven months. The wolves, it seemed, didn't like traveling through the briers any more than people did. Lucash later recalled that they showed a preference for using the paved and unpaved roads as travel corridors. Most worrisome, when a vehicle approached a wolf from behind, many wolves would continue to lope down the midline. When the vehicle got close, the animals would cut to the shoulder and wait for the car or truck to pass, as if they were common pedestrians. The biologists set their hopes on the wild-born wolves growing up more woods wary than their zoo-reared parents.

Two more red wolf pairs were released on April 12 and 14, 1988. Before being let go, all the wolves were vaccinated against rabies, distemper, hepatitis, leptospirosis, and parvovirus. Most of the newly released wolves spent from a half to a full day near their acclimation sites before venturing to explore the surrounding area. Some wandered widely, while others stuck close to their acclimation sites. The team learned from weighing recaptured wolves that it could take two to four months for the animals to learn to feed themselves. This led them to make it standard practice to provide supplemental food to captive-born wolves for about eight weeks past when they were released to the wild. By June, the team had collected 825 scats of the first ten animals released. They were able to link scats to individual wolves more than 80 percent of the time due to the radioactive tracers. Marsh rabbits, raccoons, and deer formed the bulk of the wolves' diet. After the first fifty scats, there was no sign of the supplemental food the biologists had provided in the form of carnivore logs, an indication that all of the wolves had quickly learned to hunt on their own. It was a promising sign that the wolves were able to fend for themselves.

Although there was much to celebrate with the wolves' releases and their ability to hunt on their own, the program also saw an alarming number of deaths in the early days. Within the first three months, two of the females died. Two of the remaining mated pairs birthed puppies in the spring, but only one pup survived from each litter. The Point Peter and South Lake males were killed by vehicles while crossing roads. Then the Pole Road female was also found dead. DeBlieu wrote that she had traveled back to her old acclimation pen, "crawled inside, stuck her head halfway into one of the wooden houses, and died." She had apparently been one of the wariest wolves, and the biologists had held hope for her. But she was felled by a uterine infection that likely took hold after she whelped. Her pup was assumed to have starved, according to DeBlieu, and at her death, she herself was severely underweight. A few of the now-single wolf parents were able to raise their offspring alone, an indicator of the species' resiliency. Within the first year, all of the wolves had to be caught—sometimes to remove the faulty recapture collars or to replace telemetry collar batteries, or sometimes because they strayed out of the refuge or into towns. In time, the fledgling red wolf population of Alligator River grew.

Island propagation sites saw a renaissance under Parker's oversight. He recognized the problems wrought from releasing naive zoo-born wolves and, as Carley had also foreseen, desired to have woods-wary candidates to introduce. The Bulls Island site in Cape Romain National Wildlife Refuge was soon reopened. But islands brought their own dangers. A female red wolf was killed by an alligator there in 1989, shortly after she'd birthed five pups. Her mate raised their offspring, but then he, too, was killed the following September from injuries sustained when Hurricane Hugo passed directly over the island. The Category 4 winds knocked down nearly every last tree, and the twenty-foot storm surge swished oak and pine branches around like toothpicks. The orphaned pups were collected and released to Alligator River, but one remained on the island as a breeder. Additional breeding operations were begun on Horn Island, Mississippi, where red wolves made quick work of a raccoon infestation, and wolves were also brought to St. Vincent Island, Florida. In June 1991, another female red wolf was killed by an alligator, this time on St. Vincent Island. Yearlings from the island sites were often rounded up for translocation to the refuge when vacant territories were available; and, once fostering became an established practice, island pups were sometimes fostered into wild dens in the recovery area.

Parker narrowly defined the success of the program as having second- and third-generation pups born in the wild. If they could get that far, he thought, they could overcome anything. But Parker wasn't immune to the controversy over red wolf origins. He was as surprised as the next person when Wayne and Jenks's study came out in 1991, shortly after he'd retired, declaring red wolves to be nothing more than the hybrid product of coyotes and gray wolves. He never accepted the study's conclusion, but he nevertheless mulled over the relationship between red and gray wolves. "Why the good Lord made two wolves, I never figured out," he often said. Wayne and Jenks's study triggered a lawsuit for delisting red wolves from the Endangered Species Act in August 1991. The suit, initiated by the American Sheep Industry Association, pitted the new research against the decades of research produced by the FWS on red wolves, penned mostly by Ronald Nowak, Curtis Carley, Howard McCarley, and John Paradiso. The move to delist was found unwarranted due to multiple lines of other evidence that concluded the red wolf was a unique species. (Three years later, Curtis Carley was asked if his team had X-rayed the skulls of any of the specimens used by Wayne and Jenks as red wolves in their 1991 study. He replied: "Of the sixteen 'red wolf' skins being used by Dr. R. Wayne, the Red Wolf Recovery Program selected the skulls of only five of the animals for X-ray evaluation as likely historic red wolves." Of the specimens Wayne and Jenks used, only three males (from Fallsville, Arkansas; Mena, Arkansas; and Bethel, Oklahoma) and two females (from Winn Parish, Louisiana; and Arcadia, Missouri) had been identified through cranial metrics as likely red wolves. The other eleven were considered hybrids or coyotes by Carley's assessment.)

In the first three years, the program released thirty-four wolves, eleven of which died during the same time period. But the demise of some wolves was overshadowed by the red wolves' propensity to make puppies. Without missing a beat, their breeding cycle meshed into the natural rhythms of the refuge. In spring of 1991, pups that had been born from captive-bred parents had their own pups in turn. Their births marked the second-generation of wild-born pups. The proportion of wild-born wolves slowly overtook the proportion of captive-born wolves. Incidences of wolves chasing trucks and wandering into towns declined over time. The wild-born pups were warier of people and avoided being seen. After five years, the program expanded the land available to red wolves to about 250,000 acres. The wild population stood at thirty wolves, and fifteen pups had been born in the wild. With Parker's narrow definition of success met, the program was free to dream up higher standards. Legally, the recovery plan outlined a goal of 220 wolves in the wild in at least three reintroduction sites. But to get more wolves in the first reintroduction site, the red wolf team needed more land. The third project coordinator, Gary Henry, set his sights on doubling the acreage that wolves could use in northeastern North Carolina. He helped broker deals to gain access to private land on the peninsula.

In the early 1990s, the red wolf population swelled larger, complaints by the locals declined, and all signs pointed to progress. In 1993 the program made its last release of captive bred wolves. Henry followed up on Parker's wish for a second reintroduction site. There were two bits of land that had caught Parker's eye: the Great Smoky Mountains National Park in western North Carolina and Tennessee and the Francis Marion National Forest in South Carolina. The Great Smoky Mountains offered the bonus of more land, but it also contained the eastward-bent front of coyotes that were silently pawing their way from the Midwest prairies to the Eastern Seaboard. At first glance, the Smokies seemed a perfect spot for red wolves. The park held endless miles of climax forest, including some stands of old growth. Although it was one of the most visited parks in the nation, it held few roads and a low density of people—virtually all of whom were transient tourists. There was only one livestock operator who leased land from the park to raise a few head of cattle. The picture couldn't have appeared rosier to Parker when he first visited the park with an eye toward putting wolves in it.

By the time Henry took over, the plan was nearly in place. Chris Lucash was stationed near Cades Cove, Tennessee, at the western entrance of the park (near Gatlinburg) to manage the wolves at the new site. The second reintroduction site enjoyed a deep vein of local support from two large cities nearby—Knoxville to the west and Asheville to the east. Small mountain towns around the park hoped that the red wolves would boost tourism revenue. The first packs were released in November 1992. In his book *Another Country* (1997), writer Christopher Camuto interwove the story of the red wolf reintroduction in the Smoky Mountains with a history of the Cherokee Indians who used to occupy the same lands. Between the fall of 1992 and 1999, Lucash and his assistants (who included Ford Mauney) released the same forty-one wolves more than six dozen times. (Some were captured and rereleased for things like straying outside of the park.) Every time a hiker went missing, Lucash worried that the wolves might scavenge on human remains. While that never happened, an adult wolf pair stalked and killed an orphaned black bear cub in Cades Cove in plain sight of two photographers. It was January 25, 1993, and Dick Dickerson told a reporter for the *Knoxville News-Sentinel* that after the adult wolves made the kill, the pups joined them in feeding from the carcass for more than an hour. It was unusual behavior. In hindsight, it provided insight as to the lack of prey available to the wolves in the mountains. Fifteen wolves died from fights with other wolves, starvation, getting hit by cars, and random bad luck, such as lapping up antifreeze. Out of thirty-three pups born in eight different litters, only four survived past six months of age.

The FWS employed computer models to assess the probability of success for a wolf's release and modeled the program's continuation in the Smoky Mountains. It didn't look favorable. Without pups surviving to adulthood, the project was not inching the wolves toward recovery. Although low pup survival due to parvovirus was the primary reason they gave for closing the Smoky Mountain reintroduction site in October 1998, starvation, heavy parasite loads, pressure from bears and coyotes, and straying outside of the park boundaries were equal concerns. The forest did not contain enough small prey after all, at least where the wolves could get to it. It's now thought that the mountain slopes in some areas were much too rugged, and the wolves wandered widely trying to find food at lower, flatter elevations. Lucash often tracked them down drainages that led out of the mountains to small settlements where folks kept chickens and goats, or to where the wolves found flat land across which they could pursue deer. One wolf dispersed clear south to Fontana Dam. Lucash and his assistants rounded up their charges from the rugged slopes of the Smokies and either moved them to Alligator River for reintroduction there, where eighty red wolves thrived, or put them back into captivity. But about thirty wolves that were once known to be in the park were never found. The FWS considered their fates "unknown." About twenty-five were pups that had probably died young. One or two may have bred themselves into the coyote population, according to Lucash; or, given their last known age, they may have simply died in isolation.

The biological failure of the reintroduction in the Smoky Mountains was the red wolf program's first serious setback. But nature had an even more deeply rooted challenge brewing.

The last year of the millennium was a landmark point in the red wolf's recovery trajectory. Not only had the second reintroduction site failed the previous fall, but in April 1999, the FWS also formally recognized hybridization with coyotes as a serious threat to wild red wolves. The recovery area had now come to engulf the majority of the Albemarle Peninsula, thanks to pivotal agreements brokered with private landowners. The red wolf's narrative had come full circle: after the animal had been plucked from the wild two decades before, its genome—due to inevitable genetic swamping by coyotes—was once more under siege. In April the program's fourth coordinator, Brian Kelly, presented information at a Population and Habitat Viability Assessment (PHVA) workshop in Virginia Beach, Virginia. Each year, representatives from the captive breeding side of the program met face-to-face with the field biologists to discuss the project's progress and challenges. But this year, the Conservation Breeding Specialist Group of the International Union for the Conservation of Nature was in charge of running the meeting. They wanted to examine everything that had been learned about red wolf captive breeding and reintroduction and brainstorm ways to better integrate the two programs, as well as prioritize what kind of data should be collected from each program. They also wanted to identify key threats to the wolf, good strategies to mitigate those threats, and what kinds of studies were needed to optimize recovery goals.

But the meeting agenda was quickly reset when Kelly presented key findings about hybridization with coyotes. Since 1987, the red wolf program had documented fifty-three litters of red wolves born in the wild, Kelly told them. An additional six litters were known to be hybrids, and five more were suspected. Program biologists removed all hybrids from their dens and destroyed them. Preliminary modeling done at the workshop showed what would have happened if they had not taken that step: in three to six generations, the red wolf in northeastern North Carolina would be rendered unrecognizable due to hybridization. The process could take as few as twelve to twenty-four years. (Lucash later said that he got the impression that his boss believed that the situation may already have been insurmountable.) Several PHVA meeting participants said they felt the meeting's agenda was hijacked by the hybridization issues. No one could concentrate or talk about anything except ways to deal with introgression. The organizers quickly reset the agenda, and a lively discussion ensued about how to deal with the hybridization issues. Eric Gese, an ecologist from Utah, suggested that using adaptive management to unite science with the on-the-ground management would assist them in coming up with workable solutions, and from there, the ideas flooded forth. Michael Stoskopf, a professor of veterinary medicine from N.C. State University, suggested they consider sterilizing the invading coyotes to use them as infertile "placeholders" on the landscape — an idea that became a key management protocol.

Until that meeting, the biologists had known that hybridization with coyotes was an abstract threat, but no one had considered that hybridization might thwart recovery entirely. It was a sobering possibility, one that likely counted among the many unofficial reasons that the FWS pulled the plug on the Smoky Mountain reintroduction the previous October. No more reintroduction sites would be considered, the workshop participants concluded, until they knew what kind of a beast they were dealing with in hybridization. Based on the information, the participants decided to reset the priorities of the entire red wolf program. Nothing else mattered, they decided, if they couldn't solve the hybridization issue.

Coyotes first appeared in Swain County in far western North Carolina in 1947. Things may have played out differently if coyotes had been left to bridge the distance between the mountains and the sea on their own. But the proliferation of fox pens in the eastern part of the state is said to have opened up a black market for live coyotes. For the most part, fox pens were located almost exclusively east of Raleigh, practically at the front door of the red wolf recovery area. Some coyotes likely escaped the pens, which were built to contain foxes, and roamed free. Perry Summer, a former program coordinator for fur-bearer surveys for the N.C. Wildlife Resources Commission, mapped geographic instances of early reports of coyotes in the state and locations of fox-pen operations. Summer spoke to writer Craig Holt of the N.C. *Sportsman* magazine:

> Where there's fox pens in the east, there's high concentrations of coyotes. At one point I could take a map and put pins in it where there were hunter-killed coyotes and fox pens; they were clustered together. . . . As time went on, two things started happening—coyotes began to expand their territories, then during late the 1980s and early 1990s, they started to move into western N.C. counties on their own, expanding from Virginia and South Carolina. We didn't have 'em in the middle of the state, but as as time went on, it all ran together.

In 1983 coyotes were still only in a handful of North Carolina counties, the farthest east of which were Wake and Johnston. In many areas, the reported coyotes were considered rare wanderers; they weren't thought to be established or to be breeding. In 1987 the red wolf biologists estimated that it would take coyotes at least a decade to travel from where they were documented to have become established in the western part of the state to the recovery area. But by 1990, coyotes were known to be in every county in the entire Albemarle Peninsula. By 1998 they were documented in all but fourteen of the state's 100 counties. Then, in 2003, the state legislature approved a bill that legalized the sale of live coyotes to licensed fox-pen operators. Once the transaction was legal, it sped the artificial movement of coyotes farther east, where fox-pen operators clustered.

Speaking with the blessing of hindsight, Lucash said his team ought to have been more on the ball. "We knew in the mid-1990s that there were coyotes coming in. There was missing information, though, in terms of how we incorporated that with our management," he reflected. "We should have presumed that if we had a solo, mature wolf out there, it was running with *something*. The thing is, we were dealing with issues that were rare to the rest of the world."

The participants at the 1999 PHVA meeting in Virginia Beach were evenly split over whether to try and wipe the peninsula clear of coyotes or to study their interactions with red wolves. If history was any cue, the red wolf program had no chance of categorically keeping coyotes out of the red wolf recovery area. They didn't have the manpower to even try, and the species had proven resilient to eradication in the past. The idea of a canid-proof fence was once more floated and ultimately rejected. Their best bet would be to monitor each red wolf so closely that they always knew who its mate was. The meeting attendees decided, with the help of the IUCN breeding specialist group, to clear the peninsula of as many coyotes as they could. But killing them off posed an overwhelming challenge. Gese and Stoskopf suggested that the red wolf program ought to partition the recovery area into three management zones in which management efforts would vary in intensity for preventing hybridization, in part by culling hybrids and in part by sterilizing coyotes. These preliminary ideas, of using sterilization as a management tool and implementing a zone-management system, laid the groundwork for the formation of the Red Wolf Recovery Implementation Team (RWRIT), which Stoskopf eventually chaired. The team was conceived as a group of academics that would meet twice a year (on an all-volunteer basis) and advise the recovery program using scientifically vetted information to help them design management protocols to adaptively manage the red wolves. (Adaptive management, in scientific parlance, means trying something and testing to see if it's working; if it's not, a new management protocol is tried. It requires a constant process of implementation, monitoring, analyzing, and assessing whether changes are needed.)

The program designated Dare County as zone one, and with the sea at their backs, the biologists systematically caught every canid within the zone and cleared it of coyotes. With their work in zone one complete, they moved west and started cleaning house again in zone two. There, they also radio collared some of the coyotes they caught and then released them with the intention of learning how they interacted with the red wolves. After releasing a few collared-but-still-fertile coyotes, they began to sterilize *all* their radio-collared coyotes. In zone three, they took a more opportunistic approach, removing, collaring, and sterilizing coyotes as chance allowed. For the most part, they trapped and euthanized the coyotes, but they also used rifles if the opportunity presented itself. They systematically worked their way from Dare County south and west through Hyde and Tyrrell Counties, then through Washington and Beaufort Counties.

Their hope was that with the coyote population thinned, the red wolves would be more likely to pair with their own kind. But if they did run with a coyote, at least it would be sterile, and they couldn't produce a litter. Because the peninsula was not fully saturated for wolves and because coyotes were likely to utilize habitat that the wolves found marginal, such as areas near towns, sterilizing coyotes that had set up a territory meant that they were keeping that space occupied and preventing fertile coyotes from moving in. The program biologists had long theorized that once the red wolf population was established, "other wild canids will honor or respect home ranges established by respective family groups," according to a 1987 report authored by Warren Parker. Because gray wolves in intact family units killed intruding coyotes, the biologists expected that once the red wolf population reached a critical mass and had an intact social network in place with wolf territories bumping up against one another, they would respond similarly and kill or kick out the smaller canids. But what they didn't anticipate was that red wolves simply couldn't make a living in some of the habitat on the peninsula. And in those areas, coyotes did fine. Roadless areas of the tall-tree pocosin stretches were too thick with briars for wolves to be able to catch the prey that was there, Lucash surmised. Large swaths of marsh had the same effect, though some wolves had figured out that they could live off a bounty of frogs there in certain times of year. There were some areas, the biologists noticed, where red wolf pups simply could not survive. In fact, a large portion of Dare County's pocosin, where the wolves had first been placed, was not useful to the species. But coyotes could weasel through some of these areas and, with their comparatively leaner energy requirements (and ability to consume vegetative matter), eke out a living. This resulted in a mosaic of canid territories with red wolves and coyotes living sympatrically on the peninsula.

In the meantime, the red wolf program made a sincere effort to not merely manage the red wolf–coyote hybridization but to understand it. Eric Gese — along with RWRIT members Fred Knowlton, of the U.S. Department of Agriculture Animal and Plant Health Inspection Service (APHIS) Wildlife Services, and Todd Fuller, a professor of environmental conservation at the University of Massachusetts — refined the management plan and worked to develop ways to better understand how canids were using habitat within the red wolf recovery area. Both the implementation team and the field team worked with veterinarians to explore the biology of red wolves and coyotes and studied the red wolves' habitat preferences using a geographic information system (GIS). The implementation team also solicited help from geneticists and wildlife professionals at research universities. Not long after the PHVA workshop, they recruited wildlife geneticist Lisette Waits to help the program develop ways to identify red wolves, coyotes, and hybrids through molecular techniques. She, too, became a part of the RWRIT. At the time, the field team suspected they had another hybridization event on their hands. Some puppies in a single litter that year had displayed coat color variation that seemed indicative of a red wolf–coyote cross, but the team needed a concrete way to analyze individuals in order to confirm their suspicion. Up until 1998 or so, the red wolf team had operated off the assumption that any canid they caught in the recovery area was a wolf unless it was unusually small or looked coyote-like or doglike. But when it became apparent that coyotes had infiltrated the area and were actively living within the peninsula, the team needed more stringent criteria with which to assess their animals. In other words, they needed a red wolf litmus test. Waits came up with just such a test by developing a database of hypervariable regions of nuclear DNA developed from dogs. Eventually, Waits and Jennifer Adams and Craig Miller, her graduate students at the time, used seventeen different microsatellite markers to distinguish red wolves, coyotes, and hybrids. They also found a unique mtDNA control region haplotype when they studied the four matrilineal lines of the red wolf founders. They compared its sequence to coyote populations across the nation and determined that it was completely unique to the red wolf. Using these two types of markers in tangent, Waits and Adams began reconstructing a pedigree of the wild red wolf population. It was an animal-by-animal genetic analysis that traced which red wolf begot which and evaluated whether coyotes or hybrids had bred with pure red wolves. The project became Adams's dissertation. The need for a red wolf pedigree, including a genetic assessment of the red wolf founders used in captive breeding, had been previously determined by the RWRIT.

Using the genetic database of seventeen microsatellite markers for red wolves and coyotes, Waits and Adams discovered that the suspected hybrid litter that the field team discovered in 1999 was not the first hybridization event to have occurred. They found evidence that in 1993 a red wolf female and a coyote male bred, and their male offspring backcrossed into the red wolf population, bringing coyote genes with them. "The animals that turned out to be hybrids looked like big, robust red wolves," Waits recalled. They had not been detected morphologically, even though the animals were first-generation hybrids. And because these hybrids matured and later bred with true red wolves, they produced offspring that also produced offspring. There were soon individuals within the red wolf recovery area that were classified (at the time) as 50 percent red wolf, 75 percent red wolf (second generation, backcrossed) and 87.5 percent red wolf (third generation, backcrossed). The hybrid litter from 1993 is believed to be the only one to have ever backcrossed back into the wild red wolf population.

The red wolf program initially wanted to wipe every trace of hybridization from the wild population. But when it became clear that this action might crash the population, they fell back on the zone management system and, with the help of the RWRIT, slowly bred the coyote genes out. This meant selectively culling animals that they determined were not red wolves. Years later, when additional red wolf genetic markers were identified, scientists realized they had inadvertently removed animals that would today be classified as red wolves. This happened because some of the wild canids targeted for culling harbored alleles that were initially interpreted to belong to coyotes, but further scrutiny revealed they were rare red wolf alleles that could be traced back to founders from the captive breeding program and that were not well represented in the ensuing lineage. Unfortunately, this discovery didn't occur until after many of the animals with these rare alleles had already been killed. RWRIT chair Michael Stoskopf claimed he was one of the first to press the program, out of sheer caution, to stop removing canids with these unusual alleles. His implementation team realized that "overaggressive culling had the potential for removing the alleles we most wanted to retain in the red wolves," he said.

As Adams worked out the parentage and genetic pedigree for every red wolf in the wild population, Waits turned her eye to devising noninvasive ways that the field biologists could sample large areas of land and determine what kind of canid was living within it in order to better deal with the invading coyotes. Traditionally, the field team had trapped areas where they suspected an undocumented canid might be. But sometimes traps failed to catch anything, even though the biologists found tracks and scat that indicated that some sort of canid was present. Scat was like gold for Waits. She developed a method that used DNA from the scat to reveal the genotype of the animal that had deposited it. The accuracy of Waits's fecal analysis was so good that her lab could determine if a red wolf, a coyote, or a hybrid had produced a specific scat. They could also obtain individual genotypes from each scat, which meant they could match genotypes discovered from scat to existing genotypes known from their reconstructed pedigree, which was based off of blood-derived genotypes. (Because the field team had collected blood samples for all of their known red wolves to create the reconstructed red wolf pedigree, Waits and her lab were able to cross-reference the scat genotypes against known genotypes derived from blood samples to verify the accuracy of their method.) The scat genotyping also allowed them to detect previously unknown individual red wolves, hybrids, and coyotes. In one case, she even detected an individual red wolf that had died four months before its scat was collected, though usually the method demanded scat less than a week old.

When combined together, the pedigree and scat genotyping bestowed a unique power upon the field team: the ability to understand the wild population at the discrete level of an individual wolf's genetics. After the work of reconstructing the red wolf pedigree, the field team needed only to obtain blood samples from new offspring of known breeding pairs in order to keep tabs on the purity of the population as a whole. Today, according to Waits, "the wild red wolf gene pool is currently equal to or greater than 96 percent red wolf ancestry, [with] only 4 percent recent introgression from coyotes." Waits said she's not worried about the extremely small level of recent coyote introgression that exists. Under current management methods, she explained, the percentage will only decrease over time. And Waits gave another reason to be confident: "This sort of hybridization likely happened historically where coyote and red wolf populations came into contact, under certain conditions. I think it's actually probably good for the red wolf to have a little introgression, to help prevent inbreeding depression." (When populations experience bottlenecks like the red wolf has, they often deal with reduced genetic fitness because related individuals breed; it's the loss of genetic variability under these circumstances that is often referred to as inbreeding depression.)

Because of the long shadow cast by the research saying red wolves were recent hybrids, the FWS was extremely guarded about their work to breed the coyote genes out of the wild red wolf population. They knew that if it wasn't properly communicated, the public could be left with the wrong idea about today's wild red wolves. By 2007 the program appeared to have rescued the red wolf from its second brush with genetic swamping, and the Association of Zoos and Aquariums recognized the red wolf program's efforts across the years with their highest honor, the North American Conservation Award. The recovery implementation team continued to advise the red wolf program from just a few months after the 1999 PHVA meeting until the fall of 2008; but it's now unclear whether the team will continue to work with the red wolf program, which no longer has the funding to support them.

When I first visited the recovery area in summer of 2009, the aftermath of hybridization control and the heavy-handed technique of managing individual wolf pairs and coyotes was the reality that the red wolf biologists were wrestling with. Just as they had begun to evaluate their hybridization management tools for success, the program became bogged down with illegal gunshot mortality problems. The problem had emerged around 2004, and by 2006 the biologists recognized it as a clear trend that they felt threatened their management techniques. This led them to step up their management efforts considerably because of the association they were observing between anthropogenic killings and hybridization. More than a decade after the zone management concept was introduced, the day-to-day management of the red wolves still required nearly constant vigilance against *Canis latrans*. On one particularly hard winter day, Ryan Nordsven had confided to me that he often felt they were engaged in hand-to-hand combat against the invading coyotes.

When I first began researching the red wolf, a part of me held hope that these canids could be fully recovered to the point that they would not need to be managed into the future. But as I came to better know the red wolf's story, I also came to see how vital the current management methods are, despite the remoteness of the animal making a full, unmanaged, comeback throughout even a portion of its historic range. The current techniques have resulted in fewer hybrid litters being produced and have ensured the production of greater numbers of pure red wolf litters. But at the same time, red wolf recovery has become synonymous with coyote management.

What does the future hold for this conservationally challenged wolf, which requires constant hands-on tending and near-invasive management?

A pair of red wolves were released experimentally to Bulls Island in Cape Romain National Wildlife Refuge in South Carolina on December 13, 1976. The pair, nicknamed Buddy and Margie, had been trapped from the wild near Sabine Pass, Texas, in January of the same year. (Curtis J. Carley Personal Archive)

(top) Red wolves were moved in kennels by boat to acclimation pens before being released experimentally on Bulls Island, S.C. (Curtis J. Carley Personal Archive)

(bottom) John runs over a beach at low tide while being chased by a helicopter with a gunner using a tranquilizer dart. Curtis J. Carley, the red wolf field project coordinator at the time, dubbed John the "wolf that ran on water." (Curtis J. Carley Personal Archive)

Curtis J. Carley holds a wolf after it was darted and tranquilized on the beach of Bulls Island. Carley was responsible for the early stages of the Red Wolf Recovery Program and for establishing island propagation sites, one of which is still in use today. (South Carolina Game and Fish Department/Curtis J. Carley Personal Archive)

(top) Red wolves mate in a field within Great Smoky Mountains National Park. (Barron Crawford/U.S. Fish and Wildlife Service)

(bottom) Two wolves eat at a "kill site" within Great Smoky Mountains National Park. (Barron Crawford/U.S. Fish and Wildlife Service)

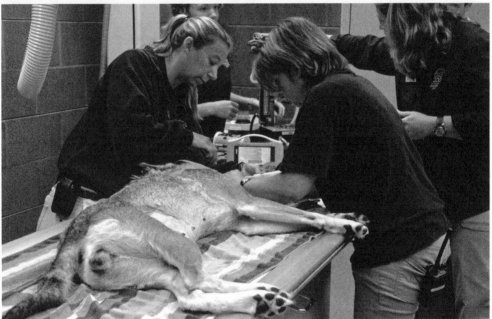

(top) A red wolf watches and stalks a deer within Great Smoky Mountains National Park. (Barron Crawford/U.S. Fish and Wildlife Service)

(bottom) Veterinarians and technicians at the Point Defiance Zoo and Aquarium in Tacoma, Washington, carefully prepare and monitor a captive female wolf during a procedure that will assess the health of her uterus. Captive breeding efforts are aimed at preventing inbreeding by getting wolves with underrepresented lineages to reproduce. Will Waddell, the Red Wolf Species Survival Plan coordinator, wants pups from this particular female. (T. DeLene Beeland)

Sea-level rise driven by climate change is a major threat to the red wolf's current habitat because the species has only one reintroduction area, the Albemarle Peninsula. The Nature Conservancy is pairing with the Alligator River National Wildlife Refuge to test climate-change mitigation strategies that aim to slow the effects of sea-level rise. Here, a ditch plug along Point Peter Road prevents wind-driven sound water, which is salty, from shooting inland up a ditch that was originally designed to bleed freshwater from the land into the sound. (T. DeLene Beeland)

Canals in the Albemarle Peninsula are much wider and deeper than ditches and are often interconnected. Though originally designed to drain freshwater from the swamps into the sounds, sea-level rise means that salt plumes often push inland along the canal bottoms, even as freshwater flows above them in the opposite direction. Simple flap-board risers allow for the water levels to be manipulated, holding freshwater back and allowing it to soak into the surrounding peat, while check valves on the opposite side prevent salt plumes from shooting inland. (T. DeLene Beeland)

(top) In recent years, canals in the Albemarle have been hijacked by saltwater intrusion, and their ubiquitous presence on the peninsula has sped the arrival of saltwater miles inland. Here, healthy pocosin (right) grows up to the edge of Highway 264 near Point Peter Road. On the left side of the highway, a wide canal has sped the arrival of salt to the land due to rising sea levels and wind-driven tide events. Saltwater intrusion has caused the retreat of a pond pine forest. (T. DeLene Beeland)

(bottom) Unhealthy pond pines retreat from a canal that allows saltwater to leach into the surrounding peat along Highway 264. They will eventually be replaced by salt meadow and then salt marsh. This transition from one ecosystem to another, due to sea-level rise and climate change, means that rapidly changing habitat may displace many creatures, from birds to red wolves. (T. DeLene Beeland)

# PART III
## The Red Wolf Tomorrow

The reinsertion of red wolves into a peopled North Carolina landscape has raised thorny questions about what physically, behaviorally, and genetically constitutes the red wolf.

CHRISTOPHER MANGANIELLO, "From a Howling Wilderness to Howling Safaris: Science, Policy, and Red Wolves in the American South," *Journal of the History of Biology* 42 (2009): 325–59

# CHAPTER 13
# The Long Road Ahead

Red wolves and humans are now inextricably, perhaps irrevocably, entwined. Humans were the cause of red wolves' near demise, but we may also be the engine of their future survival. Our country's early pioneers and settlers decimated what may have been the red wolf by transforming their forest habitat and pursuing them with wolf hounds, traps, poisons, and every sort of wolf-killing method imaginable. But concerned biologists, naturalists, and citizens also worked to save the last wild red wolves from sure extinction when hybridization and genetic swamping would have been the final death blow to their kind. Like the recent past, when humans victimized the red wolf, the future of the red wolf is also in human hands.

If the past few decades are a predictor of the red wolf's future trajectory, I'd wager a guess that the road ahead will be a continual struggle to prove this animal's conservation worthiness. Though the program has a history of working at the leading edge of wildlife management, the heated controversy over the animal's origins still clouds its future. Still, for those like me who believe the red wolf to be a unique representative of the canid that historically occupied the Southeast, there is hope that these enigmatic wolves will survive for many years to come. Current research might help guide the red wolf's future management, both in the wild and in captivity.

Many studies are in the pipeline that will hopefully help the red wolf program biologists better understand how to manage *Canis rufus*. The program is currently cooperating with graduate students to study ways to avoid inbreeding depression, the potential effect upon red wolf mortality from the widening of Highway 64 to four lanes, management techniques to reduce red wolf and coyote interactions, detailed predation patterns in red wolves and coyotes that live near each other in the recovery area using stable isotopes, and the shape and motility of red wolf sperm.

But it's not just the wild population that is under scientific scrutiny, the captive breeding program also sees its fair share of studies. In 2010 David Rabon published a paper in *Zoo Biology* that analyzed reproductive trends within the captive-bred population. He found that over the past thirty-five years, litter sizes shrank as inbreeding levels increased. While this may seem worrisome in the long run, Rabon also found that more of the young born today are surviving to adulthood than in the past. In the study, Rabon analyzed 554 instances between 1977 and 2006 in which captive red wolves were paired for the intention of mating. Of these, 192 litters were born, resulting in 797 offspring. Litters ranged from one to nine puppies. In the early years of the program, the mean litter size was 5.143 puppies. Today, it is only 3.391. Over this same time span, the average level of inbreeding has increased. Smaller litters may be a consequence of inbreeding, but Rabon's results also show that this biological setback may be offset by the improved husbandry methods and care that today's captive wolves receive.

Will Waddell, the Red Wolf Species Survival Plan coordinator who oversees the captive breeding program, was a coauthor of this study. As part of his job, Will maintains something called the red wolf studbook, which is a master document that includes each wolf's pedigree and medical history. It lists their identification number, which male sired them and which female birthed them, medical problems or surgeries they experienced, when they were born, and when and how they died. Will uses a computer program called SPARKS (Single Population Analysis and Records Keeping System) to calculate how inbred each captive red wolf is. Because the current captive population of about 200 animals all came from just fourteen founders, they are all related to each other to a certain degree. This relatedness is measured with a calculation called an inbreeding coefficient. This is the probability that alleles for a given gene may be exactly the same between two individuals in a given population. The closer the coefficient is to 0.0, the less inbred an individual is; but the closer the coefficient creeps to 1.0, the more inbred it is. SPARKS takes into account each red wolf's pedigree and inbreeding coefficient and then calculates a mean kinship value, which expresses how related an individual red wolf is to the captive red wolf population as a whole. Each year, Will looks at a list of the mean kinship values and draws a line halfway through them. All red wolves with a mean kinship value of 0.5 or less are considered for breeding, but all red wolves with a mean kinship greater than 0.5 are not allowed to breed. This method protects against the loss of genetic diversity and staves off inbreeding depression. Based on SPARKS calculations, the Fish and Wildlife Service estimates they have retained 89.52 percent of the genetic diversity that existed in the fourteen red wolves that founded the captive breeding program.

In August 2011 I travel to Tacoma, Washington, to meet Will Waddell.

He has worked in his current position for twenty-three years, and no one knows the state of the captive breeding population better than him. The largest holding of captive red wolves in the nation is affiliated with Point Defiance Zoo and Aquarium, where Will works. He's near retirement age, with blue eyes and a balding scalp that he keeps covered with a cap. He is the type of person who listens carefully, then, only after much internal deliberation, doles out brief, to-the-point responses. Point Defiance Zoo manages two offsite captive breeding facilities filled with thirty-four red wolves, and when I visit, they have an additional three red wolves on display in the zoo. The older site is known as the Graham facility. It's located in Douglas fir–dominated woods on the edge of a mink farm near the town of Graham. The second site is called the Northwest Trek facility.

When I arrive, Will and his crew are in the process of phasing out the Graham facility, which only has four wolves left in it. They are merging all the wolves to the much newer Northwest Trek facility. They are also in the middle of treating a female red wolf with a troubled uterus. In this program, not all red wolf uteruses are considered equal. This particular wolf comes from a founding lineage that is not well represented in the captive population. Will wants to increase the underrepresented lineages, and he really wants pups from this particular female. She is five years old, weighs 54.2 pounds, and has birthed at least two previous litters. But the only evidence of these were found by Sue Behrns, a red wolf caretaker since the early 1970s, as bits of fur, bones, and a tiny puppy paw in the mother's feces. Consuming newborn pups is not typical behavior for red wolves. It is a strong indication that something is very, very wrong. (On rare occasions, Sue has removed pups from their red wolf mothers and hand raised them. If they get pups out of this wolf the following spring, this is what she plans to do.) After the gory discoveries of the previous two years, Sue was hypervigilant this season. Her attentiveness clued her in to easily missed signs that this wolf suffers from a condition called pyometra. Her uterus is infected, and chronic infection may have contributed to her previous lost litters. An ultrasound six weeks earlier showed that the interior lining of her uterus was coated with pus. The Point Defiance Zoo vets, Karen Wolf and Alison Case, gave her a round of antibiotics and flushed her uterus with a saline and antibiotic solution. They, along with Sue and Will, were hopeful that the treatment would clear up her infection and allow her to birth a healthy litter the following year. Pairing her with a certain male red wolf would help improve the captive population's mean kinship score. (And yet, when pairing wolves based on their mean kinship values, Will told me he had never seen the population's functional genome equivalent increase by more than .01 in a given year. He was trying to nudge it up from 8.5 to 10.) Every pairing counted, as did the reproductive health of the individuals chosen.

When I visit the zoo, the two vets and Sue are prepping the female for a follow-up ultrasound. Simply getting the wolf into the clinic today meant that Sue had to capture her in her pen at Graham this morning using a giant salmon net, maneuver her into a kennel, and drive her to the zoo. Once there, the wolf was unloaded, sedated, and heaved onto an exam table. When I enter, the vets are busy trimming bits of belly fur from her sides. Tubes are slid down her throat, and her tongue, which hangs limp from her mouth, is carefully tied off to the side with gauze. One of the vets administers anesthesia and monitors her breathing and heart rate. An ultrasound technician, the same one who performed this wolf's first ultrasound six weeks before, rubs a wand across the wolf's lower abdomen and squints at a monitor screen.

"See this? The tissue is thickening along her uterine wall," she says to the vets. "Not what I wanted to see." She takes a few screenshots of cysts and thickened areas, and then they flip the wolf to her other side and continue the examination. Though the technician no longer sees pustules in the uterine lining, as she had previously, she sees a biofilm that she compares to the consistency of cheese. She takes a few samples using a needle to aspirate the filmy substance and then smears it onto glass slides.

At the beginning of the exam, everyone hoped for good news. But the mood sours. Sue stands off to the side and bites her lip.

"What's going to happen to her if she can't breed?" I ask.

"We'll probably still try with her again next year," Sue replies. "I'm not ready to give up on her yet."

Will nods his head in agreement.

The vets decide to flush her uterus again. It takes about twenty minutes for them to reposition her, snake a scope up to her cervix, and then insert a plastic tube into her uterus. She hemorrhages slightly, and red clouds fill the scope's view. After a few fits and starts, they transfer the antibiotic solution into her, though none flushes back out. It will likely leak out over time, and they hope it will slough off some of the biofilm with it.

Uterine infection is not an uncommon cause of death in the wild for female red wolves. But in the captive population, Sue and Will had witnessed an uncanny correlation between the birth-control drug they used and pyometra occurrences. It may sound counterintuitive that contraceptives are used in a breeding program, but sometimes space is tight and animals are penned together for long periods even though the program doesn't want them to breed. Will says that the particular drug they use, Deslorelin, seems to coincide with an uptick in pyometra cases. However, the wolf that I observe them treating is one of the few cases of a captive female red wolf not on Deslorelin that still developed pyometra.

"I just don't know what her breeding future is going to be," the ultrasound technician says.

"We don't either, but we'll hope for the best," Will replies.

Since space is a major constraint at the two satellite facilities, a captive wolf without a breeding future will likely be euthanized. They simply didn't have the resources to house, feed, and water a red wolf that wasn't going to help inch them toward their recovery goals. Perhaps in the future, improved medical care, such as the kind this wolf is receiving, will help to boost litter production.

Will, Sue, and I decide to visit the zoo's red wolf exhibit after the ultrasound procedure. Will guides us through the summer crowd of parents and young children. We amble past several vertical signposts, arranged in a timeline and imprinted with large images of a red wolf and brief text about moments along its journey. The final marker ends at the red wolf exhibit. Sue strolls up to a translucent barrier and gazes at a grassy embankment.

"There she is, same place as yesterday," Will says and points at a female wolf sprawled in the grass midway up a knoll. The wolf favors lying in this spot and has flattened the surrounding grass. Sue smiles, as if greeting an old friend. The wolf's rib cage moves up and down rhythmically as she half dozes. Her ears, however, pick up sounds like a pair of roving satellite dishes. Will tells me that this exhibit is new and was designed with multiple viewpoints in mind. The previous exhibit only allowed one vantage point to watch the wolves, and it was stationed at a low point below the knoll, which effectively cut off the uphill half of the exhibit from visitors because of its peculiar perspective. Not too many people lingered if there was nothing to see. The new exhibit holds four different vantage points in a loose L shape, which allows people to gaze onto the top of the hilly knoll and down into the lower reaches. The zoo's informal surveys had found that visitors spent more time at the new red wolf exhibit, and more time reading the information panels, than they had at the previous exhibit. Perhaps updated exhibits with purposeful designs will be part of the red wolf's future. After all, the species relies on the goodwill of the public to support its conservation, and the education outreach of zoos is just as important as their staff's expertise in animal physiology and breeding.

We walk around to the lower vantage point, where two man-made streams empty into a small pool.

"Let's see if Graham recognizes you," Sue giggles. Graham is the nickname of a male wolf from the Graham facility that Sue tells me is most atypical.

"Why would Graham recognize Will?" I ask.

"When Will walks by, often Graham will run up to the fence and jump around," Sue says. "He's boisterous. Crowds like him. He'll get up on that rock and strike poses for them." She points at a rocky outcrop jutting up about twenty feet from the water pool. As we approach, a lanky wolf walks slowly along the outcrop's rim. A breeze picks up and carries our scent right to his nose. Though he's not even looking in our direction, Graham tenses. He turns his head, faces the three of us, and sniffs the air. Without breaking his gaze, he leaps down the rock face and runs a well-worn trail through the grass. He catapults across the stream and bucks his hind legs with a flourish in midair. He stops below the translucent barrier, glares up at us, and whines. The whine devolves into a throaty growl. He stamps the grass, leaps and jumps, tears at the earth and lands ankle deep in the water. He glares directly at Will.

"Oh yeah, he sees you all right," Sue laughs. "That wolf wants a bite out of your rump."

Passersby have stopped to watch Graham's antics. A small crowd forms. He runs across the rocky outcrop again, back over the stream, and down to the pool, then tears at the grass again with broad paws. He runs this loop repetitively and stops each time to stand off against Will. One of the visitors jokes that he must smell the barbecue at a nearby lunch truck, but they misunderstand his body language. He isn't hungry. He is agitated.

"I think it's just misplaced aggression," Will says when I ask if Graham is exhibiting excitement or anger. "Usually when he sees me, I'm restraining him or helping to examine him. The wolves can't do much when they are restrained, so he acts out later."

Safe in the exhibit, Graham stares at Will. Without breaking eye contact, he walks to a bush and gnaws on its thick branches. It's as if he's saying, "Check out my canines. See how big they are?" There was nothing overtly threatening about his behavior, but it was a change from the docile nature I'd seen in other penned red wolves. Sue is right: he is definitely atypical, charismatic even.

Graham is also one of the few living products of artificial insemination experiments in red wolves, a technique that Will wants to further hone.

Artificial insemination may be useful to the program in the future in case the captive breeding efforts to create matched pairs based on mean kinship falls short of reproductive goals. In some cases, the captive female wolves were so aggressive to males that they were paired with that breeding never took place. Artificial insemination and securing red wolf sperm from all of the founding lines of the captive breeding program were identified in the 1990 Red Wolf Recovery/Species Survival Plan. Not long after, workers began collecting red wolf sperm. According to Will, there happened to be a fellow outside of Portland who had an international canid semen bank. The captive breeding program contracted him to help explore the viability of using electroejaculation on wolves. In the 1990s, Will helped develop protocols for immobilizing, catheterizing, and stimulating the wolves they sampled. They went through the captive population and methodically collected and evaluated sperm from male red wolves. If the sperm met certain criteria, it was processed and frozen. Eventually, the cryopreserved red wolf semen bank held samples from sixty individuals, which collectively represented thirteen of the fourteen founding lines. The work died down when a grant ran out and one of the main reproductive physiologists switched jobs.

Today, the early efforts to cryopreserve red wolf sperm and artificially inseminate females have proven their value—not just through Graham and his antics at the exhibit, but because a wolf named Stubs, one of the last living representatives from one of the fourteen founding lines, died in 1998. With Stubs's death, the unique diversity of his founding lineage died within the captive population. However, his semen was collected and banked before he died. Will would like nothing more than to resurrect Stubs's line. The only challenge, he says, is that the previous two cases of artificial insemination, in 1992 and 2003, were done using fresh sperm. In the first case, a six-year-old red wolf birthed two females and one male. Graham was born into a different litter of five.

"Clearly, we know artificial insemination using cryopreserved sperm works. It's been done in other animals," Will says. "We just need to pick this research up again and see where it might lead." If male red wolves experience a decrease in sperm quality, or if females are behaviorally uncooperative with their male counterparts, then artificial insemination may move from the realm of research to that of necessity. It's always nice to have a backup plan.

Given the length of the measures that have been taken to conserve red wolves—both in captivity and in the wild—combined with the uncertainty over the animal's origins, people have questioned whether the red wolf is worth saving. It's a question everyone has to answer for themselves; and it's one that is laden with subjective value judgments about what defines a species, which species are worth saving, and how we make these determinations both scientifically and in terms of legal policy. The red wolf has a very complicated history, one that I'm not convinced we fully understand. I have come to believe that it shouldn't matter *how* the red wolf originated. No matter which origin model you ascribe to, it's an animal that historically arose in the East. Like Susan Jenks, I wouldn't value the red wolf any less if it was formed through recent hybridization processes that were amplified by human-induced environmental disturbances. After all, aren't humans a part of nature too? And if there was an as-yet undescribed subspecies of gray wolf in the East, as Robert Wayne suggests, then the red wolf may be our last link to what that animal once was. However, my personal thoughts are more aligned with those of Lisette Waits: I think red wolves represent a creature that was historically present in the Southeast, a canid that was more closely related to coyotes than to gray wolves. I think Waits described it best when she conceived of the red wolf as having a core southeastern population but also a hybrid zone, or zones, where it interbred with coyotes, and that this interbreeding was probably a natural process that took place throughout their evolutionary history.

In my mind, the lack of consensus over what this animal may have once been underscores the urgency of conserving it. Rather than denigrate what we don't fully understand, I think we should elevate the red wolf because these creatures are living connections to our continent's past and its rich history of canid evolution. I also see red wolves as living lessons: they have shown us what happens when we force an animal too far in the direction of extinction and how hard it is to pull it back from that one-way exit. And while debates persist about what the red wolf once was, debate also swirls over what the red wolf ought to become.

The red wolf's future as the Fish and Wildlife Service now envisions it is genetic preservation a few hundred years into the future. But some researchers believe that orienting the red wolf's recovery objectives to genetic preservation misses a larger point. They assert that conservation of evolutionary processes should be the ultimate goal, and that letting red wolves hybridize with eastern coyotes might not be a bad thing. When I spoke with Paul Wilson of Trent University, he compared the state of the red wolf and the Algonquin wolf populations today. Whereas the red wolf population is intensively managed, he said, the Algonquin wolf population has not been managed at all. In a way, the history of Algonquin wolves reads as one huge

natural experiment in hybridization processes. Although hybridization between *C. lycaon* and coyotes occurred in recent times, he said that eventually
some breeding barriers emerged between wolves within Algonquin Provincial Park and their hybrids with coyotes external to the park. Some people
attribute this to a policy that ended trapping and hunting of wolves in a
buffer zone around the park. This might have resulted in wolf packs remaining stable instead of being frequently broken apart due to human-caused
deaths.

Whereas some may view the resulting eastern coyote hybrids as animals
of low conservation value, Wilson takes a different view. "These are the
canids that have been selected *for* in a human-modified landscape," he told
me. Without the helping hand of man, they bred and multiplied and even
invaded New England. What he was getting at is that human settlements
and activities aren't going to dwindle from the landscape in the future; they
are here to stay. And where the eastern wolf itself can't adapt to living in a
human-modified landscape, its coyote hybrids have proven they can; and
they've carried wolf genes with them back into areas where wolves have not
been in decades or even centuries. Now these hybrids are dining on white-
tailed deer. In his view, the exact same historic animal may not be present
in the Northeast now, but this new animal, this new hybrid, is performing a
similar ecological function that the eastern wolf of yesterday did. In short,
Wilson valued the role that the new predator plays in the landscape more so
than preserving the exact genetic state of the historic predator that was once
there. This stance can be viewed as a philosophical one that pits supporting
ecosystem function against preservation of an ecosystem's individual historic species components.

But is the eastern wolf's story truly interchangeable with the red wolf's?
While I understand the point about managing for evolutionary processes, I
can't make the leap to abandoning conservation of the red wolf as it is. Not
for emotional reasons, but because I think there are still many unanswered
questions that the red wolf program, on its current track, could help to
illuminate. For example, what behavioral, biological, or ecological factors
drive its hybridization with coyotes? Are the lessons of how to manage for
hybridization in a small and wild population transferrable to other threatened species? Are there still secrets in the red wolf's genome that have been
missed—secrets that might better illuminate its evolutionary relationship
with the coyote lineage?

As we have seen, the FWS can't envision a future for the red wolf that
is absent of human intervention. "These are the measures we have to go

to when we've been so careless with natural resources in the past," David Rabon said, speaking to the intense level of management the red wolf program demands. Ryan Nordsven had also told me on numerous occasions that the biologists wished they could stop doing so much management and just sit back and observe the red wolves or do research on them. But with such a small population, the threat of hybridization loomed too large, given the invasion of coyotes to the Albemarle Peninsula and the program's problem of too much churn and turnover in their breeding pairs. This threat lurks even in a human-managed future. However, the program biologists also expressed confidence to me that the tools they'd developed to deal with hybridization seemed to be working—so long as the illegal cases of gunshot mortality didn't continue to increase. Given that the FWS has decided they intend to preserve the red wolf in its current genetic state, a better understanding of exactly what drives the occurrence of hybridization is essential to managing the red wolf in the near future.

One of Lisette Waits's graduate students, Justin Bohling, has studied whether a red wolf's age, sex, social circumstances, and ancestry play a role in its susceptibility to hybridization. The field team had originally thought that it was only red wolf males that forced female coyotes to breed. They didn't think their she-wolves would tolerate mating with a male coyote, because they had observed female red wolves chasing and killing coyotes from their home ranges. But Bohling and Waits's genetic studies overturned that hypothesis and showed that modern hybridization was not directional in terms of the wolves' sex. They found that red wolves with a hybrid ancestry were more likely to breed with a coyote and that younger, inexperienced red wolf breeders were more likely to switch their fealty to a coyote. But perhaps the most interesting driver of hybridization that they found was social. If a pack was disrupted due to human-caused reasons—such as the breeding male or female being shot, poisoned, or hit by a car—then hybridization was much more likely to occur in that pack. Limiting the human-caused deaths of red wolves, seemingly a separate issue, turns out to be the most important factor of all in preventing future hybridization. "I think we've shown over the past few years that hybridization in the wild can be managed, and I think we've developed the tools to virtually eliminate it as a threat to the red wolf," Waits told me.

Another graduate student, Joey Hinton from the University of Georgia (and formerly with Louisiana State University), has spent several years studying coyote and red wolf interactions within the recovery area. He used data obtained from radio-collared animals to better discern if perhaps habitat preferences of specific individuals drive hybridization. But another kernel of an idea blossomed in his mind. He knew from ecological theory that allometric scaling, or the scaling of animals' body sizes, was used to explain resource partitioning, which is how animals divvy up limited resources. Hinton wondered if perhaps the close body sizes of coyotes in northeastern North Carolina (twenty-five to thirty pounds on average) and red wolves (forty-five to eighty-five pounds) led the two species to overlap their resource use. If so, then perhaps that overlap was a factor as to why some red wolves and coyotes paired together—and stayed paired over time—even though the sterilized coyotes mean that the pairs never produced pups. He'd heard the red wolf biologists discuss that perhaps red wolves chose coyote mates to avoid inbreeding depression, but that didn't necessarily explain why coyotes would go along with the cross-species pairing.

Hinton designed a project to study the home-range sizes of coyote pairs, red wolf pairs, and red wolf–coyote pairs. He then factored in individual animals' body sizes. He suspected that body sizes correlated roughly to home-range sizes because they support the energy requirements of the animal defending it. He hypothesized that animals that are closely matched in terms of body size are more likely to pair. In other words, a very small female red wolf of, say, thirty-eight pounds and a large male coyote of, say, thirty-two pounds would approach each other in their total body mass. Perhaps they'd be more likely to pair than a sixty-pound female wolf and a twenty-five-pound male coyote. Hinton suspects that similarly sized cross-species pairs have similar energy requirements, which means that they may be better paired to run long distances together, defend a territory together, and hunt sufficiently to sustain growing pups. In his preliminary data, Hinton found a home-range threshold of about fifteen and a half square miles. He found only red wolf pairs defending territories above this number, while below it, he found red wolves and coyotes paired together. As of the fall of 2011, his work was still in progress.

Understanding what drives hybridization will help red wolf management in the future, but one point of concern is *who* will manage the wolves, because the FWS will eventually need to hand control of the red wolf program over to the state of North Carolina. Yet historically, the N.C. Wildlife Resources Commission has not been involved in red wolf recovery efforts. For twenty-five years, the FWS has held the reins.

When I spoke with Perry Sumner, a section manager within the division of wildlife management at the Wildlife Resources Commission, he offered little evidence that the state planned to help conserve red wolves in the future. In fact, he took the stance that perhaps they were not a real species at all, and he expressed doubt that the FWS had truly learned to control the coyote hybridization issues. "I'm not sure it's even possible to maintain the purity of red wolves as long as there are coyote populations out there," Sumner said. I asked him if he'd read any of the recent evolutionary studies on red wolves. He replied that he'd reviewed some of it in the 1970s and 1980s, when the newly minted red wolf program was looking at the Land Between the Lakes for reintroduction; but he was disinterested in the more-current studies published since 2000. However, he was interested in questioning the red wolf's modern role. "The concern is, for this particular species, what *was* it? As far as ecology and the landscape today, we have a medium-sized canid now in the coyote. So I'm not sure what purpose the red wolf serves that the coyote doesn't."

Given Sumner's stance, I was almost afraid to ask what the state's vision was for taking over the red wolf program someday. There was a long pause. "We don't have any funds to manage red wolves," he replied. "I guess the Fish and Wildlife Service would be restricted to managing the red wolf on the federal lands they have out there on the peninsula. Or maybe they'd have to capture their pure red wolves and put them all back in captivity." If the FWS restricted red wolves to federal land, this would mean a more than 60 percent reduction in the area where wild red wolves exist, not to mention a complete truncation of the connectivity between these scattered federal lands. Sumner clearly viewed the red wolf program as hopeless. "It's not that different a picture out there today than how it was in the 1970s in Texas, in terms of the hybridization that's going on," he said. I was sorely tempted to argue with him on that last point, because things are *very* different today in terms of how hybridization is detected and managed.

Sumner's stark negative take on the red wolf, and his depiction of the state's lack of interest in managing the animal, left me wondering what allies the "doubly damned" red wolf will have in the future, other than the program biologists and a handful of academics and conservationists. Sumner left me with little doubt that the N.C. Wildlife Resources Commission would be just as content to see the program fade from the Old North State as they would be to see red wolves go extinct.

When I asked David Rabon about North Carolina's lack of support, he replied that it largely boiled down to the state's interpretation of the Endangered Species Act's nonessential experimental population (NEP) status. While there is a great deal of coordination between federal and state agencies concerning NEP species in other states, he said North Carolina's Wildlife Resources Commission has consistently taken the position that red wolves with the NEP status have no protections. "They feel they don't have to deal with it," he told me. "They hide behind the deficiencies of the [NEP] language, and use it to say they don't have to recognize red wolves as a listed species within the state." Worse, based on the 1986 "Final Rule" for reintroducing the red wolf in North Carolina, the wolves were only granted NEP status when they were on national wildlife refuge and national park lands. When not on those lands, they are treated as a proposed species rather than a listed species (meaning that they are treated as a species that is proposed for listing on the Endangered Species Act but not a species that is actually listed). This renders the red wolf's protection status on private and state lands a very murky gray. In the past, the red wolf program has successfully argued that the NEP protections must stay intact on any lands that connect the federal lands that red wolves use, but this patchwork mosaic of differing protection levels allows the state to ignore the spirit of federal protection that the ESA listing originally conferred on red wolves.

Rabon felt that the NEP status was originally designed in good faith, and that its flexibility was a boon to cooperating landowners; but he said that the state's "willful ignorance" of the spirit of the law led state leaders to subvert and misuse it. An example of this surfaced in early 2012, when the N.C. Wildlife Resources Commission proposed a rule to expand the current open daylight season on coyotes to include nighttime spotlighting and hunting with no bag limit and no season statewide. The move, which came at the behest of predator-hunter lobbyists, angered many red wolf conservationists and put the red wolf field team on edge. In the originally proposed rule, the state offered no concessions to protect red wolves within the recovery area.

Will doubling the opportunities to shoot coyotes double the number of red wolves shot illegally each year in cases of mistaken (or supposed mistaken) identity? And if hunters are already having trouble distinguishing coyotes and red wolves during full daylight, how well might the distinction be made at night, even with the use of spotlights? When I spoke with eastern coyote researcher Jonathan Way about the effect of the proposal upon red wolves, he replied: "To allow hunting of one species that is so closely related to, and so similar looking to, a second species that is fully endangered is just bizarre." Kim Wheeler of the Red Wolf Coalition was a little more blunt when she said that the Wildlife Resources Commission's rule put "people in a position to shoot an endangered species, and that's against the law."

While the shortcomings of the state's indifferent, even belligerent, attitude toward one of the world's most globally endangered wild canids is disheartening, it's not the only seemingly intractable threat to the red wolf's future. Perhaps the most unpredictable wild card for the red wolf in the long term is the looming problem of climate change.

## CHAPTER 14

# A Dire Threat from the Sea

The area where red wolves are being restored is entirely flat, low-lying coastal habitat that is surrounded on three sides by sounds that connect to the Atlantic Ocean. Large swaths of the recovery area's eastern section are no more than two or three feet above current sea level. If the sea rises in the future, as anticipated, what will happen to the red wolves of the Albemarle? The effects of sea-level rise here are not limited merely to higher water levels. Already, saltwater intrusion into the region's extensive canal system is poisoning peat soils and transforming former forests to salt meadows and marshes—miles inland from the sounds and the river mouths that define the peninsula's watery perimeter. Climate change will likely drive a variety of other ecological disturbances in the wolves' reintroduction area, including an increase in the frequency and intensity of wildfires and hurricanes.

In 2011 I witness several of these threats menace the peninsula in tandem.

In early May, a giant wildfire, which became known as the Pains Bay fire, spreads from private land onto Alligator River National Wildlife Refuge. Over the next few weeks, it affects areas between the Dare County Bombing Range and the coastal community of Stumpy Point. Its smoke plume snakes south and chokes Wilmington. Over the next three months, it burns 45,294 acres. Luckily, no red wolves are lost or injured. The fire is fueled in part, ironically, by the peninsula's system of dikes and canals, which were originally built to drain the region's wetlands. But the consistent and large-scale loss of freshwater has also meant that large peat deposits have dried out over time in some places. Peat is formed from decomposing vegetation. It's also an early form of what eventually will become coal—and when it's dry, it's highly flammable. Draining pocosins of their water sentences their organic soil to transform into a substance not unlike charcoal briquettes. This explains why fire here sometimes jumps across traditional firebreaks by creeping through the dried-out subterranean peat *beneath* them. Wendy Stanton, a biologist at Pocosin Lakes National Wildlife Refuge, tells me that while frequent fires were a part of the historic ecological cycle of pocosins, they never burned as intensely or across as large of an area as today's fires do, and that has quite a lot to do with the draining influence of the area's canals.

"A few hundred years ago," she says, "if lightning sparked a fire here, you could probably stand in the forest and watch it pass by you. We think it was carried along by grasses and small shrubs, but it wouldn't have been so hot as to burn the tree trunks and crowns severely, like we see today."

Today's wildfires also ravage seed banks in the soil, which means they burn so aggressively that they retard the future growth of plants that drop their seeds, some of which can take a decade to germinate. Combine these negative effects with predictions of a drier, hotter climate to come, as well as rising seas, and it's not hard to envision a future in which more frequent or more intense wildfires burn in the red wolf recovery area, even while the sea threatens to swamp parts of it. How long can the forests here maintain the deep vegetative cover the red wolves need for denning and refuge?

One afternoon, the year before, Ryan Nordsven and I were driving through the Pocosin Lakes refuge and he showed me a recovering burned area that stretched as far as my eyes could see. A lightning-sparked fire had swept through the refuge in June 2008. Six months and $20 million in fire-suppression measures later, the Evans Road fire had transformed 40,704 acres from woods to charred and smoldering open space. Smoke from the wildfire trailed west and inland all the way to Raleigh and Charlotte. When the wind changed, it billowed offshore in a braided plume visible in images relayed from NASA satellites.

So much peat burned that pond pine trees still standing afterward appeared to be perched precariously on their tippy toes, like ballerinas dancing on point. As the peat burned, soil levels dropped as much as a few feet around these pines, which tend to form soil hummocks at their base. This left their normally subterranean roots exposed, splayed sideways, and plunging downward into the still-smoking earth. Firefighters pumped more than 2 billion gallons of water from Lake Phelps, New Lake, and the Alligator River. They used helicopters capable of carting 1,500 gallons of water and bulldozers that dug up hot spots smoldering deep underground. With the help of well-timed late summer rains, the flames were eventually drenched. Officials declared the fire to be finally out on January 5, 2009, and they claimed it had burned up to 12,000 acres in a single twenty-four-hour period. Ryan is a volunteer wildfire fighter, and he helped fight the Evans Road fire. At least one red wolf succumbed to the blaze. In places where it had burned very hot, the charred trunks of burned-out trees lay across the land like downed telephone poles. Those that were still standing were hollowed and blackened brittle shells. A year and a half later, when we passed through it, only the faintest glimmer of new growth indicated the area was recovering. All the wildlife that formerly used this land, including red wolves, black bears, red-cockaded woodpeckers, and marsh rabbits, had relocated elsewhere.

One strategy that may help to mitigate the intensity and scale of future wildfires is work by the the staff of the Pocosin Lakes refuge that seeks to restore hydrologic function to the landscape. They hope to reverse or ameliorate the system of dikes and canals that drain their freshwater wetlands to the sounds. At a broad scale, their project consists of control structures that manipulate water levels in major canals by preventing their seaward flow. "The best way to think of this is that we're holding water back," Stanton tells me. By slowing the arrival of freshwater from the land to the sounds, some of the area's vast peat deposits stay moist longer, and moist peat won't burn. This action mimics historic hydrologic sheet flow, in which water only an inch or two deep slowly crept across a landscape that changes mere inches in elevation per mile.

A few weeks after the Pains Bay fire is extinguished, a large Category 4 hurricane, Irene, sweeps across the Bahamas and menaces the Eastern Seaboard. I watch its projected track for days, and my stomach sinks when model after model depicts its huge eye tracking directly over the heart of the red wolf recovery area. While I know that the wild red wolves will seek shelter, I also know that when Hurricane Isabel swept over the peninsula in 2003, a captive male red wolf was killed at Sandy Ridge. He'd sought shelter in his metal dog box, but a tree cracked and fell over his pen. He peeked out right before it fell, and his skull was crushed. When Irene makes landfall on August 27, its winds subside to about eighty-five miles per hour, which knock it down to a Category 1 hurricane. This time, thankfully, no red wolves are lost, despite massive flooding from the sound waters being pushed inland from the winds.

Suffering a major hurricane hit is a long-held worry for the red wolf field team due to the recovery area's vulnerable coastal position. But if climate change unfolds as scientists predict, then northeastern North Carolina can expect not only more intense wildfires and hurricanes, but also a rise in sea level between one and three feet within a century, and perhaps even more. If the sea rises by three feet, then about one-third of the current red wolf recovery area will drown, with most of the submerged land located in the easternmost part of the peninsula. The Alligator River refuge is particularly vulnerable. Nearly 90 percent of the refuge is less than twenty-four inches in elevation, and the refuge forms the core of what the red wolf biologists consider their pure wolves. If nature conforms to predictions, then the ocean might sway atop large swaths of the refuge by this century's end. It's a process that has played out again and again on the peninsula over millions of years, and yet scientists are still trying to understand exactly *how* sea-level rise may affect specific localities here.

Stanley Riggs, a geologist at East Carolina University (ECU), has studied coastal processes in North Carolina for forty-seven years. About two decades ago, he became hooked on the question of how North Carolina's coastal shorelines originated and evolved. He spent decades drilling sediment core samples all along the Albemarle Peninsula and the Outer Banks and shooting seismic pings from boats up and down the sounds. From this, he and his colleagues pieced together evidence of where ancient shorelines and ancient barrier islands once were. Some ancient shorelines indicate a time when sea level was much higher than today, like the 125,000-year-old Suffolk shoreline that lies nearly seventy-five miles inland on the peninsula, near the modern-day town of Plymouth. Others, like the ancient Roanoke River mouth that lies miles offshore at the base of the continental shelf, represent a period when sea levels were much lower than today.

I pay Riggs a visit at ECU in Greenville three weeks after Irene has made landfall. Riggs has published predictive maps showing the Outer Banks largely gone as we know them, reformed in a different configuration at some future point in time, and the Albemarle and Pamlico Sounds reshaped as open bays. The land, too, is shown altered in an attempt to depict what may stay high and dry after the seas rise.

"I don't like to show these maps anymore," he confesses. "People start to wonder why they should care at all if it's all just going to change or go away." It can be shocking for someone unfamiliar with the issue to see their county replaced by water. I have the opposite reaction, though, when Riggs shows me the maps of water covering what is now prime habitat for the red wolves. All I can think is, *Where will they go?* If anything, the maps make me care more.

Riggs and three colleagues have recently published *The Battle for North Carolina's Coast* (2011), which contains summaries from decades of their coastal research. He sees it as a resource for laypeople to understand not just future sea-level rise in North Carolina but also the ways that changing shorelines have shaped the state in the past. "We're frequently asked, 'How well do you know what you say you know in this book?'" Riggs says. "And the answer is: 'We know it *damn* well.'" He practically growls the last part at me, a marked contrast to his otherwise grandfatherly and professorial persona.

Riggs says that the reason he's done so much work on the Albemarle Peninsula and in the coastal northeastern part of the state is because the area is basically one giant basin. The Albemarle Peninsula just happens to lie smack-dab in the middle of this area. It's been collecting sediments for millions and millions of years, which means that there is a lot of muck he can sample to elucidate the state of environments now long past. The basin formation is a result of rifting that created the Atlantic Ocean 225 million years ago and caused what is now Senegal, Africa, to pull apart from what is now North Carolina. The basin's accumulation of sediments allows scientists like him to drill cores that date back 180 million years (though he is more interested in the last 24 to 36 million years). In a weird catch related to past glaciation, the Albemarle is also within a portion of coastal plain that is slowly sinking. In contrast, if you were to draw a line from Raleigh to Bogue Banks in the extreme lower portion of the Outer Banks, you would find that the swath of coastal land that falls roughly south of this line is moving in an opposite trajectory: it is slowly rising. Sediments are unable to accrue there before they are eroded away. Cores from this area only go back 3,000 to 5,000 years before they strike bedrock; they aren't very useful for piecing together a detailed look at how the coasts have changed through time. The southern zone also has a steeper average slope of three feet per mile, whereas the flat northern zone of the Albemarle barely registers a change in elevation of 0.2 to 0.3 feet per mile. While no one knows for sure the exact rate at which the basin in the northern zone is sinking—it's been roughly estimated at a rate of eight inches per century—it's definitely sinking at a slower rate than that of sea-level rise. Similarly, no one knows the exact rate at which the coast along the southern zone is rising, but Riggs says the difference amounts to slightly higher rates of sea-level rise occurring in the northeastern zone versus the southeastern. This is not simply theory; it has been measured. In a 2008 publication, Riggs reported that actual rates of sea-level change measured by the National Oceanic and Atmospheric Administration ranged between 1.78 to 4.32 millimeters annually, with a cline that clearly increased from south to north. The effects of this rise are not the same as simply turning on a tap and watching water creep up the side of your bathtub. It's much more nuanced, and it depends upon the type of shoreline that interfaces with the sounds and sea, in addition to the types of sediments and vegetation that the shoreline contains.

Within this rough framework of understanding, Riggs set about to learn how the varied shorelines that form the edges of the Albemarle Peninsula function in relation to active storm seasons and a sea-level rise scenario of about two to three millimeters per year. He recognized that accelerated erosion caused by increased storm intensity and frequency, which is also predicted to occur in future climate change, could spur some ecosystems to slowly change into others. It's already happening in some areas. Biologist Dennis Stewart of the Alligator River refuge has watched the land transform before his eyes. He's seen pond pines wither and die from saltwater intrusion, and he's witnessed an entire forest retreat half a mile inland away from Alligator River's swelling shores. He's watched woodlands near Mashoes Marsh, north and west of Manns Harbor, dissolve away into shrubs and invasive grasses. One pocosin patch morphed into a sawgrass marsh. All of this happened in two decades or less. When I visited Stewart at his refuge office, he showed me proof: aerial images of the changing shoreline along Alligator River that were taken across decades. Forests grow right up to the water in some areas, but where tall woods retreated over time due to saltwater intrusion, invasive phragmites (a type of reed) and low-growing shrubs have filled in. The new habitat is of little to no use to the birds, bats, and mammals that rely on the taller forest canopy for refuge and food.

For red wolves, the retreat of the forests inland signals a corresponding contraction of the vegetative cover on which they depend. But how large of a threat does this actually pose to the wolves? Do they have time to adjust and move elsewhere within the recovery area? In order to quantify the magnitude of this threat, we first need to know how fast the shorelines are changing and how fast the forests are retreating.

Riggs has classified the four main types of shorelines around the Alligator River refuge and the peninsula and meticulously recorded erosion and accretion rates for each. Swamp forests, bluffs, beach, and platform marsh can be found in a mosaic pattern here. His research shows that swamp forests, where the trees grow right up to the water, are least common and form only about 7 percent of northeastern North Carolina's shores. They are found mostly along drowned rivers. By measuring their shifting underwater sediment banks, Riggs found that these can erode at about −2.3 feet per year. Bluffs form about 8 percent of the area's shorelines and erode at a similar rate as the swamp forests. Platform marshes are the most common shoreline a visitor will see, forming nearly 85 percent of northeastern North Carolina's shores. They are also the most vulnerable to erosion and the most typical shoreline type encircling the red wolf recovery area. Riggs calculated an average accretion rate of +0.6 feet per year to an average erosion rate of −3.3 feet per year. Some areas, like Point Peter Road on the eastern side of the Alligator River refuge, proved even more vulnerable and lost up to 7.5 feet per year. During a very active storm year, Riggs recorded a loss of twenty-six feet of platform marsh on the northern tip of Roanoke Island.

Marshes are most affected because of their sediment structure. When high-energy wave action encounters the marsh's leading edge, it laps at the platform of sediments that the marsh has accrued. The initial layer of this platform is dense with the matted and interwoven roots of grasses, but below this, it is loose sediment that can be the consistency of thick pancake batter. Once the lower sediment begins to erode and undercut the roots, entire shelves of the mat will collapse. Riggs predicts that with increased storm intensity, there is a high probability that this erosion rate will increase. While the degradation of coastal habitat from shoreline change is not good for today's red wolves because it chips away at their usable habitat, it pales in comparison to the projected effects of sea-level rise.

While it's natural for the marshes to shift boundaries over time, one of the effects of rising seas in this area is saltwater intrusion into pond pine forests. Pond pines are extremely sensitive to salinity. Simply spraying the crown of a pond pine with saltwater, as happens during nor'easters, causes the needles to brown. But the whole tree dies when the roots sit in soil that is periodically flooded by saltwater, or if the soil surrounding it increases in salinity due to leaching. This saltwater intrusion causes the forest to retreat, and the land then grades into salt meadow or marsh.

But predicting exactly what forest retreat and sea-level rise will look like at a scale localized to the peninsula is tricky. For one thing, bathtub models don't always take into account the effect of the network of roads, canals, and ditches upon the progress of rising water. Many roads, like Highway 264, will act as large dams that hold water back. Meanwhile, the area's ubiquitous canals, initially dug to flush freshwater off the land (or to build raised road beds, as many of the canals are simply borrow pits), are being hijacked by rising seas. They help speed the arrival of saltwater deep into inland areas when wind-driven storms push sound water up their channels. This is not only changing vegetative communities by rapidly purging them of salt-intolerant plants; it's also changing the inland soil chemistry. Saltwater, when mixed with freshwater pocosin peats, causes sulfate-reducing bacteria to initiate a reaction that then causes the peat to collapse and subside. (Peats that form under salt marshes do not collapse this way, because they formed in the presence of salt.) This reaction also releases mercury, nitrogen, and carbon dioxide as by-products. Models that simply consider the elevation of the land may show tattered remains where peat domes poke up like thousands of tiny islands. But in reality, these domes might drown faster than surrounding soils that are not composed of peat.

Past sea levels are well documented in the vicinity of the Albemarle Peninsula. Riggs has taken cores of salt-marsh peat around Roanoke Island that indicate that sea-level rise rates have been accelerating, increasing from three inches per century from 0 to 1800 A.D. to seven inches over the course of the 1800s and sixteen inches during the 1900s. What this means to people living in the area is perhaps symbolized by the recent death of an island known as Batts Grave. Starting in the mid-1700s, an entire forty-acre island began drowning within sight of the mainland in the Albemarle Sound. It housed a home and orchards just three-quarters of a mile offshore from Drummond Point, on the northern side of the sound. Within a century, the island shrank to ten acres. Within two centuries, it was marked by buoys and a "lone cypress skeleton," according to a report Riggs wrote in 2008.

Still, it can be difficult for a person living in the area to notice month-to-month and year-to-year changes in shoreline migration and swamping. Part of the beauty of the marshes, salt meadows, and swamp forests here is their nearly unvaried repetition. "Unless you work off the aerial photographs, you can't necessarily tell that the shoreline is changing. It all looks the same," Riggs tells me. "Erosion and accretion are happening all the time. It's natural for changes to occur here. But basically what we're seeing now is that the rate of erosion and the rate of shoreline change is accelerating in some areas."

"Are you talking about the rate of erosion from wave action at the shoreline, or from storms?" I ask.

"Well, both," he replies. "Because you have wave energy all the time, it's just more forceful during a storm. For example, in a single storm in 2003, Point Peter Road receded 100 feet in half an hour."

I know the road that Riggs is referring to. It is on the Croatan Sound side of the Alligator River refuge, and it forms a straight line between Highway 264 and the water. Ryan and I had often passed it when we were headed south to sites near Lake Mattamuskeet. Point Peter Road is also the location of my appointment the following day with a Nature Conservancy employee who is implementing climate-change mitigation strategies.

I ruminate on Riggs's research as I depart ECU in the middle of a powerful downpour that soaks me to the bone. The storm chases me as I drive north from Greenville, then east across Highway 64 into the red wolf recovery area. Rain comes down so hard that I pull over to let it abate before crossing the narrow concrete bridge spanning Alligator River. I think about what Riggs has just told me regarding marshes and storms, and I wonder what this one tiny event is doing to them. It's too dark to see if there are waves on the river, but judging from the horizontal cant of the rain streaks, I conclude that there must be. As I wait, whitecaps are probably pounding against the platform marshes and lashing at the forest's edge.

The next morning, I meet Brian Boutin at a Nature Conservancy office tucked so far into the scrub woods of Kill Devil Hills that I unwittingly drive past it—twice. Boutin is dark haired and appears to be in his thirties. He exudes a youthful and optimistic energy. He's a marine biologist by training but has boned up on terrestrial ecology since joining the conservancy two and a half years ago, specifically to discover climate-change mitigation strategies. Whereas Riggs sees little opportunity for society to make changes, Boutin sees tiny cracks where changes can be implemented that can then ratchet the cracks wider and wider. He's not so naive as to think that the climate adaptation project he's working on will hold back the sea, but he believes that by slowing shoreline erosion and saltwater intrusion, the conservancy can help to hold onto habitat for just a wee bit longer— long enough to give species time to adjust and migrate inland. For him, it's all about slowing the rate of change and giving species time to adapt.

His project is a joint effort born from collaboration between Alligator River biologist Dennis Stewart and a scientist formerly with the Nature Conservancy, Sam Pearsall. The two organizations have shared close ties over the years as the conservancy helped to broker the deal that established the refuge. Stewart and Pearsall first began chatting about ways to mitigate sea-level rise and other climate-change effects in 1998. Stewart shared with him the changes he'd noticed on the refuge over the years: forests retreating inland from river shores and mature pine forests morphing into salt meadows and then salt marshes. Then they tossed around ideas for how to slow the saltwater intrusion and reduce shoreline erosion. It took a decade, but Pearsall secured funding from Duke Energy to get the project rolling. Today, the Alligator River refuge provides a benchmark for creative thinking about how coastal areas can prepare for and mitigate the effects of climate change. While it's not the first refuge in the nation to adopt on-the-ground mitigation strategies, it is among the first to implement these strategies along with a commitment to gather long-term monitoring data to assess how well the strategies are working. The intent is to buy time for the species that use its lands, such as the red wolf. Refuge manager Mike Bryant told me that other refuges regularly seek advice from people actively working on the project shared by Alligator River and the Nature Conservancy. The refuge is widely viewed as being on the cutting edge of this sort of mitigation work, and not only because of its precarious position on the land that juts farther out into the Atlantic Ocean than any other point on the East Coast.

When we reach Boutin's experimental site at Point Peter Road, hundreds of mosquitoes bob and weave around the closed truck windows. Boutin eyes them warily. "Yeah, we're not getting out today," he says. "You'll just have to look at the project site from the truck." Even though we are wearing backwoods clothing, the insects are so thick that we'd have needed head nets and gloves duct taped to long-sleeve shirts to be able to move around outside. It wasn't much different from the Everglades. Hurricane Irene had dumped so much water on the refuge a month earlier that the blackwater swamps belched hordes of young mosquitoes for weeks after the storm dissipated. Now, they hang in hungry swarms.

Point Peter Road is flanked on its southern side by a smallish canal and on its northern side by a shallow ditch. If you were to walk from Highway 264 to the sea through the vegetation here, you'd pass through pocosin that gives way to a salt meadow dotted with pines, which in turn gives way to a cordgrass marsh. Nearer to the sound, the pocosin appears straggly at the transition to salt meadow and scrub. The pond pines are stunted and twisted. Many are barely taller than me. Their needles are a characteristic auburn-orange hue that belie the presence of salt. Because Hurricane Irene had moved a storm surge of about six feet of salty sound water up and onto this area a month ago, much of the scrub vegetation we gaze upon has browned and withered. The shrubs will bounce back, Boutin says, but the pond pines will not.

While this isn't habitat that most red wolves would readily use, it is highly valuable land because it takes the first pounding from storm surges when hurricanes and nor'easters come ashore. In essence, this is the type of land that protects the inland areas that red wolves do use.

There are four elements to the Point Peter project, Boutin explains. First, they are testing the effectiveness of planting salt-tolerant trees to replace the forest cover where pond pines have retreated rapidly due to saltwater intrusion. In 2010 the conservancy hired professional silvaculture contractors to plant 21,000 saplings over the course of two days. At this site, they are experimenting with a mix of bald cypress and black gum trees, which can tolerate freshwater flooding and seem to be more resilient than pond pines against saltwater intrusion. Today, the saplings are only chest high, and monitoring includes recording their growth rates and survivability. "That's something that can't be figured out in two years," Boutin says. "They are trees, it's going to take time." But so far, he's not noticed large-scale die-offs, and their growth doesn't appear stunted. "The goal is to get them to a mature-enough point that by the time the shoreline reaches them, they are able to tolerate flooding and saltwater for as long as they can to hold onto that sediment."

The scenario Boutin describes is complicated by the area's ditches and canals. Invisible to us from our low vantage point in the truck are a series of ditches perpendicular to the road. Originally cut to drain the land, they have since been hijacked by the salty waters of the sound. During wind-driven storm events, and even during high spring tides, sound water pushes up the canal and ditch along the road. In the deeper canal, it forms a dense wedge that pushes inland along the bottom even as freshwater flows toward the sound above it in the opposite direction. When the salty plumes reach the cross ditches, they carry salt into broad swaths of the landscape. The saltwater stands in the ditches for weeks or months until it is flushed out by a heavy rainstorm. During that time, salt leaches into the pocosin peat. It is a perfect design to poison the land. Now, multiply this scenario by the hundreds, if not thousands, of ditches and canals that lace the peninsula.

To halt this arrival of salt deep into inland areas, Boutin worked with Stewart to refine designs to plug ditches and build special water-control features for the deeper and wider canals. The result is sixteen feet of nylon piling driven into marsh mud near the mouth of the Point Peter Road ditch, only yards from the sound. "The ditch plugs have to be level with the surrounding land," Boutin says. "We can still get overwash that puts salt behind it, but for the most part, we haven't seen that." The plug holds freshwater back within the ditch, where it is allowed to seep into the surrounding peat deposits. This helps to rehydrate the pocosins while preventing sound waters from entering the ditches and speeding inland.

But the canals require more finesse. "We can't refill them because we don't have enough material," Boutin explains. "Even if we dug up this road we're sitting on and dumped the roadbed into the canals, it wouldn't be enough. Because once you remove this material, it dries out and compresses." Nor could they plug the canals. So he and Stewart designed a low-tech solution to the problem. Existing culverts connect the canals to cross ditches or other canals. At these junctures, existing pipes set in earthen dams are often used to allow water to flow from one canal or ditch to the other. Stewart and Boutin modified these by building simple structures of wood lapboard set side by side vertically to allow the water level of one canal to be held artificially higher than the earthen dam and pipe system allowed. Called flashboard risers, these, too, held freshwater back and rehydrated the peat. But the flashboard risers did nothing to stop the saltwater plumes from shooting inland. To thwart those, Boutin crafted what he calls a check valve. It's a flexible neoprene valve that extends from the sound side of a canal's pipe at the earthen dam juncture. It allows freshwater to flow out to the sound, but when water pushes in from the sound side, the pliable flap simply folds in on itself and flops to one side. Pressure from the outward-flowing freshwater keeps the valves filled and slightly open but unidirectional, while pressure from the incoming salt plume keeps it bent to one side just enough that the plume itself is thwarted.

"With the one-two punch of the check valves and these flashboard risers, this is pretty much the last stand against saltwater intrusion," Boutin says. His initial data from stratified water-quality loggers (a type of sensor) stationed just behind the check valves showed they were working. The loggers test salinity, flow direction, and velocity. They showed a drop in salinity directly after the check valves and risers were installed, and they didn't detect any plumes moving inland along the canal bottom. "But what we didn't count on was the Pains Bay fire," Boutin says. When the fire broke out, the firefighting operation began pumping groundwater from a nearby area. The pumping lowered the groundwater table locally, which caused salty water to move upward from below. Boutin's water-quality loggers showed a corresponding spike, and the incident taught him a lesson about the interconnected nature of the ditch and canal systems with the groundwater. He's already planning how to better isolate the experimental site.

At the end of Point Peter Road, the Nature Conservancy has worked to build oyster reefs to help mitigate the wave energy absorbed in the marsh's leading edge. But because the sediments are so soft directly in front of the marsh, they had to place the oyster reefs 100 yards offshore, or seventy-five yards further than Boutin wanted. Despite the freshwater, which is highly anoxic (lacking in oxygen), pouring out from the canal mouth and seeping off the marsh, Boutin says the reefs are doing just fine. "What we're trying to do with the marsh restoration is to keep a band of marsh as a buffer between the forests and the sea," he explains. "So when we have something like Hurricane Irene come through with a big storm surge, the marsh takes the pounding, not the pocosin."

For the most part, Boutin says the response from the local community has been neutral—except for the time someone shot his buoys that marked the oyster reefs and the time someone stole $4,000 in equipment. Gill-net fishers like the reefs because it fosters a productive habitat. Boutin says he sees them running nets by the reefs, where they catch shad, croakers, and flounder. But some people complain about anything that manipulates the area's water levels, and Boutin received complaints his project was flooding someone's land—even before the flashboard risers or ditch plug were installed.

The initial assessment of Boutin's project has been positive. The Nature Conservancy signed an agreement with nine area refuges to implement similar climate-change mitigation strategies on their lands. "We're taking what we know from this area and moving on," Boutin says. "We don't have the luxury of waiting five or ten years to monitor these strategies. We kind of have to go with our gut and move fast." Still, people like Nancy White, executive director of the University of North Carolina Coastal Studies Institute, question if the whole venture isn't an exercise in spitting into the wind. Others, like Riggs, question if they have enough hard data to say it's working.

While Boutin's mind is often occupied with the minutiae of his projects, he never loses sight of the fact they are simply a means to a goal: to extend the life of habitat in order to buy time for species.

As we drive back across the refuge, Boutin points out the legacy of saltwater intrusion elsewhere. On the eastern side of Highway 264, healthy pocosin grows right up to the road in a chaotic tangle of healthy pond pines, briers, gums, and myrtles. But a large canal is on the western side of the road, and pond pines have retreated up to an eighth of a mile from the canal. In their wake, a marsh dotted with invasive phragmites is filling in. Boutin immediately begins drawing a mental map for how to fix it. I can almost hear him thinking: *Plug this ditch, put a water control structure with check valves there, plant saplings here . . .*

I can almost hear Riggs, as well, groaning and telling him not to bother. In truth, you probably can't find scientists with more opposite views of the future than Riggs and Boutin. But I believe both of their perspectives are necessary. We need the Boutins of the world to tinker with short-term mitigation measures that work on the order of decades and acres, and we need the Riggses of the world to show us how changes in climate have shaped our environments for millennia, and how they will continue to be shaped for millennia to come.

But what of today's wild red wolf? Despite the valiant efforts of people like Boutin and Stewart, in time, the sea will reclaim large swaths of the

Albemarle Peninsula. While species like black bears and foxes can migrate inland, red wolves face a continent's worth of coyotes to their west, north, and south. Red wolves that stay on the peninsula will be squeezed within the recovery area as the coastal habitat around them degrades. They will have nowhere left to run. Since it is unlikely that red wolves will evolve blowholes or fins by the century's close, they will need additional reintroduction sites in the coming decades. Additional recovery sites will reduce the single wild population's vulnerability to natural disaster. Boutin's project may benefit red wolves by helping to hold their recovery area habitat together for a little while longer. But it's clear that plans need to be made now to figure out where a second and third recovery area—called for in the red wolf's recovery plan—will be sited. David Rabon says he is highly interested in finding new reintroduction sites and conservation partners. How or where this might play out is yet to be seen.

Up until now, the red wolf program has focused exclusively on a kind of triage biology, determining if red wolves can be reintroduced and if they can be managed to prevent hybridization. The answer to both questions appears to be "yes," with the caveat that they will always need to be managed.

A large part of me yearns to know that the red wolf will be fully recovered in the future and will reclaim its former southeastern range. But the rational side of my brain realizes that this is only a fantasy: the red wolf is too conservationally challenged to ever be recovered to such a degree. Its former habitat has changed fundamentally in ways that render major parts of its historic range unsuitable for its survival. And the little patch of land it now occupies ranks high among landscapes most threatened by sea-level rise on our Atlantic coast.

There are those in the Fish and Wildlife Service who believe that red wolves will never be unmanaged, and I agree. To maintain wild red wolves into the future with their present genetic diversity will always require human hands. This is, to a certain extent, a sad realization. At times, it has conjured images in my mind of an entire species on artificial life support. In this regard, the story of the red wolf is a cautionary tale of what happens when we push a species too far into the twilight of extinction.

Yet the permanent management of red wolves also prompts a realization tinged with hope: we *have* the tools and the knowledge to preserve them. All that is needed is the funding and the political will.

Yet the question remains: what will happen to red wolves in the future? This creature has such a storied and complicated past and present; for as much as we know about them—or think we know—there is still so much about their natural history that we've yet to uncover. As research continues to investigate what red wolves may once have been, I hold hope that conservation efforts will continue to preserve what they are today, both in the wild and in captivity. I am deeply intrigued by the concept of red wolves representing a distinct southeastern wolf that was part of a North American–evolved canid lineage leading to coyotes. I can only hope to see the debate over red wolf origins resolved in my lifetime.

I am hopeful, too, that future generations will come to know, understand, and value the red wolf's tremendously complex and inspiring story. I am hopeful that if the sea continues to rise, our society will carve out a new space for this undeniably unique canid. Above all, I am hopeful that future scientists and citizens will see fit to conserve what we have left of *Canis rufus* as a living reminder of both what was and what still can be.

# ACKNOWLEDGMENTS

Throughout the odyssey of this project, I was amazed at how well everything fell into place. People were eager to share information with me, and sources seemed to come into the picture just when the story most needed them. The story of the red wolf was waiting to be told, but it never would have been told so thoroughly without the help of several key people. The good-natured and sincere cooperation of the Red Wolf Recovery Program biologists allowed this book to blossom in a way that I could not have imagined at the start. I thank each of them, and I hope to continue working with them for red wolf conservation in the future. The book may be written, but the work is unfinished.

I especially thank Ryan Nordsven for the enormous amount of time he spent and patience he showed hashing out details of the red wolf biologists' management routines. He recounted numerous anecdotes and demonstrated integrity and dedication in his daily job. Ryan's consistent willingness to work with me went well beyond what his position requires. I am humbly indebted. I also especially thank biologist Chris Lucash for his long-time commitment to the red wolf program and the hours he spent sharing information from his twenty-seven-year career. I thank Art Beyer, red wolf biologist and field team coordinator, for helping to verify facts and figures. David Rabon, the Red Wolf Recovery Program coordinator, also deserves heartfelt thanks for giving me access to freely shadow the program's biologists. Ryan received an advance copy of part I of this book and corrected errors I had inadvertently made regarding pack names, places, and wolf life-history details. David received an advance copy of the semifinal draft and provided valuable feedback on historic and scientific accuracy relevant to the program.

I also thank Sara Hanson Carley, widow of Curtis J. Carley. Her husband was one of the first muddy-boots Fish and Wildlife Service biologists to actively work on recovering the red wolf. She allowed me access to his field notes and records not long after his death in 2010. Hers was the most unexpected of kindnesses. Words cannot express my deep gratitude. She opened a window of information that made the past come to life.

I thank the Albemarle citizens who agreed to speak with me about what it's like to live with red wolves. I also thank Ronald Nowak, Linda Rutledge,

Lisette Waits, Bob Wayne, Susan Jenks, Steve Fain, and Paul Wilson for their time in helping me to understand competing models of red and eastern wolf origins.

I thank Cornelia Hutt, chair of the board of directors for the Red Wolf Coalition and a board member of the International Wolf Center; Cornelia patiently read draft after draft after draft and offered her knowledgeable perspective on various issues.

I also thank Linh, Kristina, and Katharine Nguyen for allowing me use of their guest room in my forays to Albuquerque to learn more about wolves. Their hospitality to a researcher/writer of meager means has been amazingly generous and very much appreciated. Likewise to my cousin Carolyn Vemulapalli in Tucson.

I am also deeply grateful for the support and encouragement of my husband, Matt Ertl. Matt sacrificed his dream of hiking the Appalachian Trail in 2010 so that I could embark on my dream: writing my first book. His support made the production of this work possible. I also thank my parents for supporting me when I announced my intentions to head to graduate school and pursue science writing.

Last, but certainly not least, I give special thanks to my UNC Press acquisitions editor, Mark Simpson-Vos, for taking a chance on an unknown writer, and to Jay Mazzocchi for his patience in editing my work. Hearing "yes" from the Press was not only one of the most euphoric moments of my life, but it also gave the green light for the complete telling of the red wolf's important story.

If you would like to help support
the conservation of wild red wolves, please
visit the website of Friends of the Red Wolf:

WWW.FRIENDSOFREDWOLVES.ORG.

# BIBLIOGRAPHY

The following includes sources used in my research. Not all works were referenced directly in the book, but all shaped my understanding of the red wolf or helped to frame my thoughts on particular points.

## Museums and Archives

Elizabeth City, N.C.
   Museum of the Albemarle
Manteo, N.C.
   Outer Banks History Center
Raleigh, N.C.
   North Carolina State Archives

## Professional Sources

Sue Behrns, red wolf caretaker, Point Defiance Zoo and Aquarium, Tacoma, Wash.
Arthur Beyer, biologist and field team coordinator, Red Wolf Recovery Program
Justin Bohling, Ph.D. candidate (now graduated), University of Idaho
Brian Boutin, climate-change adaptation director, the Nature Conservancy
Curtis Carley (deceased; past red wolf field project coordinator), personal archives (1973–2005)
Sarah Carley, widow of Curtis Carley
Steven Chambers, senior scientist, U.S. Fish and Wildlife Service Division of Ecological Services, Albuquerque, N. Mex.
Kelly Davis, citizen, Hyde County, N.C.
John Dorsett, former red wolf field team member
Steve Fain, geneticist, U.S. Fish and Wildlife Service Forensic Laboratory
Camilla Fox, president, Project Coyote
Joey Hinton, Ph.D. candidate, University of Georgia
Aaron Jenkins, postdoctoral researcher in environmental economics, Duke University
Susan Jenks, professor of psychology and biology, The Sage Colleges, Troy, N.Y.
Mike Johnson, commissioner, Dare County, N.C.
Melissa Karlin, Ph.D., University of North Carolina at Charlotte
Roland Kays, biodiversity and earth observation lab director, N.C. Museum of Natural Sciences
Chris Lucash, biologist, Red Wolf Recovery Program
Ford Mauney, biologist, Red Wolf Recovery Program
Ryan Nordsven, field technician, Red Wolf Recovery Program
Ronald Nowak, mammalian biologist, retired from U.S. Fish and Wildlife Service

Warren Parker (deceased), former red wolf recovery program coordinator
David Rabon, coordinator, Red Wolf Recovery Program
Troy Respess, citizen, Beaufort and Hyde Counties, N.C.
Stanley Riggs, coastal geologist, East Carolina University
Linda Rutledge, postdoctoral researcher with the Natural Resources DNA
    Profiling and Forensic Centre at Trent University
Sherry Samuels, animal caretaker, Museum of Life and Science, Durham, N.C.
Jamin Simmons, citizen, Hyde County, N.C.
Wendy Stanton, biologist, Pocosin Lakes National Wildlife Refuge
Dennis Stewart, biologist, Alligator River National Wildlife Refuge
Michael Stoskopf, chair of Red Wolf Recovery Implementation Team and
    professor at N.C. State University College of Veterinary Medicine
Perry Sumner, wildlife management section manager, N.C. Wildlife Resources
    Commission
Will Waddell, director, Red Wolf Species Survival Plan
Lisette Waits, wildlife geneticist, University of Idaho
Xiaoming Wang, vertebrate paleontology curator, Natural History Museum of
    Los Angeles
Robert Wayne, population geneticist, University of California, Los Angeles
Kim Wheeler, executive director, Red Wolf Coalition
Nancy White, executive director, UNC Coastal Institute Studies
Paul Wilson, biology professor, Trent University

## Books, Articles, and Dissertations

Adams, Jennifer. "A Multi-Faceted Molecular Approach to Red Wolf (*Canis Rufus*)
    Conservation and Management." Ph.D. diss., University of Idaho, 2006.
Adams, Jennifer, Brian Kelly, and Lisette Waits. "Using Faecal DNA Sampling and
    GIS to Monitor Hybridization between Red Wolves (*Canis Rufus*) and Coyotes
    (*Canis Latrans*)." *Molecular Ecology* 12, no. 8 (2003): 2175–86.
Adams, Jennifer, Chris Lucash, Leslie Schutte, and Lisette Waits. "Locating
    Hybrid Individuals in the Red Wolf (*Canis Rufus*) Experimental Population Area
    Using a Spatially Targeted Sampling Strategy and Faecal DNA Genotyping."
    *Molecular Ecology* 16, no. 9 (2007): 1823–34.
Adams, Jennifer, and Lisette Waits. "An Efficient Method for Screening Faecal
    DNA Genotypes and Detecting New Individuals and Hybrids in the Red Wolf
    (*Canis rufus*) Experimental Population Area." *Conservation Genetics* 8, no. 1 (2007):
    123–31.
Allendorf, Fred W., Robb Leary, Paul Spruell, and Jon Wenburg. "The Problems
    with Hybrids." *Trends in Ecology and Evolution* 16, no. 11 (2001): 613–22.
American Association of Zoological Parks and Aquariums. "Annual Conference
    Proceedings." Milwaukee, Wisc., September 25–29, 1988.
American Zoo and Aquarium Association. "Red Wolf Fact Sheet." 2000.
Bailey, Vernon. "Biological Survey of Texas." *North American Fauna* 25 (1905): 9–222.
Banks, Vic. "Red Wolf Gets a Second Chance to Live by Its Wits." *Smithsonian* 18,
    no. 2 (1988): 101–6.

Barcott, Bruce. "Grolar Bears and Narlugas: Rise of the Arctic Hybrids." *OnEarth*, December 15, 2010.

Bartram, William. *Travels through North and South Carolina, Georgia, East and West Florida.* Savannah, Ga.: Beehive Press, 1973. First printing, London, 1791.

Beck, Karen. "Epidemiology of Coyote Introgression into the Red Wolf Genome." Ph.D. diss., North Carolina State University, 2005.

Beck, Karen B., Christopher F. Lucash, and Michael K. Stoskopf. "Lack of Impact of Den Interference on Neonatal Red Wolves." *Southeastern Naturalist* 8, no. 4 (2009): 631–38.

Bohling, Justin. "Exploring Patterns and Mechanisms of Red Wolf (*Canis Rufus*) Hybridization in North Carolina." Ph.D. diss., University of Idaho, 2011.

Bohling, Justin, and Lisette Waits. "Assessing the Prevalence of Hybridization between Sympatric *Canis* Species Surrounding the Red Wolf (*Canis Rufus*) Recovery Area in North Carolina." *Molecular Ecology* 20 (2011): 2142–56.

Brickell, John. *The Natural History of North Carolina.* Murfreesboro, N.C.: Johnson Reprint Corp., 1969.

Bromley, Cassity, and Eric Gese. "Effects of Sterilization on Territory Fidelity and Maintenance, Pair Bonds, and Survival Rates of Free-Ranging Coyotes." *Canadian Journal of Zoology* 79, no. 3 (2001): 386–92.

Brownlow, Alexander. "Molecular Taxonomy and the Conservation of the Red Wolf and Other Endangered Carnivores." *Conservation Biology* 10, no. 2 (1996): 390–96.

Camuto, Christopher. *Another Country: Journeying toward the Cherokee Mountains.* New York: Henry Holt and Company, Inc., 1997.

Carley, Curtis. "Discussion and Recommendations on the Experimental Translocation of a Pair of Red Wolves (*Canis Rufus*) to Bulls Island, Cape Romain National Wildlife Refuge, S.C." Edited by Southwest Region Department of Interior, U.S. Fish and Wildlife Service, Albuquerque, N.Mex. 1977.

———. Red Wolf Recovery Program Field Records for Canids Questioned by Will Waddell and Gary Henry. Document from Will Waddell's archives, September 20, 2000.

———. "The Red Wolf (*Canis Rufus*) Recovery Program: Things They Didn't Tell Me in School." In *Reflections of a Naturalist: Papers Honoring Professor Eugene D. Fleharty,* edited by J. R. Choate, 125–41. Hays, Kans.: Fort Hays State University, 2000.

———. "Report on the Successful Translocation Experiment of Red Wolves to Bulls Island, South Carolina." Presented at the Portland Wolf Symposium, Lewis and Clark College, Portland, Ore., August 13–17, 1979.

———. "Status Summary: The Red Wolf (*Canis Rufus*). Endangered Species Report 7." Albuquerque, N.Mex.: U.S. Fish and Wildlife Service, 1979.

Carroll, Sean B. "Hybrids May Thrive Where Parents Fear to Tread." *New York Times,* September 13, 2010.

Chadwick, John, Bud Fazio, and Melissa Karlin. "Effectiveness of GPS-Based Telemetry to Determine Temporal Changes in Habitat Use and Home-Range Sizes of Red Wolves." *Southeastern Naturalist* 9, no. 2 (2010): 303–16.

Chambers, Steven M., Steven R. Fain, Bud Fazio, and Michael Amaral. "An Account of the Taxonomy of North American Wolves from Morphological and Genetic Analyses." *North American Fauna* 77 (2012): 1–67.

Coleman, Jon. *Vicious: Wolves and Men in America*. New Haven, Conn.: Yale University Press, 2004.

Corbett, D. Reide, J. P. Walsh, Lisa Cowart, Stanley R. Riggs, Dorothea V. Ames, and Stephen J. Culver. "Shoreline Change within the Albemarle-Pamlico Estuarine System, North Carolina." Greenville, N.C.: East Carolina University Institute for Coastal Science and Policy, 2009.

Cronin, Matthew. "In My Experience: Mitochondrial DNA in Wildlife Taxonomy and Conservation Biology: Cautionary Notes." *Wildlife Society Bulletin* 21, no. 3 (1993): 339–48.

Cronon, William. *Changes in the Land: Indians, Colonists, and the Ecology of New England*. New York: Hill and Wang, 1983.

Crooks, Kevin R., and Michael Soulé. "Mesopredator Release and Avifaunal Extinctions in a Fragmented System." *Nature* 400 (1999): 563–66.

Custer, Jay W., and Danny B. Pence. "Ecological Analysis of Helminth Populations of Wild Canids from the Gulf Coastal Prairies of Texas and Louisiana." *Journal of Parasitology* 67, no. 3 (1981): 289–307.

DeBlieu, Jan. "The Wolves of Alligator River." In *Meant to Be Wild: The Struggle to Save Endangered Species through Captive Breeding*. Golden, Colo.: Fulcrum Publishing, 1991.

———. "Could the Red Wolf Be a Mutt?" *New York Times Magazine*, June 14, 1992, 30–31, 42–46.

Dowling, Thomas E., W. L. Minckley, Michael E. Douglas, Paul C. Marsh, and Bruce Demarais. "Response to Wayne, Nowak, and Philips and Henry: Use of Molecular Characters in Conservation Biology." *Conservation Biology* 6, no. 4 (1992): 600–603.

Drye, Wille. "Vast Peat Fire May Burn for Months in North Carolina." *National Geographic News*, June 13, 2008.

Dunlap, Thomas. *Saving America's Wildlife*. Princeton, N.J.: Princeton University Press, 1988.

Ferrel, Robert, Donald C. Morizot, Jacqueline Horn, and Curtis J. Carley. "Biochemical Markers in a Species Endangered by Introgression: The Red Wolf." *Biochemical Genetics* 18, nos. 1–2 (1980): 39–49.

Flood, Joseph, and Christopher Parker. "Stakeholder Meeting on Red Wolf Ecotourism in North Carolina." Unpublished white paper, 2006.

Fogleman, Valerie. "American Attitudes toward Wolves: A History of Misperception." *Environmental Review* 13, no. 1 (1989): 63–94.

Fritts, S. H., R. O. Stephenson, R. D. Hayes, L. Boitani. "Wolves and Humans." In *Wolves: Behavior, Ecology, and Conservation*, edited by L. David Mech and Luigi Boitani, 289–316. Chicago: University of Chicago Press, 2003.

Fuller, Todd, and Lloyd Keith. "Non-Overlapping Ranges of Coyotes and Wolves in Northeastern Alberta." *Journal of Mammalogy* 62, no. 2 (1981): 403–5.

Gale, Christopher. "Christopher Gale, Major, Personal Letter." In *The Colonial*

Records of North Carolina, edited by William L. Saunders. Wilmington, N.C.: Broadfoot Publishing Company, 1993.

Goldman, Edward A. "Part II: Classification of Wolves." In The Wolves of North America, edited by Stanley P. Young and Edward A. Goldman. Washington, D.C.: American Wildlife Institution, 1944.

———. "The Wolves of North America." Journal of Mammalogy 18, no. 1 (1937): 37–45.

Hammer, Michael F., August E. Woerner, Fernando L. Mendez, Joseph C. Watkins, and Jeffrey D. Wall. "Genetic Evidence for Archaic Admixture in Africa." Proceedings of the National Academy of Sciences USA 108, no. 37 (2011): 15123–28.

Hoagland, Edward. "Lament the Red Wolf." In Red Wolves and Black Bears. New York: Lyons and Burford, 1972.

Holt, Craig. "Howl." North Carolina Sportsman, March 12, 2007.

International Union for the Conservation of Nature. "IUCN Red List." International Union for the Conservation of Nature, 2009.

James, Erin. "Feds Investigate Killings of Endangered N.C. Red Wolves." Virginian-Pilot, October 15, 2010.

Karlin, Melissa, and John Chadwick. "Red Wolf Natal Dispersal Characteristics: Comparing Periods of Population Increase and Stability." Journal of Zoology 286, no. 4 (2011): 266–76.

Kays, Roland, Abigail Curtis, and Jeremy Kirchman. "Rapid Adaptive Evolution of Northeastern Coyotes via Hybridization with Wolves." Biology Letters 6, no. 1 (2010): 89–93.

———. "Reply to Wheeldon et al.: 'Colonization History and Ancestry of Northeastern Coyotes.'" Biology Letters 6, no. 2 (2010): 248–49.

Kellert, Stephen R. "Public Perceptions of Predators, Particularly the Wolf and Coyote." Biological Conservation 31 (1985): 167–89.

Kellert, Stephen R., Matthew Black, Colleen R. Rush, and Alistair J. Bath. "Human Culture and Large Carnivore Conservation in North America." Conservation Biology 10 (1996): 977–90.

Kramer, Randall, and Aaron Jenkins. "Ecosystem Services, Markets, and Red Wolf Habitat: Results from a Farm Operator Survey." Unpublished white paper, 2009.

Kyle, C. J., A. R. Johnson, B. R. Patterson, P. J. Wilson, K. Shami, S. K. Grewal, and B. N. White. "Genetic Nature of Eastern Wolves: Past, Present, and Future." Conservation Genetics 7 (2006): 273–87.

Kyle, C. J., A. R. Johnson, B. R. Patterson, P. J. Wilson, and B. N. White. "The Conspecific Nature of Eastern and Red Wolves: Conservation and Management Implications." Conservation Genetics 9 (2008): 699–701.

Lanfear, Robert, John Welch, and Lindell Bromham. "Watching the Clock: Studying Variation in Rates of Molecular Evolution between Species." Trends in Ecology and Evolution 25, no. 9 (2010): 495–503.

Lash, Gail Y. B., and Pamela Black. "Red Wolves: Creating Economic Opportunity through Ecotourism in Rural North Carolina." Unpublished white paper, 2005.

Lawson, John. A New Voyage to Carolina. Edited by Hugh Talmage Lefler. Chapel Hill: University of North Carolina Press, 1967.

"Letter from a Carolina Planter: North Carolina Gazette, Nov. 28 1777." In *The State Records of North Carolina*, edited by Walter Clark. Winston and Goldsboro: State of North Carolina, 1993.

Lewis, M. A., and J. D. Murray. "Modeling Territoriality and Wolf-Deer Interactions." *Nature* 366 (1993): 738–40.

Lugo, Ariel E., Edward C. Fritz, Gerald Kuchling, Thomas E. Dowling, Bruce DeMarais, W. L. Minckley, Michael E. Douglas, and Paul C. Marsh. "Letters: Use of Genetic Characters in Conservation Biology." *Conservation Biology* 6, no. 1 (1992): 7–8.

Mallett, James. "Hybridization as an Invasion of the Genome." *Trends in Ecology and Evolution* 20, no. 5 (2005): 229–37.

Manganiello, Christopher. "From a Howling Wilderness to Howling Safaris: Science, Policy, and Red Wolves in the American South." *Journal of the History of Biology* 42 (2009): 325–59.

McCarley, Howard. "The Taxonomic Status of Wild Canis (Canidae) in the South Central United States." *Southwestern Naturalist* 7, nos. 3–4 (1962): 227–35.

———. "Vocalizations of Red Wolves (*Canis Rufus*)." *Journal of Mammalogy* 59, no. 1 (1978): 27–35.

McCarley, Howard, and Curtis J. Carley. "Recent Changes in Distribution and Status of Wild Red Wolves (*Canis Rufus*)." Albuquerque, N.Mex.: U.S. Fish and Wildlife Service, 1979.

McIntyre, Rick. *The War against the Wolf: America's Campaign to Exterminate the Wolf.* Osceola, Wisc.: Voyageur Press, 1995.

Mech, L. David. "Non-Genetic Data Supporting Genetic Evidence for the Eastern Wolf." *Northeastern Naturalist* 18, no. 4 (2011): 521–26.

———. "Whatever Happened to the Term Alpha Wolf?" *International Wolf* (Winter 2008): 4–8.

———. "What Is the Taxonomic Identity of Minnesota's Wolves?" *Canadian Journal of Zoology* 88 (2010): 129–38.

Mech, L. David, Richard C. Chapman, William W. Cochran, Lee Simmons, and Ulysses Seal. "Radio-Triggered Anesthetic-Dart Collar for Recapturing Large Mammals." *Wildlife Society Bulletin* 12, no. 1 (1984): 69–74.

Mech, L. David, and Ronald M. Nowak. "Systematic Status of Wild Canis in North-Central Texas." *Southeastern Naturalist* 9, no. 3 (2010): 587–94.

Miller, Craig, Jennifer Adams, and Lisette Waits. "Pedigree-Based Assignment Tests for Reversing Coyote (*Canis Latrans*) Introgression into the Wild Red Wolf (*Canis Rufus*) Population." *Molecular Ecology* 12, no. 12 (2003): 3287–301.

Mills, L. Scott, Michael E. Soulé, and Daniel Doak. "The Keystone Species Concept in Ecology and Conservation." *BioScience* 43, no. 4 (1993): 219–24.

Nature Conservancy. "Climate Change Adaptation on the Albemarle Peninsula." Edited by the Nature Conservancy, 2010.

North Carolina General Assembly. "An Act to Prohibit the Placing of Live Foxes or Coyotes in Enclosed Areas for the Purposes of Field Trials or the Training of Dogs." Senate Bill 515, sess., March 11, 2009.

———. "Chapter 9: An Act for Destroying Vermin in This Province." In *The*

State Records of North Carolina, vol. 23, edited by Walter Clark. Winston and
Goldsboro: State of North Carolina, 1993.

———. "Chapter 6: An Act to Amend an Act (1748)." In The State Records of North
Carolina, vol. 25, edited by Walter Clark, 312. Winston and Goldsboro: State of
North Carolina, 1993.

———. "Chapter 6: An Act for Destroying Vermin in This Province." In The State
Records of North Carolina, vol. 23, edited by Walter Clark, 288. Winston and
Goldsboro: State of North Carolina, 1993.

———. "Chapter 16: An Act to Encourage Destroying Vermin in the Several
Counties Therein Mentioned." In The State Records of North Carolina, vol. 23, edited
by Walter Clark. Winston and Goldsboro: State of North Carolina, 1993.

———. "Chapter 3: An Act to Encourage the Destroying of Vermin in the Several
Counties Mentioned Within." In The State Records of North Carolina, vol. 23, edited
by Walter Clark, 784. Winston and Goldsboro: State of North Carolina, 1993.

———. "Chapter 3: An Act to Encourage the Destroying of Vermin in This
Province." In The State Records of North Carolina, vol., 23, edited by Walter Clark,
784. Winston and Goldsboro: State of North Carolina, 1993.

———. "Chapter 3: An Act for Destroying Wolves, Wildcats, Panthers, Bears,
Crows, and Squirrels in the Several Counties Therein Mentioned." In The State
Records of North Carolina, vol. 24, edited by Walter Clark, 749. Winston and
Goldsboro: State of North Carolina, 1993.

———. "Chapter 24: An Act to Encourage the Destroying of Vermin in the
Several Counties of This State." In The State Record of North Carolina, vol. 24,
edited by Walter Clark, 133. Winston and Goldsboro: State of North Carolina,
1993.

Nowak, Ronald M. "Hybridization: The Double-Edged Threat." Canid News, IUCN
Canid Specialist Group 3 (1995): 2–6. Accessed online at http://www.canids.org/
PUBLICAT/CNDNEWS3/hybridiz.htm. June 10, 2010.

———. "Louisiana Protects Wolf, Cougar, and All Birds of Prey." Defenders of
Wildlife News, Fall 1971, 278

———. "The Mysterious Wolf of the South." Natural History 81 (1972): 50–53,
74–77.

———. "North American Quaternary Canis." Monograph no. 6, 1–154. Lawrence,
Kans.: Museum of Natural History, University of Kansas, 1979.

———. "The Original Status of Wolves in Eastern North America." Southeastern
Naturalist 1, no. 2 (2002): 95–130.

———. "Red Wolf: Our Most Endangered Mammal." National Parks and
Conservation, August 1974, 9–12.

———. "The Red Wolf in Louisiana." Defenders of Wildlife News 42, no. 1 (1967):
60–70.

———. "The Red Wolf Is Not a Hybrid." Conservation Biology 6, no. 4 (1992): 593–
95.

———. "Wolf Evolution and Taxonomy." Chap. 9 in Wolves: Behavior, Ecology, and
Conservation, edited by L. David Mech and Luigi Boitani, 239–58. Chicago:
University of Chicago Press, 2003.

Nowak, R. M., and N. E. Federoff. "Validity of the Red Wolf: Response to Roy et al." *Conservation Biology* 12, no. 3 (1998): 722–25.

Paradiso, John, and Ronald M. Nowak. "A Report on the Taxonomic Status and Distribution of the Red Wolf." Washington, D.C.: U.S. Fish and Wildlife Service, 1971.

Parker, Warren T. "A Plan for Reestablishing the Red Wolf on Alligator River National Wildlife Refuge, North Carolina." Asheville, N.C.: U.S. Fish and Wildlife Service, 1987.

Parker, Warren T., and Michael K. Phillips. "Application of the Experimental Population Designation to Recovery of Endangered Red Wolves." *Wildlife Society Bulletin* 19, no. 1 (1991): 73–79.

Pence, Danny B., Jay W. Custer, and Curtis J. Carley. "Ectoparasites of Wild Canids from the Gulf Coastal Prairies of Texas and Louisiana." *Journal of Medical Entomology* 18, no. 5 (1981): 409–12.

Phillips, Michael K. "Conserving the Red Wolf." *Canid News, IUCN Canid Specialist Group* no. 3 (1995): 13–35. Accessed online at http://www.canids.org/PUBLICAT/CNDNEWS3/consredw.htm. June 10, 2010.

———. "Measures of the Value and Success of a Reintroduction Project: Red Wolf Reintroduction in Alligator River National Wildlife Refuge." *Endangered Species Update* 8, no. 1 (1990): 24–26.

Phillips, Michael K., and Gary Henry. "Comments on Red Wolf Taxonomy." *Conservation Biology* 6, no. 4 (1992): 596–99.

Phillips, Michael K., Brian Kelly, and Gary Henry. "Restoration of the Red Wolf." In *Wolves: Behavior, Ecology, and Conservation*, edited by L. David Mech and Luigi Boitani, 272–88. Chicago: University of Chicago Press, 2003.

Phillips, Michael K., and Warren T. Parker. "Red Wolf Recovery: A Progress Report." *Conservation Biology* 2, no. 2 (1988): 139–41.

Plott, Bob. *A History of Hunting in the Great Smoky Mountains*. Charleston, S.C.: The History Press, 2008.

Point Defiance Zoo and Aquarium. "Red Wolf Newsletter Collection." Tacoma, Wash.: Point Defiance Zoo and Aquarium, 1988–99.

Powell, William S. "Creatures of North Carolina from Roanoke Island to Purgatory Mountain." *North Carolina Historical Review* 50, no. 2 (1973): 121–68.

Rabon, David R. "Factors Affecting Reproduction in the Red Wolf (*Canis Rufus*)." Ph.D. diss., North Carolina State University, 2009.

Rabon, David R., and William Waddell. "Effects of Inbreeding on Reproductive Success, Performance, Litter Size, and Survival in Captive Red Wolves (*Canis Rufus*)." *Zoo Biology* 29 (2010): 36–49.

Red Wolf Coalition. "The Value of Red Wolf Conservation." Unpublished white paper, 2008.

Red Wolf Recovery Program. "Five-Year Status Review: Red Wolf (*Canis Rufus*)." Alligator River National Wildlife Refuge, Manteo, N.C., 2007.

Reich, D. E., R. K. Wayne, D. B. Goldstein. "Genetic Evidence for a Recent Origin by Hybridization of Red Wolves." *Molecular Ecology* 8 (1999): 139–44.

Rennie, John. "Howls of Dismay." *Scientific American* 265, no. 4 (1991): 18–20.

Riggs, Stanley, and Dorothea Ames. "Drowning the N.C. Coast: Sea-Level Rise and Estuarine Dynamics." Edited by Ann Green, 152. Raleigh: North Carolina Department of Environmental and Natural Resources, 2003.

Riggs, S. R., S. J. Culver, D. V. Ames, D. J. Mallison, D. R. Corbett, and J. P. Walsh. "North Carolina's Coasts in Crisis: A Vision for the Future." Greenville, N.C.: East Carolina University, 2008.

Riley, Glynn A., and Roy McBride. "A Survey of the Red Wolf (Canis Rufus)." Washington, D.C.: U.S. Fish and Wildlife Service, 1972.

Rogers, Lynn L., L. David Mech, Deanna K. Dawson, James M. Peek, Mark Korb. "Deer Distribution in Relation to Wolf Pack Territory Edges." Journal of Wildlife Management 44, no. 1 (1980): 253–58.

Rowland, Buford. "Some Observations on the Low Parts of North Carolina." North Carolina Historical Review 15 (1938): 156–57.

Roy, Michael S., Eli Geffen, Deborah Smith, and Robert K. Wayne. "Molecular Genetics of Pre-1940 Red Wolves." Conservation Biology 10, no. 5 (1996): 1413–24.

Rutledge, Linda Y., Kirsten I. Bos, Robert J. Pearce, and Bradley N. White. "Genetic and Morphometric Analysis of Sixteenth-Century Canis Skull Fragments: Implications for Historic Eastern and Gray Wolf Distribution in North America." Conservation Genetics 11, no. 4 (2010): 1273–81.

Schlyer, Krista. "Refuges at Risk: The Threat of Global Warming; America's Ten Most-Endangered Wildlife Refuges." Unpublished white paper, 2006.

Simmons, Morgan. "Cameramen Capture Wolves' Attack on Cub." Knoxville News-Sentinel, March 7, 1993.

Skogen, Ketil, and Olve Krange. "A Wolf at the Gate: The Anti-Carnivore Alliance and the Symbolic Construction of Community." Sociologia Ruralis 43, no. 3 (2003): 309–25.

Snyder, Noel F., Scott R. Derrickson, Steven R. Beissinger, James W. Wiley, Thomas B. Smith, William D. Toone, and Brian Miller. "Limitations of Captive Breeding in Endangered Species Recovery." Conservation Biology 10, no. 2 (1996): 338–48.

Soulé, Michael, James Estes, Joel Berger, and Carlos Martinez Del Rio. "Ecological Effectiveness: Conservation Goals for Interactive Species." Conservation Biology 17, no. 5 (2003): 1238–50.

Soulé, Michael, James Estes, Brian Miller, and Douglas Honnold. "Strongly Interacting Species: Conservation Policy, Management, and Ethics." BioScience 55, no. 2 (2005): 168–76.

Sparkman, Amanda, Lisette Waits, and Dennis L. Murray. "Social and Demographic Effects of Anthropogenic Mortality: A Test of the Compensatory Mortality Hypothesis in the Red Wolf." PLoS-ONE 6, no. 6 (2011).

Stolzenburg, William. "Ecosystems Unraveling." Conservation Magazine 9, no. 1 (2008): 20–25.

Stoskopf, Michael K., Karen B. Beck, Bud B. Fazio, Todd K. Fuller, Lloyd B. Keith, and others. "Implementing Recovery of the Red Wolf: Integrating Research Scientists and Managers." Wildlife Society Bulletin 33, no. 3 (2005): 1145–52.

Tilley, Nannie May. "The Settlement of Granville County." *North Carolina Historical Review* 11 (1934): 1–19.

U.S. Department of the Interior. "Native Fish and Wildlife Endangered Species." *Federal Register* 32, no. 48 (1967).

U.S. Fish and Wildlife Service. "The Endangered Red Wolf Program Report." 2008.

———. "Evans Road Fire on Pocosin Lakes National Wildlife Refuge Officially Declared 'Out.'" Columbia, N.C.: U.S. Fish and Wildlife Service, 2009.

———. "Final Rule: Determination of Experimental Population Status for an Introduced Population of Red Wolves in North Carolina." In "50 CFR Part 17," U.S. Fish and Wildlife Service 41790–97. *Federal Register* 51, no. 223 (1986).

———. "Final Rule: Determination of Experimental Population Status for an Introduced Population of Red Wolves in North Carolina and Tennessee." In "50 CFR Part 17," U.S. Fish and Wildlife Service 56325–34. *Federal Register* 56, no. 213 (1991).

———. "Ninety-Day Finding for a Petition to Delist the Red Wolf." In "50 CFR Part 17," U.S. Fish and Wildlife Service 64799–800. *Federal Register* 62, no. 236 (1997).

———. "Red Wolf Journal, Collection." 2007–9.

———. "Red Wolf News, Collection." 1999–2004.

———. "Red Wolf Recovery Program: First Quarter Report, October–December 2009." Manteo, N.C.: U.S. Fish and Wildlife Service, 2009.

———. "Red Wolf Recovery Program: Second Quarter Report, January–March 2010." Manteo, N.C.: U.S. Fish and Wildlife Service, 2010.

———. "Red Wolf Recovery Program: Third Quarter Report, April–June 2011." Manteo, N.C.: U.S. Fish and Wildlife Service, 2011.

———. "Red Wolf Recovery Program: Third Quarter Report, April–June 2010." Manteo, N.C.: U.S. Fish and Wildlife Service, 2010.

———. "Red Wolf Recovery/Species Survival Plan." 1990.

———. "U.S. Fish and Wildlife Service, National Parks Service End Effort to Establish Endangered Red Wolves in Great Smoky Mountains National Park." Press release, 1998.

Updike, Bill. "Wolf Song of the South." *Defenders* (Spring 2005).

Venters, Vic. "Return of the Red Wolf." *Wildlife in North Carolina* (1989): 19–23.

VonHoldt, Bridgett M., John P. Pollinger, Dent A. Earl, Robert K. Wayne, et al. "A Genome-Wide Perspective on the Evolutionary History of Enigmatic Wolf-Like Canids." *Genome Research* 21, no. 8 (2011): 1294–305.

Wang, Xiaoming, Richard H. Tedford, and Mauricio Anton. *Dogs: Their Fossil Relatives and Evolutionary Origins*. New York: Columbia University Press, 2008.

Wayne, Robert K. "On the Use of Morphologic and Molecular Genetic Characters to Investigate Species Status." *Conservation Biology* 6, no. 4 (1992): 590–92.

Wayne, Robert K., and John Gittleman. "The Problematic Red Wolf." *Scientific American* 273, no. 1 (1995): 36–39.

Wayne, Robert K., and S. M. Jenks. "Mitochondrial DNA Analysis Implying Extensive Hybridization of the Endangered Red Wolf *Canis Rufus*." *Nature* 351 (1991): 565–68.

Wayne, Robert K., Michael S. Roy, and John Gittleman. "Origin of the Red Wolf: Response to Nowak and Federoff and Gardener." *Conservation Biology* 12, no. 3 (1998): 726–29.

Weaver, Jefferson. "Bill to Ban Fox Pens Advances to Committee." *Whiteville News Reporter*, March 17, 2009.

Wilson, Paul J., Sonya Grewal, Ian D. Lawford, Jennifer N. M. Heal, Angela G. Granacki, and others. "DNA Profiles of the Eastern Canadian Wolf and the Red Wolf Provide Evidence for a Common Evolutionary History Independent of the Gray Wolf." *Canadian Journal of Zoology* 78 (2000): 2156–66.

Wilson, Paul J., Sonya K. Grewal, Frank F. Mallory, and Bradley N. White. "Genetic Characterization of Hybrid Wolves across Ontario." *Journal of Heredity* 100 (2009): S80–89.

Wilson, Paul J., S. Grewal, T. McFadden, R. C. Chambers, and B. N. White. "Mitochondrial DNA Extracted from Eastern North American Wolves Killed in the 1800s Is Not of Gray Wolf Origin." *Canadian Journal of Zoology* 81 (2003): 936–40.

Yoon, Carol Kaesuk. "DNA Clues Improve the Outlook for Red Wolf." *New York Times*, December 26, 2000.

# INDEX

NWR in index refers to National Wildlife Refuge and RWRA refers to Red Wolf Recovery Area.

Bachman, John, 135
Bailey, Vernon, 135
Bartram, William, 126–27
*Battle for North Carolina's Coast, The* (Riggs et al.), 216–17
Bears. *See* Black bears
Beaufort County, N.C., 67, 71, 182
Beaumont, Texas, Red Wolf Recovery Project: and aerial photographs of region, 143; animal damage complaints to, 145, 148, 149; buffer-zone plan for, 143, 147, 148; and captive breeding, 150–52; Carley at, 143–64; Carley's work schedule at, 145–46; censusing techniques used by, 144–48, 151–52; closing of, 156, 163; and criteria for identification of red wolves, 151; founding of, 143; goals of, 150–51; howling surveys by, 143–48, 151–52; identification cards from, for tracking red wolves, 146–47; and illnesses of wolves, 149–50; staff of, 144, 145; telemetry studies by, 149; trapping by, 144–48; and veterinary care of wolves, 150
Beck, Karen, 36
Behrns, Sue, 201–3
Bertie County, N.C., 90
Beyer, Art, xiii, 38, 56–59, 64, 70–71, 80
Biological Survey, U.S., 107, 135, 136
Birds: in Albemarle Peninsula, 9, 16–17, 23, 30, 45, 53, 74, 75; and Atlantic Flyway, 9; in Bulls Island, S.C., 159–60; in colonial America, 126; endangered birds, 106; extinct birds, 85, 126; hunting of waterfowl, 81; in Louisiana, 106; migratory waterfowl, 9, 147; from Pocosin Lakes NWR, 215; quail and quail hunting, 81, 83, 84, 85
Black bears: on Albemarle Peninsula generally, 9; in colonial America, 130; evidence of, 16; folklore on, 89; future of, 226; hibernation of, 73–74; hunting of, 65, 70–71, 87, 133, 134; killing of bear cub by red wolf, 177; from Pocosin Lakes NWR, 215; prey of, 88; research on, 83; sightings of, 46, 48, 79, 83; study of dead black bear by local resident, 81; traps sprung by, 53–54, 74
Black phase red wolf, 135, 137
Blood samples: analysis of, for identification of true red wolves, 69, 185; from

red wolf puppies, 36, 40–41, 42, 98, 185; from trapped red wolves, 58
Bohling, Justin, 69, 70, 208
Bounties for wolves, 128–30, 132–35
Boutin, Brian, 221–26
Breeding pairs: age of female breeders, 29, 69; age of sexual maturity, 29, 47; behavior of, in Sandy Ridge pen, 22, 25; on Bulls Island, S.C., 157–64; copulation of, 190; deaths of one wolf in, 68–70, 174–75, 208; and definition of pack, 21, 46; displacement of male in, by bigger male, 52–53; euthanasia of captive wolves without breeding future, 203; first successful translocation of, in United States, 161–63; gunshot injuries and killings of breeding individuals, 42, 67–70, 100; hybridization events following dissolution of, 68, 69–70, 208; management efforts in creating new pairs, 26–27, 61, 70; mating and gestation period for pregnant females, 29, 79; number of, 27, 42, 70; photograph of, 187; size and number of litters from, 29, 31, 42, 52, 74, 78, 97, 200; temporary nature of, 21; and uterine infection, 9, 161, 175, 201–3. *See also* Captive breeding; Inbreeding; Red wolf packs
Brickell, John, 128, 129
Bryant, Mike, 221–22
Buffer zone, 57, 62, 143–48, 169, 207
Bulls Island, S.C., 125, 157–64, 166, 175, 187, 188
Burke County, N.C., 129

Canada, 115–20, 127
*Canis*, 9, 26, 107–11, 145. *See also* Coyotes; Eastern wolves; Gray wolves; Hybridization; Red wolves
*Canis arnensis*, 109, 110
*Canis ater*, 135
*Canis dirus*, 108, 109
*Canis etruscus*, 109, 110
*Canis floridanus*, 136
*Canis latrans*. *See* Coyotes
*Canis lepophagus*, 108, 109
*Canis lupus*. *See* Gray wolves
*Canis lupus familiaris*, 26
*Canis lupus lycaon*. *See* Eastern wolves
*Canis lupus* var. *Rufus*, 135
*Canis lycaon*. *See* Eastern wolves

tion of red wolves in the wild, 151; and
hybrids, 113; lawsuit for delisting red
wolves from, 176; and nonessential experimental population (NEP) status,
168, 210–11; and Parker, 165–67; passage of, 14, 143; and preceding legislation, 139; and red wolf reintroduction
program of U.S. Fish and Wildlife Service, 165–68; and Tennessee Valley
Authority (TVA), 166–67
Endangered Species Preservation Act
(1966), 139
Engelhard, N.C., 92
Eradication records of red wolves: from
Louisiana Department of Wildlife
Fisheries, 138; from U.S. Biological
Survey, 137
ESA. See Endangered Species Act (ESA)
Euthanasia: of coyotes, 101, 181–82; of
hybrid red wolves, 42, 47, 101, 154,
155, 156, 179, 184; of injured or ill red
wolves, 18, 41, 73, 100; reasons for
euthanasia of hybrid wolves, 47; of
wolves without breeding future, 203
Evolutionary origin theories. See Hybrid-
origin theory; Shared-ancestry theory;
Unique-origin theory

Fain, Steve, 121–22
Fairfield, N.C., 7, 82, 83, 86
Fall: home range of red wolves in, 62; tracking and trapping of red wolves during,
42, 51–64, 100
Farming: on Albemarle Peninsula generally,
5, 8, 9, 12; attitudes of farmers toward
red wolves, 30, 47; benefits of red
wolves to, 47, 65, 83; and black bears,
83; and conservation payments for red
wolves, 90; and coyotes, 13, 63; crops
grown on Albemarle Peninsula, 11, 53,
57, 65, 81; deer's damage to, 65, 83; and
hunting leases, 53, 84; and coyote–red
wolf hybridization, 63; and livestock as
wolves' prey, 77, 128, 132, 133–34, 138,
149; red wolves in farmlands, 12, 62, 63,
100, 149; in Texas, 147, 149
Fear of wolves. See Myths and folklore about
wolves
Fires. See Wildfires
Fish and Wildlife Service, U.S. (FWS): and
Beaumont, Texas, Red Wolf Recovery

Project, 145, 150, 164; and captive breeding of red wolves, 13, 150–56, 200;
Carley's relationship with, 164; and Endangered Species Act (ESA), 165–68;
endangered species section of specimen
laboratory of, 107; and extermination
of wolves, 144, 165; forensics laboratory of, 121–22; and future of red wolf,
206, 207–10, 226; Office of Endangered
Species, 107; and Point Defiance Zoo,
156, 167; on red wolf as functionally extinct in the wild, 13, 151, 156; and red
wolf population in 1960s, 138–40; and
reintroduction of red wolves into the
wild, 157–64, 166–68; Southeast region
of, 148, 165–67; Southwest region of,
148, 150. See also Red Wolf Recovery
Program, Albemarle Peninsula
Florida, 9, 91, 110, 126–27, 135, 136
Folklore. See Myths and folklore about
wolves
Fossil specimens of wolves, 107–11, 122–23
Fostering: criteria for performing, 31; first
use of, 29; of island pups, 175; and
locating den, 30–31, 33–34; neonatal
studies of impacts of, 36; pup acceptance practices, 35–37; statistics on,
29; verifying acceptance of wild female,
31–32
Foxes, 4, 9, 83, 84, 85, 88, 226
Fox pens: legalization of coyote sales to
(2003), 180; as market for live coyotes,
91–92; as market for live foxes, 91; rela-
tionship of, to coyote invasion in North
Carolina, 180; and trapper agreement
with red wolf biologists, 91–93
Francis Marion National Forest, 160, 177
Fritts, Stephen, 90
Frying Pan, N.C., 37
FWS. See Fish and Wildlife Service, U.S.
(FWS); Red Wolf Recovery Program,
Albemarle Peninsula

Genetics: alleles rare to red wolves, 184;
captive breeding and genetic diversity,
200; of coyotes, 113; of gray wolves, 113;
hybridization and backcrossing into red
wolf population, 183–84; hybrid origin of red wolves supported by, 112–15;
mtDNA haplotype unique to red wolf,
112–13, 116–21, 183; Nowak on, regard-

program, 179–86; scientific research on, 208–9; statistics on "purity" of red wolf population, 185; susceptibility to, 208; in Texas, 13, 110, 138, 140–41, 146, 210; as threat to species' recovery, 25, 27, 51, 141, 178–81, 208; Wayne and Jenks on, 112; wolf-hybrid pairs, 42. *See also* Coyotes

Hybrid-origin theory, 105, 111–15, 123, 175–76

Hyde County, N.C., 66, 67, 81–89, 93, 182

ID chips: mechanism of, 31; monitoring uses, 33, 75, 77; scanner for, 33, 56; tagging puppies with, 31–32, 33, 40–41

Illegal killings. *See* Mortality of red wolves

Illinois, 9, 110, 136

Inbreeding: inbreeding coefficient, 200; inbreeding depression, 185, 199, 200, 209; and island propagation sites, 159; and kinship score, 200, 201–2, 205; prevention techniques for generally, 191; and SPARKS (Single Population Analysis and Records Keeping System), 200

Indiana, 9, 110, 136

Infections in red wolves, 9, 149–50, 161, 175, 178, 201–3; heartworm, 149–50, 162; mange, 22–24, 26, 149, 15; pyometra, 201–3; uterine infection, 9, 161, 175, 201–3

Injuries to red wolves, 24, 51, 52, 59, 60, 70, 75–78, 144. *See also* Mortality of red wolves

Interbreeding of red wolves and coyotes. *See* Hybridization of red wolves

International Union for the Conservation of Nature (IUCN), 179, 181

Island propagation: advantages and disadvantages of, 157, 175; Buddy and Margie as first pair to be released to Bulls Island, S.C., 159–61; first experimental releases to Cape Romain NWR, 158–59; Horn Island, Miss., 175; John and Judy as second pair released to Bulls Island, 162–63; pursuit of John, 163; pursuit of Margie, 160–61; reopening of Bulls Island, 175; St. Vincent Island, Fla., 175; South Carolina Wildlife and Marine Resources Department, involvement with, 158

IUCN. *See* International Union for the Conservation of Nature (IUCN)

Jenks, Susan, 112–14, 175–76, 206

Johnson, Mike, 88–90

Kansas, 9, 137

Kansas City Zoological Gardens, 154–55

Karlin, Melissa, 61–63

Kays, Roland, 121

Kelly, Brian, 178–79

Kennels for transporting red wolves, 75–76, 188

Kentucky, 136

Kill Devil Hills, N.C., 221

Killings of red wolves. *See* Bounties for wolves; Mortality of red wolves

Kinship score. *See* Inbreeding

Krange, Olve, 86–87

Lake Mattamuskeet, 30, 37, 52, 57, 81, 82, 83, 84, 220

Lake Phelps, 214

Land Between the Lakes, 166–69, 171, 210

Lawson, John, 125–28, 158

Lederer, John, 124–25

Lincoln Park Zoo, 29–30, 31, 33

Litter sizes of red wolves, 29, 31, 42, 52, 74, 78, 97. *See also* Puppies

Little Rock, Ark., zoological gardens, 155

Livestock, 77, 128, 132, 133–34, 138, 149. *See also* Farming

Long, "Buddy" Aaron, 150, 153–54, 159

Louisiana: captive breeding of wild red wolves captured in, 13, 156, 161; Carley's interest in red wolves in, 148; coloration of wolves in, 4; diet of red wolves in, 82; early records on red wolves from, 132, 135; eradication records of red wolves in, 138; Nowak on red wolves in, xiii, 106–7, 132, 135–39; red wolf skulls found in, 110, 176

Louisiana Department of Wildlife Fisheries, 138

Lucash, Chris: on coyotes, 180–81; on hunters, 66, 70; on hybridization, 179, 180–81; and injured red wolves, 77–78; processing of red wolves by, 57–61, 78, 99; on recapture collars, 174; and reintroduction program, 127, 170–71, 173, 174, 177, 178; and springtime puppy season, 32–41; as staff member of Red Wolf Recovery Program, xii, xiii, 80

*Lupus niger*, 126–27

Plymouth, N.C., 89

Pocosin: definition and ecological description of, 9–10, 11, 168; historic description of, 125; as poor habitat for red wolves, 182; photograph of, 194; and sea-level rise, 218, 219, 222, 223; and wildfires, 213–14

Pocosin Lakes NWR: black bears in, 70, 215; conservation easement near, 32; fire in, 214–15; map location of, 7; pocosin deposits in, 11; red wolves in, 26, 57, 215; size of, 8; staff of, 213–14; wildlife abandonment of, 215

Point Defiance Zoo and Aquarium: captive breeding program of, 150–54, 156, 159, 162, 167, 170, 201–5; and Carley's morphometric criteria for classification of red wolves, 153; contraceptives used in captive breeding program of, 202–3; exhibits on red wolves at, 203–4; howling records from red wolves at, 146; and reintroduction program at Alligator River NWR, 172; satellite facilities of, 52, 201, 202, 204; ultrasound for female wolf with uterine infection, 191, 201–2; and U.S. Fish and Wildlife Service, 156, 167

Point Peter Road, 192, 194, 219–20, 222–24

Poisoning of red wolves. See Mortality of red wolves

Population, reintroduced. See Reintroduction program

Population and Habitat Viability Assessment (PHVA): and establishment of Red Wolf Recovery Implementation Team (RWRIT), 69, 181–86; and hybridization issues, 178–79, 181

Predator reintroduction. See Reintroduction program

Predatory vacuum, 138

Prey: in Alligator River NWR, 168–69, 174; of black bears, 88; on Bulls Island, S.C., 158, 159–60, 163; of coyote hybrids, 207; of coyotes, 88; deer as, 8, 55–56, 82, 84, 87–88, 121, 126, 127, 128, 158, 159, 162–63, 172, 173, 174, 178, 191; of Florida wolves, 127; in Great Smoky Mountains National Park, 178; livestock as, 77, 128, 132, 133–34, 138, 149; nutria as, 47, 84, 85, 147–50, 172; photograph of wolves eating at "kill site," 190; and

territory size, 21; and test of red wolves' ability to hunt before their reintroduction to the wild, 172; in Texas, 147–49; wild animals as, 8, 12. See also Diet of red wolves

Project Coyote, 91

Public education about red wolves, 82, 84, 169, 203–4

Pulliam, Jim, 165–67

Pungo area, 87

Puppies: and birth pulse, 29; births of, by reintroduced red wolves in Alligator River NWR, 174–76; births of, by reintroduced red wolves in Great Smoky Mountains National Park, 177; blood samples from, 36, 40–41, 42, 98, 185; in captive-bred population, 200; deaths of, 78, 174, 175, 177; decline in production of, since 2003, 27; and fear of humans while in captivity, 22; fostering of captive-born red wolves, 29–37, 175; ID chips for, 31–32, 33, 40–41; photographs of, 97, 98; processing methods for, 31–32, 33, 40–41, 42, 98; size and number of litters, 29, 31, 42, 52, 74, 78, 97, 200; in spring, 19, 29–42, 61–62, 97–98; thermoregulation of, 36

Rabon, David: as coordinator of Red Wolf Recovery Program, xii, 28, 80; and illegal killings of red wolves, 66, 70, 73; on need for management of red wolf program, 207–8; and need for new reintroduction sites and conservation partners, 226; on red wolves' NEP (nonessential experimental population) status, 210–11; on reproductive trends in captive-bred population, 199–200

Radio collars. See Telemetry

Recapture collars, 171–75; designed by 3M Corporation, 171–72, 173

Recovery goals, 42, 150–51, 175, 176, 206–7

Red Wolf Coalition, 45–50, 72, 211

Red Wolf Education and Health Care Facility, 56, 99

Red wolf packs: alpha wolf of, 46; definition of, 21, 46; members of, 21, 46–47; Milltail pack, 8–9, 73–78; names of, xiii, 173; New Lake pack, xiii, 31–32, 214; Newlands pack, xiii, 77; Northern pack, 77, 78–79; number of, 42; Phantom

Road pack, 173; Pocosin Lakes pack, 37; Point Peter pack, 173, 174; Pole Road pack, 174–75; size of, 46–47; South Lake pack, 173, 174; stable network of, 28; Swindell pack, 37–41; Timberlake pack, 57; Waupaupin pack, 52, 53, 56–57, 61, 73. *See also* Breeding pairs

Red Wolf Recovery Implementation Team (RWRIT), 69, 181–86

Red Wolf Recovery Program, Albemarle Peninsula: area of, 8; beginnings of, 142–56; "Canid Info" book of, 56; captive breeding program of, 13–14, 29; care of wounded or sick wild red wolves by, 15, 17, 22–25, 26; euthanasia of hybrid red wolves by, 42, 47, 101, 155; fall tracking and trapping by, 42, 51–64; and fostering captive-born red wolves, 29–37, 175; goal of reintroduction program of, 175, 176, 179, 203; and Great Smoky Mountains failure as reintroduction site, 177–78, 179; headquarters of, 15, 16; and hybridization as threat to red wolves, 178; hybridization management by, 20, 47, 179–86, 226; and illegal shootings of red wolves, 27–28; interns in, 17, 52, 60; and investigation of killings of red wolves, 66; last wolves released by, 176–77; locating and documenting dens by, 19, 30–31, 33–34, 37–42; map of, 7; and medication for red wolves, 60–61; North American Conservation Award for, 185; opposition to, by residents, 83–84, 87–90; and origin of red wolves, 123; pedigree database of, 19, 33, 69; population of red wolves on Albemarle Peninsula, 27–28; and private fur trappers, 91–93; processing of puppies by, 40–41, 42, 98; processing of wolves by, after trapping, 57–59, 99; quarterly reports of, 72; and radio collars for red wolves, 51, 56, 57, 59, 61–64; reintroduction program of, 3, 5, 7, 12, 14, 20, 81–82, 167–77, 226; residents' attitudes toward, 81–91; and spring puppy season, 19, 29–42, 61–62, 97–98; staff of generally, xii, 82, 104; sterilization of coyotes by, 20, 61; survey of red wolves by, 18–20; telemetry monitoring by, 18–19, 27, 30–34, 38, 43, 51, 61–63, 79, 98; tranquilizer darts used

by, 14, 171–74, 188, 189; trapping of red wolves by, 42–45, 51–64; unique aspects of, 13–14; use of privately owned and public lands, 8; and vaccination of red wolves, 23–24, 56, 58, 59, 99, 174; and veterinary care, 56, 57, 78; winter trapping by, 42, 61, 65, 73–80. *See also* Alligator River NWR; Sandy Ridge; *and specific staff members*

Red Wolf Recovery Project, Beaumont, Texas. *See* Beaumont, Texas, Red Wolf Recovery Project

Red Wolf Species Survival Plan, 191, 200–205

Red wolves: benefits of, 47, 65, 83, 84–85; conservation payments for in RWRA, 90; cranial measurements of, 152–53, 176; daily activity patterns of, 149; dispersals of, 47, 63; fear of humans by, 22, 24–25, 129; future of, 206, 209–12, 226–27; gait of, 71, 79, 163; injuries to humans from, 86; kennels for transporting, 75–76, 188; life expectancy for, 8, 9, 96; and mistaken identity issues in RWRA, 71–72, 91–93, 154–56, 211; myths and misinformation about, 3, 4, 12–13, 88–89, 169; naming of and scientific name for, 4–5, 26, 135, 137; population of, 7, 27–28, 76; problems faced by generally, 14–15, 27–28; reasons for conservation of, 206; and species problem, 14–15, 26, 138, 145, 205–6; taxonomic description of, 136; vaccination of, 23–24, 56, 58, 59, 99, 150, 174; veterinary care of, 56, 57, 78, 150, 191, 201–2. *See also* Beaumont, Texas, Red Wolf Recovery Project; Breeding pairs; Captive breeding; Captivity of red wolves; Dens; Howling; Hybridization of red wolves; Mortality of red wolves; Physical appearance of red wolves; Red wolf packs; Red Wolf Recovery Program, Albemarle Peninsula; Trapping

Reintroduction program: acclimation pens for, 26, 159, 161–63, 170–71, 174, 175, 188; at Alligator River NWR, 6, 12, 20, 29, 32, 45, 84, 167–77; area of, on Albemarle Peninsula, 8, 176, 178; behavior of wolves around roads and vehicles, 174, 176, 177; and births of puppies, 174–75; and Endangered Species Act,

165–68; first birth of red wolf in the
wild after, 83; first red wolves in Alligator River NWR, 12, 172–74; and Great
Smoky Mountains failure, 177–78, 179;
and growth of red wolf population, 7,
27, 176; and hybridization issues, 179–
86; and Land Between the Lakes failure, 166–69, 171, 210; and monitoring
of wolves' home ranges, 172; mortality
of red wolves in, 174–75, 176; and nonessential experimental population (NEP)
status from Endangered Species Act,
168; number of red wolves released in
Alligator River NWR, 172–74, 176–77;
Parker as red wolf reintroduction project
coordinator, 167–77; plateau of reintroduced population, 27, 73; proportion
of red wolf pairs to red wolf–coyote or
red wolf–hybrid pairs, 42; Rabon on
new sites for, 226; and recapture collars, 171–75; of Red Wolf Recovery Program, Albemarle Peninsula, 3, 5, 7, 12,
14, 20, 81–82, 167–77, 226; and study of
scats of individual red wolves, 172, 174;
telemetry monitoring for, 159, 162–63
Releases from captivity: behavioral issues
with captive-bred wolves, 170–74; to
Bulls Island, Cape Romain NWR, 158–
63; last release by the Red Wolf Recovery
Program, Albemarle Peninsula, 176–77;
number of red wolves released in Alli-
gator River NWR, 172–74, 176–77; re-
ported sightings during first year after,
174. See also Acclimation pens
Remote sensing, 61. See also Telemetry
Reproduction. See Breeding pairs; Captive
breeding; Inbreeding
Resource partitioning, 209
Respess, Troy, 71–72, 87–88, 90
Riggs, Stanley, 216–21, 225
Riley, Glynn, 50
Roadkill, 22–23, 53, 81, 159, 172
Roanoke Island, 15, 16, 219, 220
Roanoke River, 216
Roosevelt, Theodore, 135
Rutledge, Linda, 118, 120–23
RWRIT. See Red Wolf Recovery Implemen-
tation Team (RWRIT)

St. Vincent Island, Fla., 53, 57, 175
Saltwater intrusion, 194, 213, 218–25. See

*also* Climate change in RWRA: and Sea-
level rise
San Antonio Zoological Gardens, 155
Sandy Ridge, 15–28, 43, 48–50, 59–61, 78,
94, 215
Scent posts, 21, 55, 159, 167
Schaefer, Mr. and Mrs. Donald, 152–53
Scourge Town, N.C., 92
Sea-level rise: annual rate of, 217, 218; and
Batts Grave, 220; and canal check valves,
193, 224, 225; and canals and ditches,
219; and ditch plugs, 192, 223, 225; ecological effects of, 213; measurements of
by National Oceanic and Atmospheric
Administration, 217; mitigation strategies to slow, 221–26; and oyster reefs,
224–25; past scenarios of, 216–17, 220;
photographs of, 192–94; predictions
for, 215–16; red wolf range affected by,
215–16, 225–27; and roads, 219, 220;
and saltwater intrusion inland, 219–20;
and shoreline types, 218–19; trees affected by, 218, 219
Sexual maturity, 29, 47. See also Breeding
pairs
Shared-ancestry theory, 105, 115–23
Simmons, Jamin, 83–86, 90
Skogen, Ketil, 86–87
Smith, Roland, 172
Smoky Mountains. See Great Smoky Mountains National Park
Southeastern Endangered Species work-
shop (1974), 149
Spangenberg, August Gottlieb, 128–29
SPARKS (Single Population Analysis and
Records Keeping System), 200
Species concepts: biological species con-
cept, 26; phylogenetic tree, 117; species
problem, 14–15, 26, 138, 145, 205–6;
Spring: heat of, 17, 24, 30, 37; home range
of red wolves in, 61–62; as puppy sea-
son, 19, 29–42, 61–62, 97–98
Stanton, Wendy, 213–14
Stewart, Dennis, 218, 221, 223
*Story of the Plott Hound, The* (Plott), 134–35
Stoskopf, Michael, xiii, 68–69, 179, 181,
184
Stumpy Point, N.C., 168, 213
Summer: heat of, 30, 42, 62; home range
of red wolves in, 62; howling session
for tourists during, 43–50

Sumner, Perry, 180, 209–10
Swain County, N.C., 180

Tacoma Zoological Society, 151–52
Taxonomy of red wolves: Bailey's designation of *Canis rufus* for, 135; Goldman on, 136–37; and scientific name of *Canis lupus* var. *Rufus* by Audubon and Bachman (1851), 135; subspecies named and described, 136–37
Taylor, John, 172–73
Tedford, Richard, 109–10
Telemetry: abdominal radio transmitters, 42, 57, 98; by Beaumont Red Wolf Recovery Project, 149; determining directionality and distance with, 33–34; GPS collars, 61–64; radio collars for coyotes, 181; radio collars for red wolves, 51, 56, 57, 59, 61–64, 99, 101, 149, 159, 170; recapture collars, 171–75; by Red Wolf Recovery Program, Albemarle Peninsula, 18–19, 27, 30–34, 38, 43, 51, 61–63, 79, 98; for reintroduction of wolves into the wild, 159, 162–63; VHF collars, 61, 63
Tennessee, 110, 136–37. *See also* Land Between the Lakes
Tennessee Valley Authority (TVA), 166–67
Territories: borders of and interstitial spaces between, 62; of coyotes, 62–63, 180, 182; defense of, 62, 209; dispersal of red wolves from natal territory, 47; of gray wolves, 21, 62; and home ranges of red wolves, 61–62, 172, 182; of red wolves, 21, 27, 61–63, 149; shape of, 62; size of, and prey, 21
Texas: black phase wolf in, 135; bounties for red wolves and coyotes in, 135; *canis rufus gregoryi* in, 136; *canis rufus rufus* in, 137; capture of wild red wolves from, for Red Wolf Recovery Project, 13; Carley's work with red wolves in, 141–45, 148–62; coyotes in, 115, 135, 138, 140, 146, 149; diet of wild red wolves in, 82; farming in, 147, 149; fossil canid skulls from, 108; historic distribution of red wolves in, 9, 10; hybridization of red wolves in, 13, 110, 138, 140–41, 146, 210; killing of red wolves in, 137; naming of red wolf in, 4, 137; Predator Ecology Research Station in, 142–43, 144; red wolf skulls found

in, 110; red wolves trapped from, and released to Bulls Island, S.C., 187; wild red wolves in, during nineteenth century, 135; wild red wolves in, during twentieth century, 13, 50, 82, 110, 135, 137, 139–41, 143–44; zoos in, 155. *See also* Beaumont, Texas, Red Wolf Recovery Project
Thoreau, Henry David, 131–32
Top-down controlling effect of apex predators, 85
Tourism in RWRA, 5–6, 25, 42, 43, 45–50, 88–89, 177
Tranquilizers, 14, 144, 160–61, 171–74, 188, 189
Transmitters. *See* Telemetry
Trapping: bear-sprung traps, 53–54, 74; at Beaumont, Texas, Red Wolf Recovery Project, 144–48; behavior of trapped red wolves, 74–76; of coyotes, 61, 70, 91–92, 101, 181; and deer season, 53, 54, 56; dogs caught in traps, 54; drag attached to trap, 44; in fall, 42, 51–64, 100; of foxes for fox pens or fur market, 91–93; injuries from, 51, 52, 60, 70, 75–78, 144; leg-hold trap, 43; processing of wolves after, 57–59; and radio colors for red wolves, 51, 56, 57, 59, 61–64; risks of, 51; scent lures for, 54–55, 128; soft-jaw traps, 43–45, 51; springing trap and putting red wolves in kennel, 75–76; state law on, 51; targets of, by Red Wolf Recovery Program, 51, 61, 73; as traditional activity in North Carolina, 91, 169; tranquilizer tabs in traps, 144; in winter, 42, 61, 65, 73–80; wolves shot in, 71, 165
Trees: on Albemarle Peninsula, 11, 16, 18, 51, 168; in Alligator River NWR, 168; on Bulls Island, S.C., 158; salt-tolerant trees, 222–23; sea-level rise and forest retreat, 192–94, 213–21, 225
Trent University, 68, 118, 206
Tyrrell County, N.C., 31, 66, 85–86, 89, 182

Unique-origin theory, 105–11, 112, 114, 123, 140
University of North Carolina at Chapel Hill, 89
University of North Carolina at Charlotte, 61–62

University of North Carolina Coastal Studies Institute, 225

*Ursus americanus*, 46. *See also* Black bears

Vehicular mortality. *See* Mortality of red wolves

VHF collars. *See* Telemetry

*Vicious: Wolves and Men in America* (Coleman), 131

*Viviparous Quadrupeds of North America, The* (Audubon and Bachman), 135

VonHoldt, Bridgett, 119–20

Waddell, Will, 191, 200–205

Waits, Lisette, xiii, 68–70, 122–23, 183–85, 206, 208

Wake County, N.C., 180

Wang, Xiaoming, 109–10, 122

*War against the Wolf, The* (McIntyre), 129–30

Washington County, N.C., 87, 89, 182

Washington State, 52, 150, 191. *See also* Point Defiance Zoo and Aquarium

Way, Jonathan, 211

Wayne, Robert, 105, 111–12, 119–21, 123, 175–76, 206

Western gray wolves. *See* Gray wolves

West Virginia, 110

Wetlands Reserve Program, 32

Weyerhaeuser timber company, 87

Wheeler, Kim, 45–50, 211

Wildfires, 213–15, 224; Evans Road fire, 214–15; Pains Bay fire, 213–15, 224

Wildlife: in Albemarle Peninsula, 9, 16–17, 30, 41, 48; in Canada, 115; in colonial America, 124–26, 129, 130, 131; and mesopredator release, 84–85; and Native Americans, 130; negative attitudes toward native predators, 86–87, 129; in Norway, 86–87; in Pocosin Lakes NWR, 70, 215; trapping of, 91–93. *See also* Birds; Black bears; Coyotes; Endangered Species Act (ESA); Gray wolves; Red wolves; *and other specific wildlife*

Wildlife refuges. *See* Alligator River NWR; Mattamuskeet NWR; Pocosin Lakes NWR

Wilson, Paul J., 105, 115–18, 206–7

Winter: deer season during, 65–73; home range of red wolves in, 62; trapping of red wolves during, 42, 61, 73–80

Winterville, N.C., 87

Wolves: bounties for, 128–30, 132–35; in colonial America, 124–33; map of historic distribution of, in North America, 10; in nineteenth century, 133–35; in twentieth century, 135–41. *See also* Eastern wolves; Gray wolves; Red wolves; *and Canis* headings

*Wolves of North America, The* (Goldman and Young), 136–37

Wood, William, 130

World Wildlife Safari (Winston, Ore.), 155

Yellowstone, 5, 171

Young, Stanley P., 107, 136

Zoos, 8, 154–56. *See also specific zoos*